DIRECTOR'S FOREWORD

For over 30 years, the Art Gallery of Ontario maintained and enjoyed a close relationship with Canadian art collector Phil Lind. As a longstanding Gallery Trustee and member of various curatorial committees, he supported the building of our collections and shaped our vision—offering essential wisdom and guidance over significant periods of change at the AGO. Phil counted among the most passionate and committed collectors of contemporary art in this country. Many of our current and former curators were fortunate to have a strong working relationship with Phil, and he likewise fostered a deep friendship with Matthew Teitelbaum, former Michael and Sonja Koerner Director, and CEO from 1998 to 2015.

While Phil collaborated closely with the Rogers family to build one of the most successful companies in Canada, his passion for the arts was a central tenet of his life. Phil began collecting in the 1980s and over the following decades, he thoughtfully assembled an ambitious collection of work by artists belonging to the Vancouver School, including Jeff Wall, Rodney Graham, and Stan Douglas. He made several important and lasting financial gifts to the AGO—recognized by the naming of the Anne Lind Artist-in-Residence Room and the Philip B. Lind Galleries—in addition to significant donations of paintings, photographs, and multimedia works. In recent years, Phil generously supported the commission of Brian Jungen's bronze sculpture *Couch Monster: Sadzě? yaaghęhch'ill* (2022) at the corner of Dundas and McCaul streets, the acquisition of the Montgomery Collection of Caribbean Photographs, and the exhibition presentation of *Wolfgang Tillmans: to look without fear* (2023), among several others.

Phil's final act of generosity to the AGO was a transformative donation of 37 works of art—one of the most significant gifts of contemporary art the Gallery has received in its history. This bequest marks the first works by artists such as Ai Weiwei, William Eggleston, Antony Gormley, Philip Guston, Allan Sekula, Laurie Simmons, and Christopher Williams to enter the AGO's collection. Phil's abiding commitment to the work of these artists and their addition to our postwar collection feels nothing short of a windfall. Accompanying the exhibition *Light Years: The Phil Lind Gift*, thoughtfully curated by Adam Welch, this visually rich publication serves to document the care and attention Phil paid to assembling one of the most judicious collections of postwar art in Canada. The catalogue details not only those works that are now part of the AGO's holdings but also broadly surveys his collection as a whole—showing its evolution over time and the considerable depth of works by certain artists. While it was Phil's intention to leave a monumental gift to the AGO, it was his son, Jed Lind, who realized that wish. An artist and designer, Jed has long been a passionate supporter of the AGO's mission and has brought with him a deep appreciation for the power that encounters with art can inspire. Sarah Lind, Phil's daugher, has also stewarded his legacy here at the AGO and generously supported this project. Ellen Roland, Phil's partner for over 20 years, has similarly been a great friend of the AGO. Her appreciation for contemporary art made her an enthusiastic supporter of Phil's collecting.

For lending works to the exhibition, we thank Sarah Lind, Jed Lind, and Missy Goerner. We wish to highlight an important relationship Phil maintained with the Vancouver Art Gallery for many decades, and we are likewise grateful to Anthony Kiendl, Eva Respini, Mandy Ginson, and Kim Svendsen at the VAG for lending Ron Terada's *Entering City of Vancouver* (2002) to our exhibition. Thank you to MuseumPros for working through various logistical demands and to numerous members of our AGO staff for realizing this ambitious presentation of works. I am especially grateful for the dedication and committed stewardship of Adam Welch, Associate Curator of Modern Art, in addition to the leadership and guidance of Julian Cox, Deputy Director & Chief Curator, and Erin Prendergast, Chief, Strategic Initiatives, and the project management of Katarina Veljovic. The donation of these works was deftly coordinated by Debbie Johnsen, Manager, Modern and Contemporary Art, for which Britt Gallpen and Kaari Sinnaeve provided crucial research. I would also like to recognize the efforts of our Development team, led by Kate Halpenny, Chief Development Officer, and in particular, Andrea Orr, Senior Director, Major Gifts and Campaign. Additional thanks to our Publications team of Jim Shedden, Curator, Special Projects & Director, Publishing; Kathryn Yuen, Publishing Coordinator; and Editor Nives Hajdin-Rorabeck, along with Gilbert Li, for the beautiful design of this publication. Finally, thank you to Kitty Scott, former Carol and Morton Rapp Curator, Modern and Contemporary Art, for her long-term commitment to Phil's art connoisseurship over the years.

An ardent and excitable collector, Phil Lind always embraced the new when it came to contemporary art—nothing was too innovative for him. Thanks to Phil's unwavering advocacy for the AGO, we are fortunate to continue guiding these global conversations. His legacy as a leader in Canadian business and deeply passionate supporter of the arts has had a profound impact on our collective history at the AGO. We are honoured to recognize Phil's enormous contributions and achievements through this timely presentation of his beloved collection.

Stephan Jost

Michael and Sonja Koerner Director, and CEO
Art Gallery of Ontario

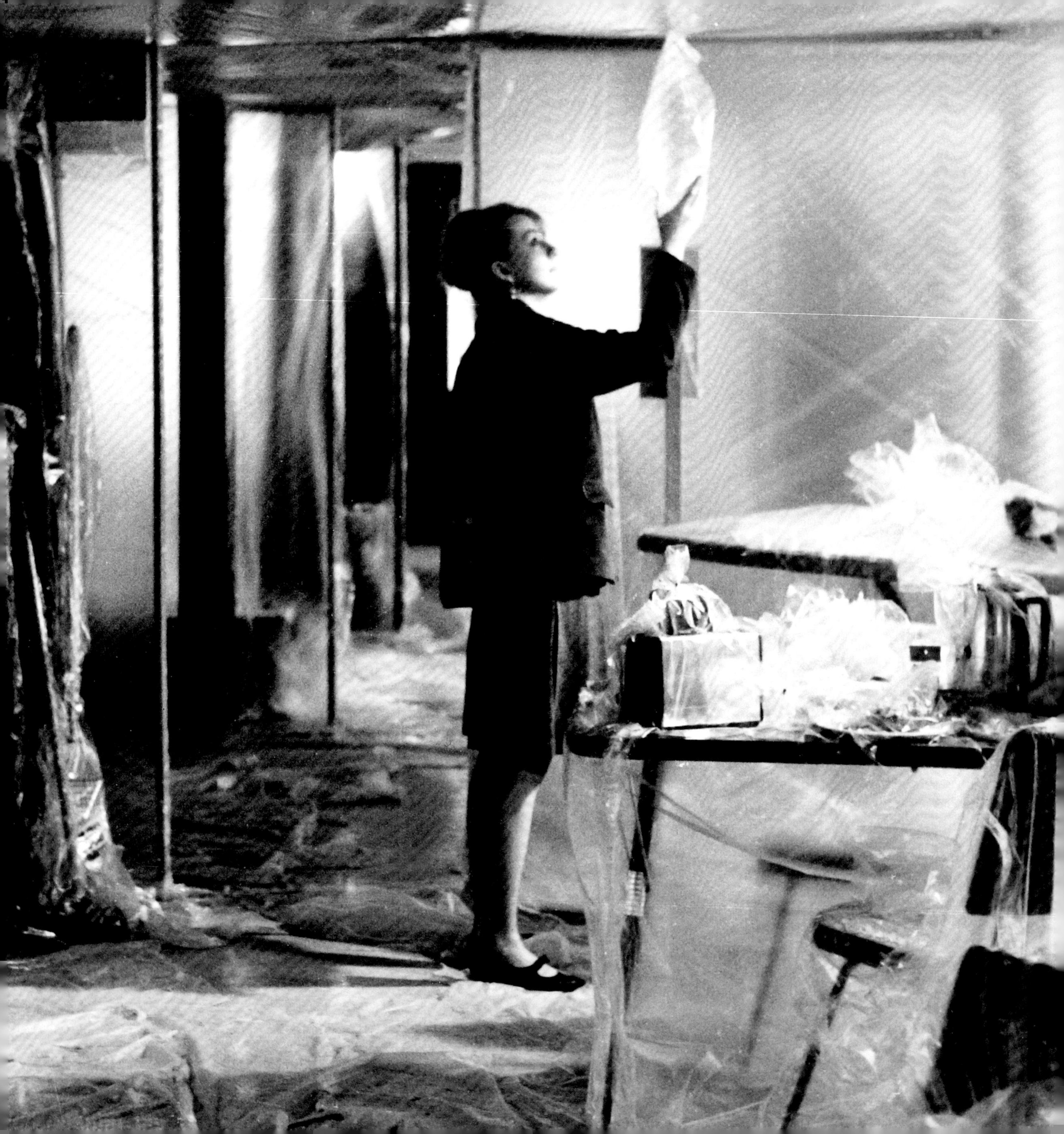

COMPANIONS: PHIL LIND'S LIFE WITH ART

Adam Welch

In February 1966, as part of the Sixth Festival of Contemporary Arts in Vancouver, a twenty-two-year-old undergraduate from the University of British Columbia spent an afternoon mesmerized by *Bagged Place* (fig. 1). The project, by the recently incorporated N.E. Thing Co. (otherwise known as the artists Ingrid and Iain Baxter), took place at the UBC Fine Arts Gallery.[1] A set of four rooms arranged as an apartment, its contents were individually bagged in plastic. The Baxters had borrowed the furniture and appliances from a local department store called Wosk's. At least one critic at the time recognized the immersive and enigmatic installation as "the first public celebration of McLuhanism."[2] "It was," the student later recalled, "the most unusual thing I'd ever seen."[3]

Some twenty years later, Phil Lind saw the installation again, reconstructed in 1987 for the inaugural exhibition at The Power Plant Contemporary Art Gallery in Toronto, where he served as a board member. In the accompanying publication, guest curator AA Bronson wrote that *Bagged Place* stood as "a monument to the consumer society… the Baxters were primary forces in investigating ways in which the artist could participate directly with the world of communications, business, and power."[4]

For the sixty years following that first encounter with N.E. Thing Co.'s *Bagged Place,* Lind passionately collected work by some of the postwar period's most innovative artists (fig. 2). When he died in August 2023, his collection was elegantly installed across two properties: an apartment in midtown Toronto and a converted mill on the Rocky Saugeen River, south of Owen Sound, Ontario (fig. 3). Unlike many ambitious collectors of contemporary art, Lind lived with everything he owned. He contemplated and reflected daily on the photographs, drawings, sculptures, and paintings that surrounded him. As with his first encounter with *Bagged Place,* Lind was undaunted by work he did not yet understand. He appreciated the untested and it was cause for excitement. On seeing new work that engaged him, a broad smile would cross his face. Lind read widely and voraciously about art, took every occasion to talk to artists, curators, dealers, and fellow collectors, and acquired works of art with zeal. His passion for contemporary art was boundless.

Phil Lind was born in 1943 into a family with deep ties to both Ontario and British Columbia. His grandfather, John Grieve Lind, was a prospector during the Klondike gold rush and later, alongside his brother, co-founded the St. Marys Portland Cement Company in 1912. The family's philanthropy went on to considerably shape the small Ontario town of St. Marys during the early twentieth century. Following studies at Ridley College, Lind briefly attended McGill University before switching to the University of British Columbia in 1963. Later, he earned an MA in political sociology from the University of Rochester.

It was then that he met with AA Bronson, Felix Partz, and Jorge Zontal of General Idea to discuss their proposal to air a "one-hour round-up [which we] would like very much to be able to run… on our system in the fall."[7] Likely a video component of the fledging group's *Light-On* work, it was never broadcast but nevertheless informed their work for television later in the decade. Lind's enthusiasm to support artists working in a new and untested medium is admirable. It also points, perhaps, to a shared understanding of Canadian media theorist Marshall McLuhan's importance. Both N.E. Thing Co. and General Idea emerged from this ground, and their fascination with communications systems and corporate models of artistic production clearly appealed to Lind. Rodney Graham's *Media Studies '77* (2016; fig. 6), a much-loved work for Lind, makes an irreverent nod to McLuhan's outsized influence on the postwar Canadian landscape. Graham, in the guise of a late '70s-era professor, is surrounded by technologies which were the stuff of Lind's daily work at Rogers. The chalkboard behind Graham, who perches nonchalantly on his desk, has been wiped clean and the television monitor is blank.

Focused mostly on collecting work by Canadian artists during the 1990s, Lind's attention turned to practices in the United States and Europe by the early 2000s. This interest beyond Canada was driven by a few factors. Ellen Roland, Lind's partner since the early 2000s, is an interior architect who shared his passion for international contemporary art. Upon seeing Lind's collection, Roland asked why he mostly collected Canadian art. With no ready answer, Lind began thinking beyond his existing networks. The two travelled together extensively, and it was often an exhibition or art fair that served as the motivation for a trip. With over

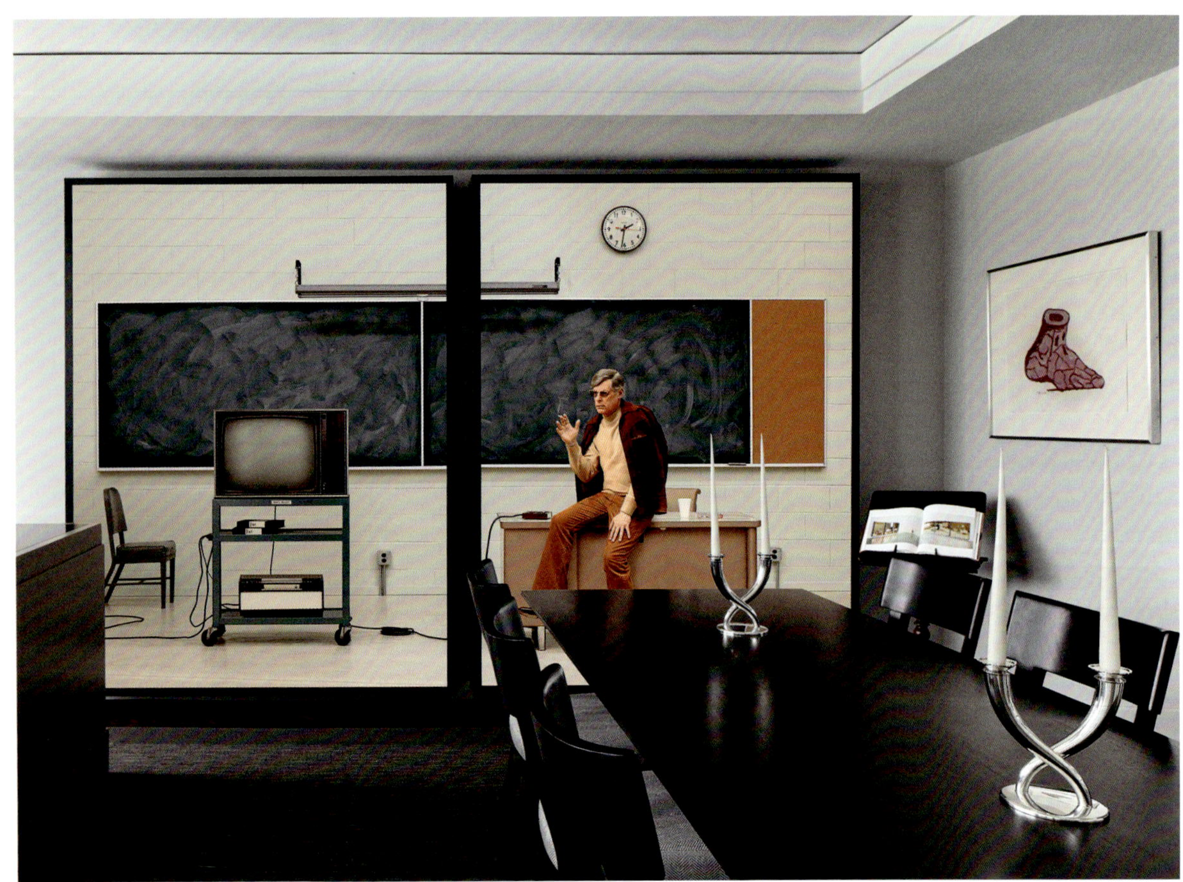

FIG. 6
Installation view of Rodney Graham's *Media Studies '77* (2016). © Estate of Rodney Graham, Courtesy Lisson Gallery. With Philip Guston's *Rome* (1971) on right. © The Estate of Philip Guston, courtesy Hauser & Wirth. Photo: Gieves Anderson.

two decades of collecting under his belt, he also found a degree of success in business that allowed him the means to expand his collection internationally.

Around this time, Lind also met a new guide through the Canadian—and international—art world. Lind's ties to Vancouver stemmed not just from his family's history but his own happy memories at UBC. In 2002, Kathleen Bartels took up the directorship of the Vancouver Art Gallery and the two quickly formed a friendship of mutual respect. Bartels led a highly ambitious travel circle for the museum's patrons, which strengthened Lind's ties to the VAG and brought him into regular contact with artists, collectors, and dealers throughout Europe, the United States, and Asia. (Lind joined the board of the VAG in 2012 as a Trustee and served as Vice-Chair between 2019 and 2021.)

In October 2005, Lind and Roland travelled with Bartels to London, where Lind was introduced to the work of Antony Gormley, Julian Opie, and Philip Guston—artists with whose work he would engage deeply throughout the rest of his life. Lind first saw Gormley's sculptures at the home of a collector in St. John's Wood, and then again at Regent's Park as part of the Frieze Art Fair. The fair would become a regular destination for Lind and Roland. Following a major stroke in July 1998 that left Lind with limited mobility, the London fair afforded him an opportunity to meet easily with many dealers and artists. It was at Lisson Gallery's booth that Lind saw Opie's work, for instance, which soon after led to the 2006 Rogers commission with Jeanne Parkin.

During this same trip, Lind and Roland were invited to the home of architect Richard Rogers and chef Ruth Rogers—whose collection of Guston paintings was installed in the converted Chelsea townhouse Richard had designed (fig. 7). The couple's connection to the artist was profound: Guston had been a close friend of Ruth's parents, Fred and Sylvia Elias, and Richard met frequently with the painter while designing the Centre Pompidou. Guston's decisive turn to figuration gave many creatives motivation to make a late-in-the-day change. That courage to reinvent himself also resonated with Lind. It wasn't only Guston's biography that resonated with Lind, but also the painter's resolution to address the racism embedded in American life; the banal everydayness of Guston's hooded figures was an affront to easy postwar optimism.

Following this introduction to Guston's work, Lind asked David Moos, then-Curator of Modern and Contemporary Art at

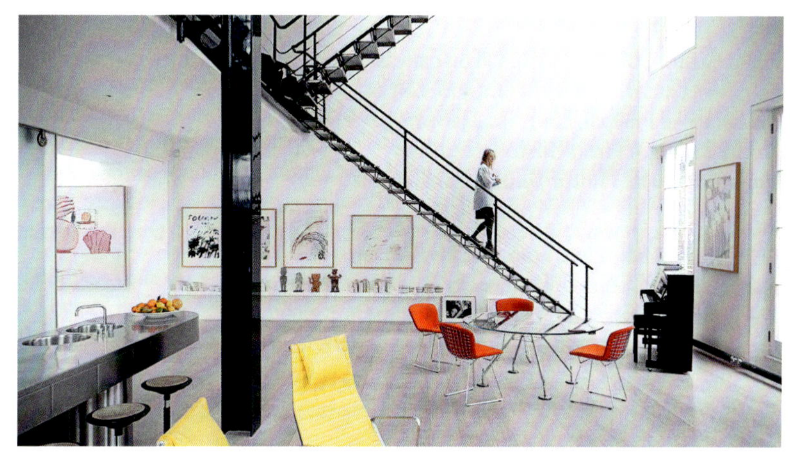

FIG. 7
Ruth and Richard Rogers' house, Chelsea, London. Designed by Richard Rogers, 1983. Image courtesy of The Modern House, London.

the AGO, how to find available work. Moos introduced him to gallerist David McKee, who cut his teeth at Marlborough Gallery when it represented Guston and, in 1974, had opened his own space with an exhibition of work by the artist. Lind began acquiring work by Guston from McKee in 2006, purchasing two drawings from 1968 and 1969. In 2008, Lind bought the painting *Untitled* (1979; fig. 8), and the following year, a smaller oil on board, *Untitled* (1970). McKee and Lind formed a friendship that extended beyond their shared interest in Guston's work. Indeed, Lind formed abiding friendships with many dealers in Canada and abroad. His zeal for Vancouver art was nurtured by Monte Clark, Daniel Faria, and Catriona Jeffries. Later, as his collecting grew toward international artists, David Zwirner, Marian Goodman, and Lisson Gallery played a critical role.

More than spending time in collectors' homes or art fairs, however, what Lind really valued was being with artists in their studios. Shortly after arriving at the VAG, Bartels brought Lind into closer contact with photographer Jeff Wall, and Lind acquired several of his works between 2001 and 2002. Lind was drawn to Wall's inscrutable images and chose photographs that sustained his interest for many decades. With artists such as Wall—whom he would visit often on trips to Vancouver—Lind shared a creative intelligence. It was his engagement with artists in Vancouver that led him to collect works by the so-called Dusseldorf School: Hilla and Bernd

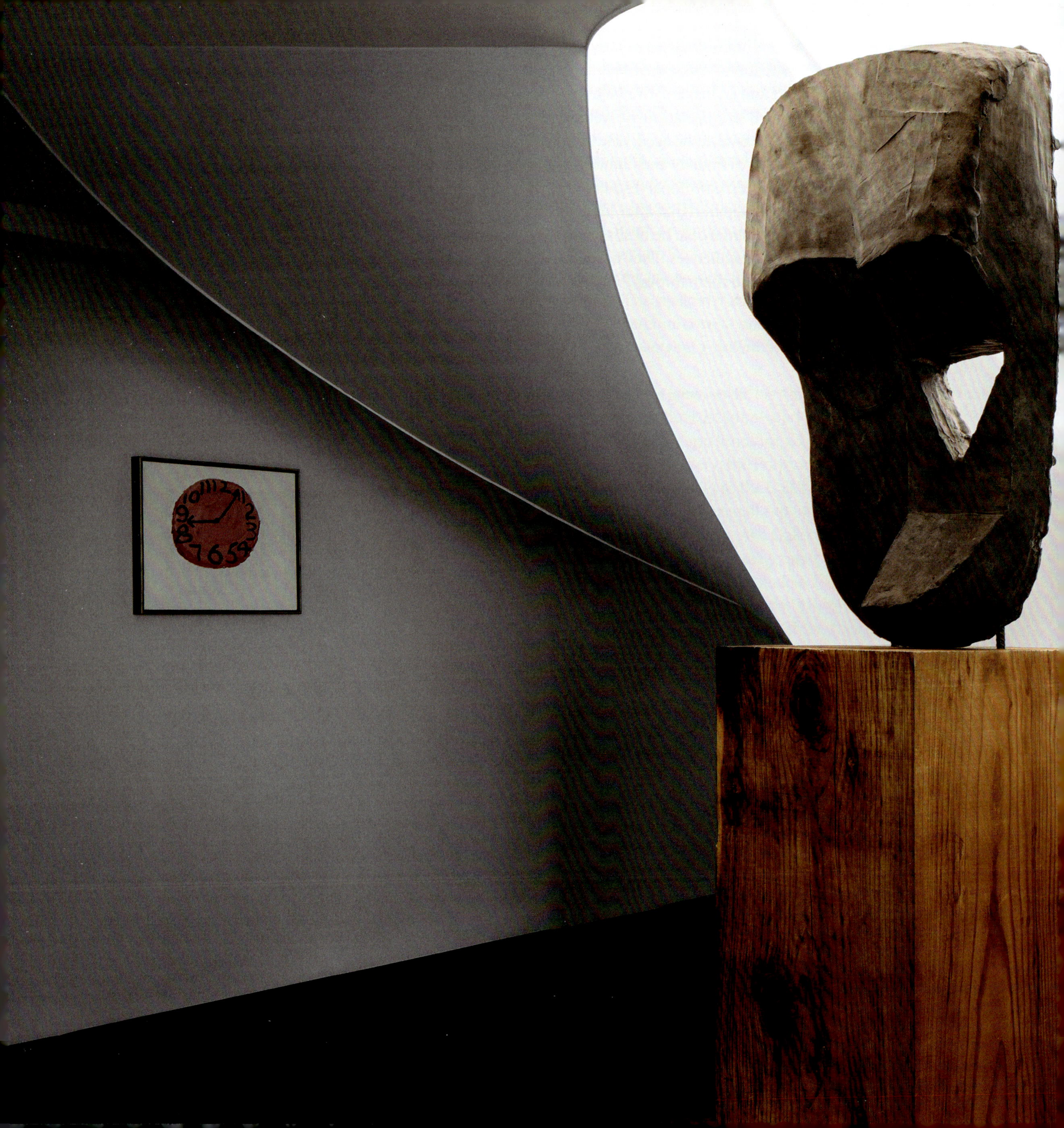

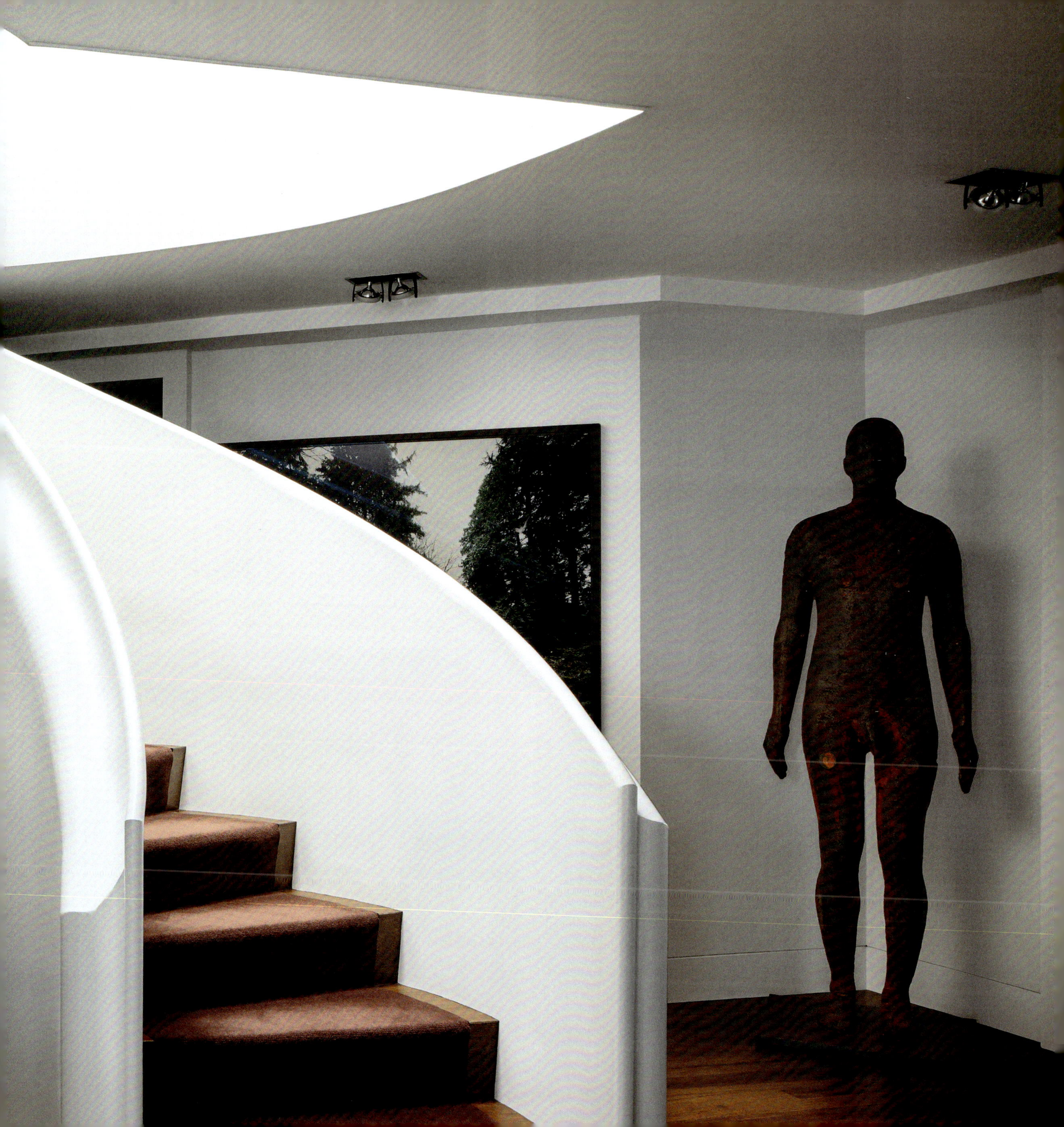

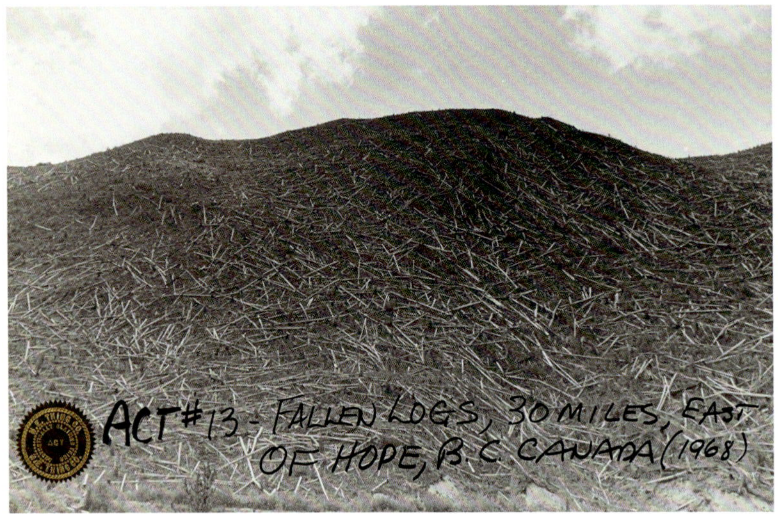

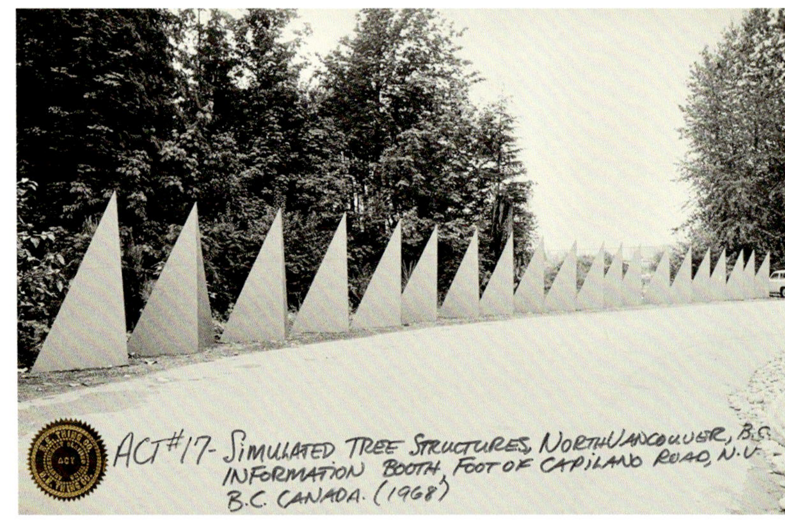

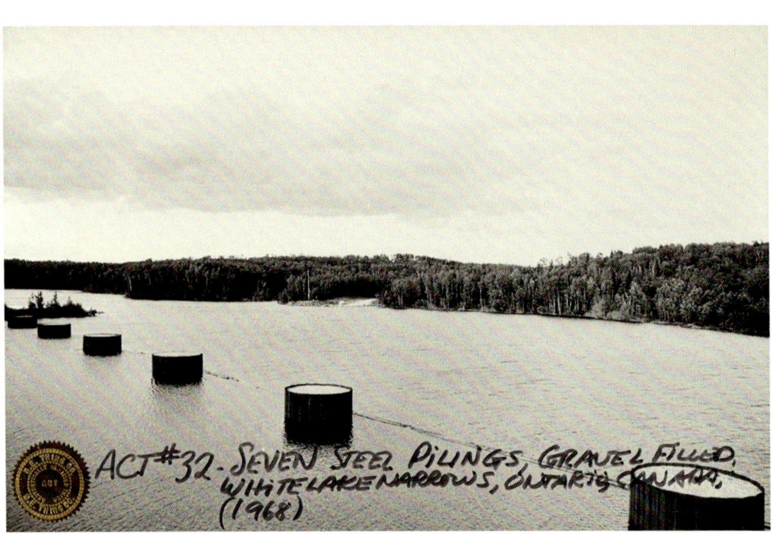

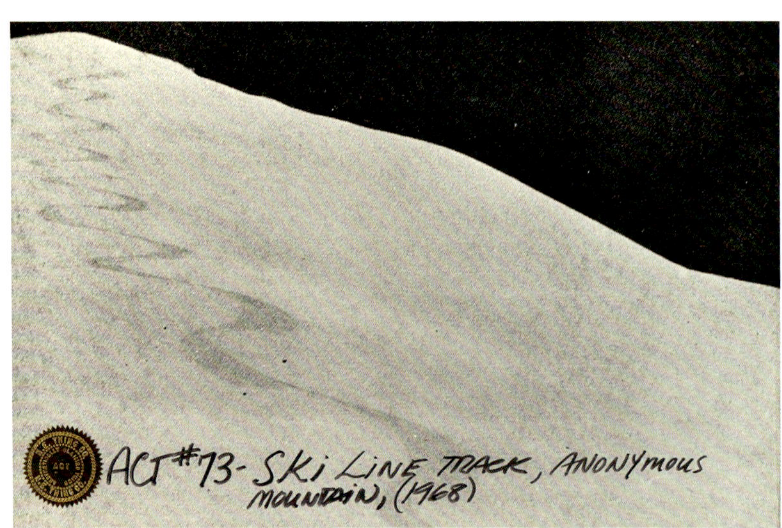

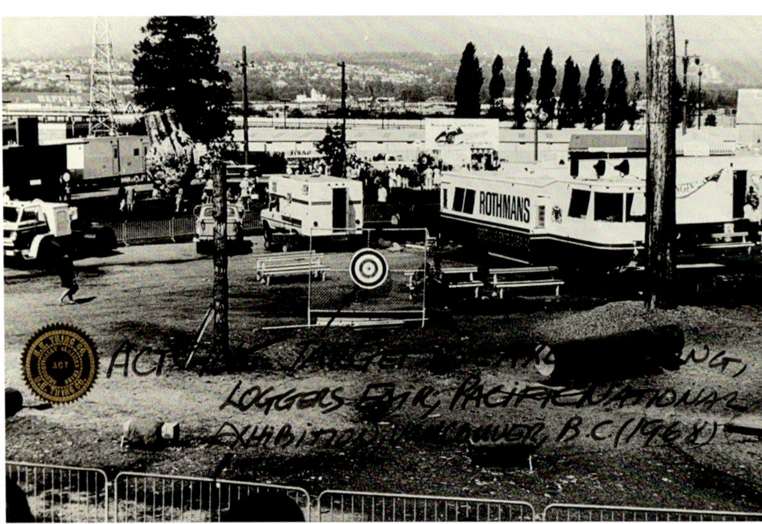

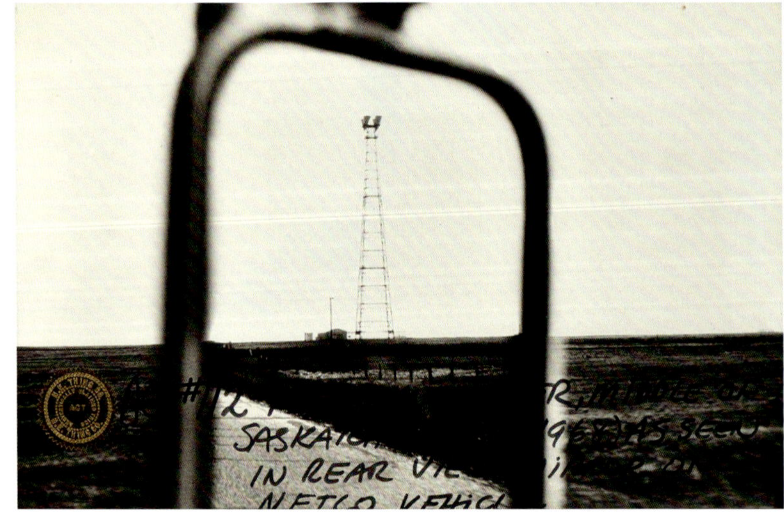

N.E. Thing Co. *ACT # 13, 17, 32, 73, 74, 106, & 112, 1968*

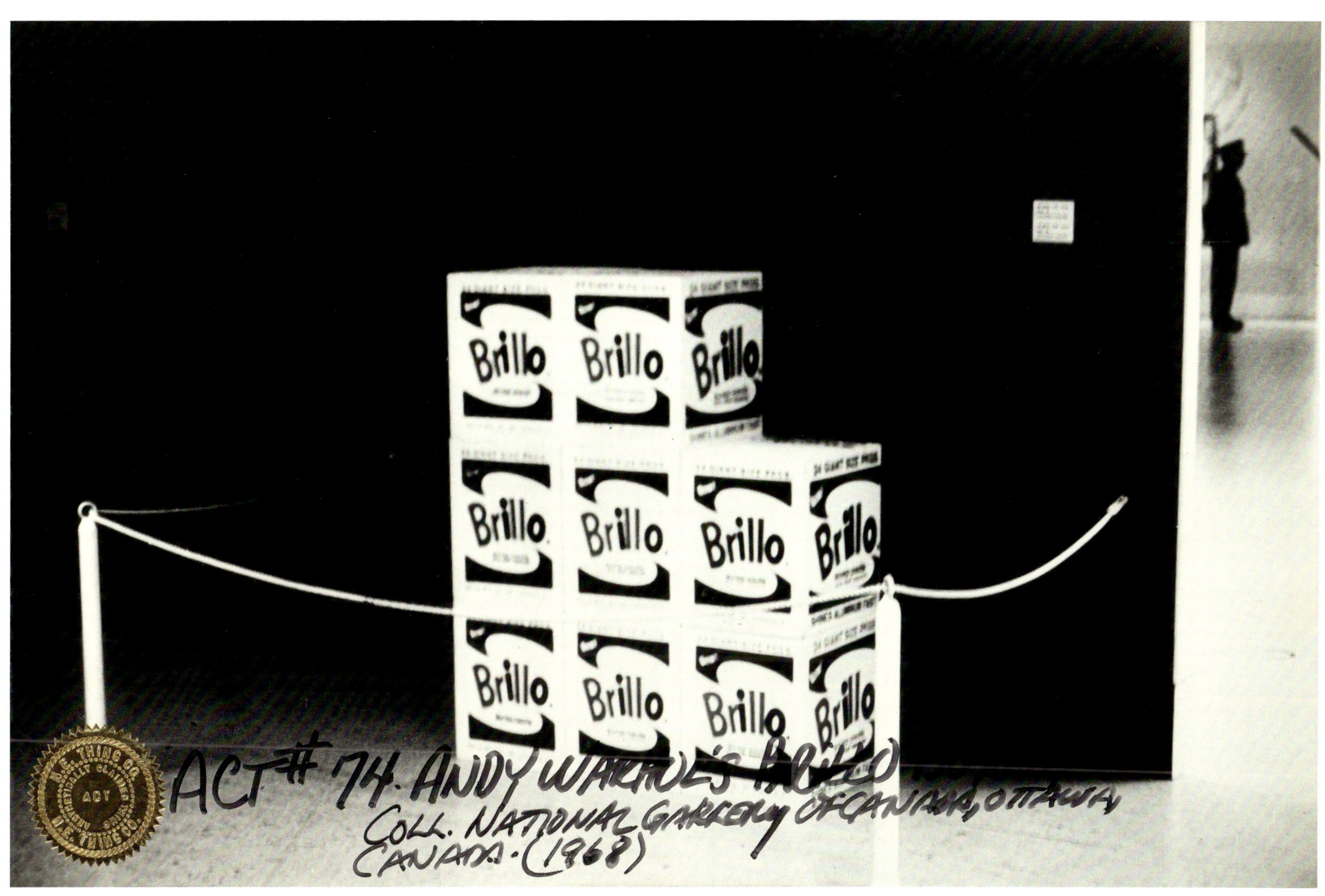
N.E. THING CO.
ACT
Brillo
ACT # 74. ANDY WARHOL'S BRILLO.
COLL. NATIONAL GALLERY OF CANADA, OTTAWA,
CANADA. (1968)

N.E. Thing Co. *Double Light Casts – 1969 Seymour River N. Vancouver, B.C.*, 1968–1969; assembled 1981

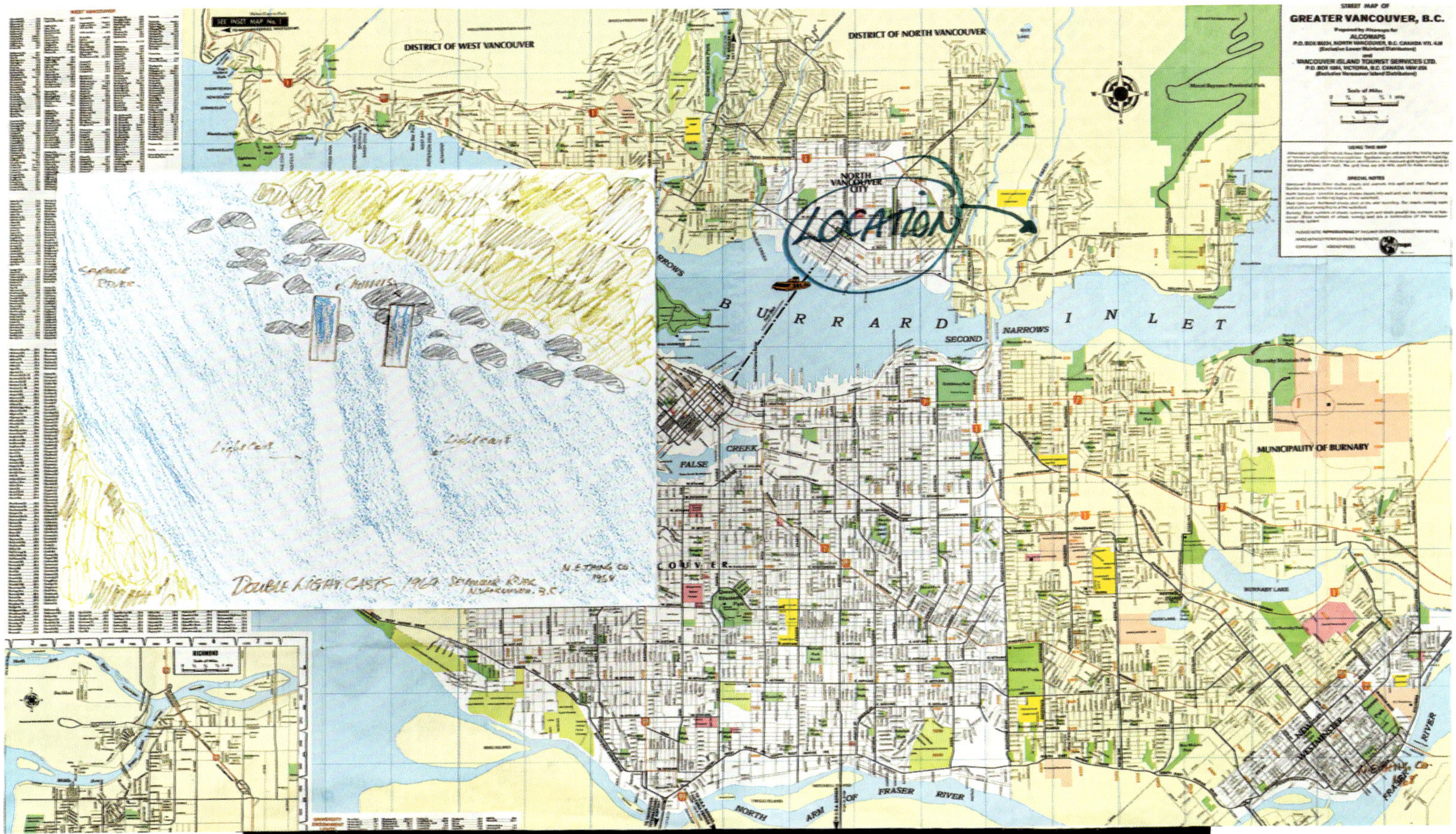

STREET MAP OF
GREATER VANCOUVER, B.C.

DISTRICT OF WEST VANCOUVER

DISTRICT OF NORTH VANCOUVER

NORTH VANCOUVER CITY

LOCATION

B U R R A R D I N L E T

SECOND NARROWS

MUNICIPALITY OF BURNABY

NORTH ARM OF FRASER RIVER

RICHMOND

DOUBLE LIGHT CASTS 1968 SEYMOUR RIVER N. VANCOUVER, B.C.

N.E. THING CO. 1968

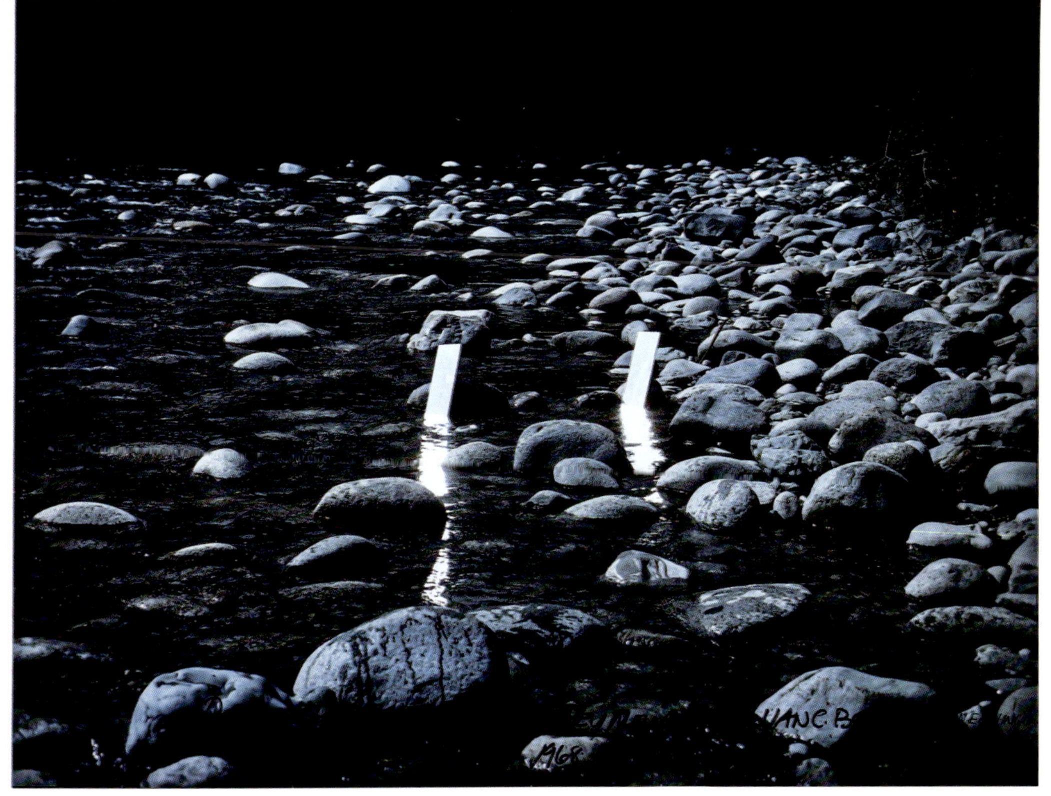

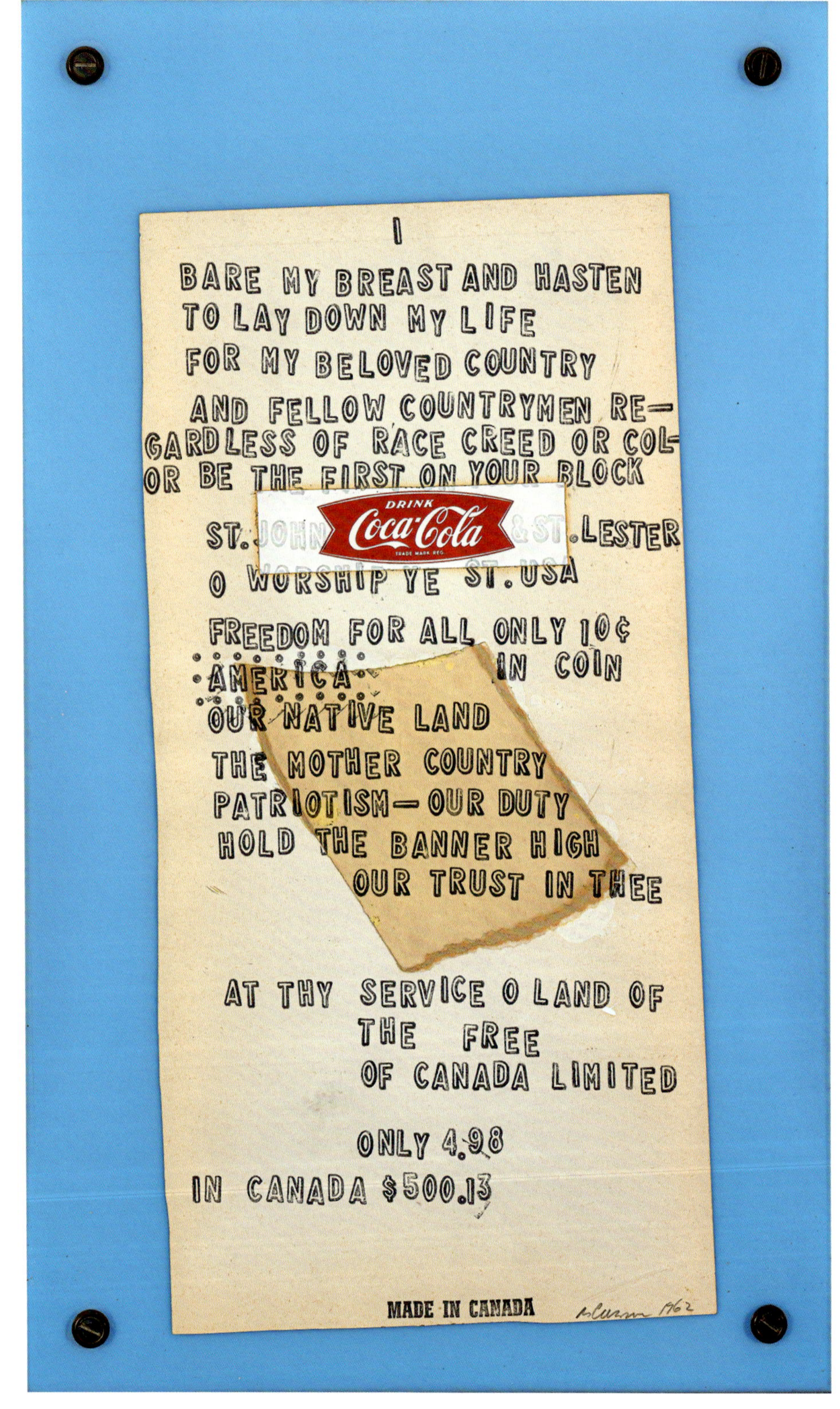

Greg Curnoe *Canada,* 1962

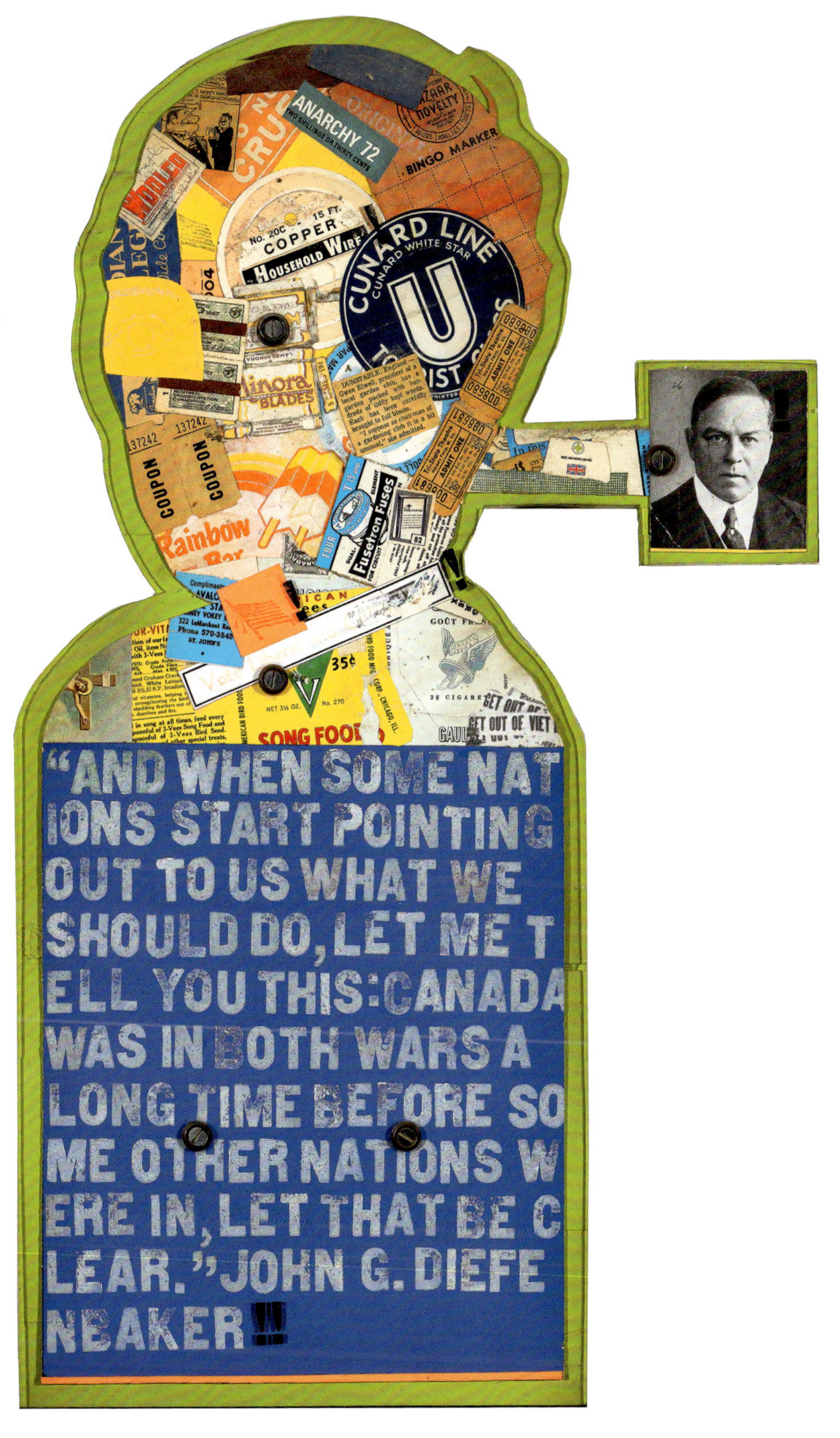

Greg Curnoe *Diefenbaker, Canada,* 1962

Ron Terada *Entering City of Vancouver*, 2002

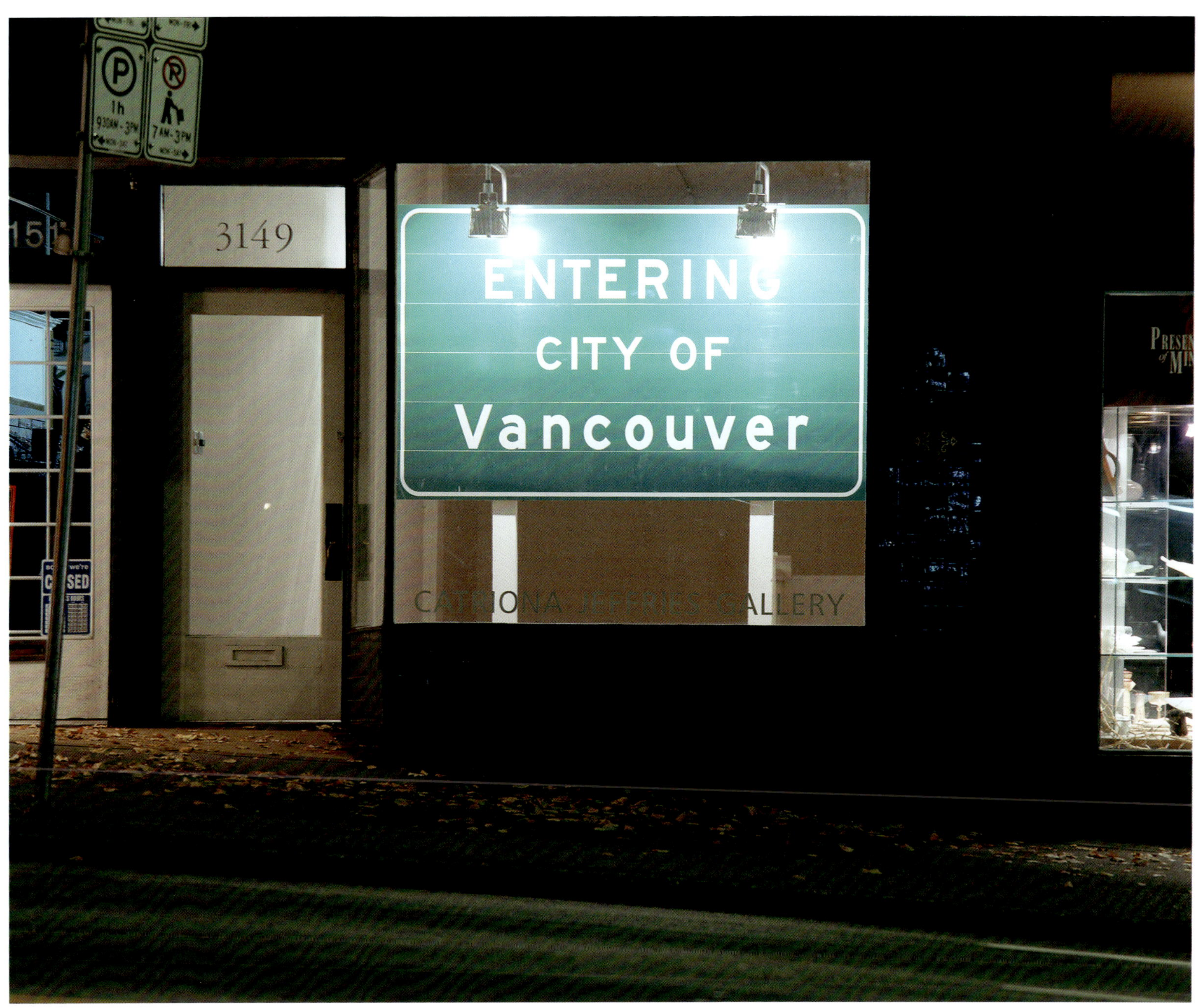
3149
ENTERING
CITY OF
Vancouver
CATRIONA JEFFRIES GALLERY

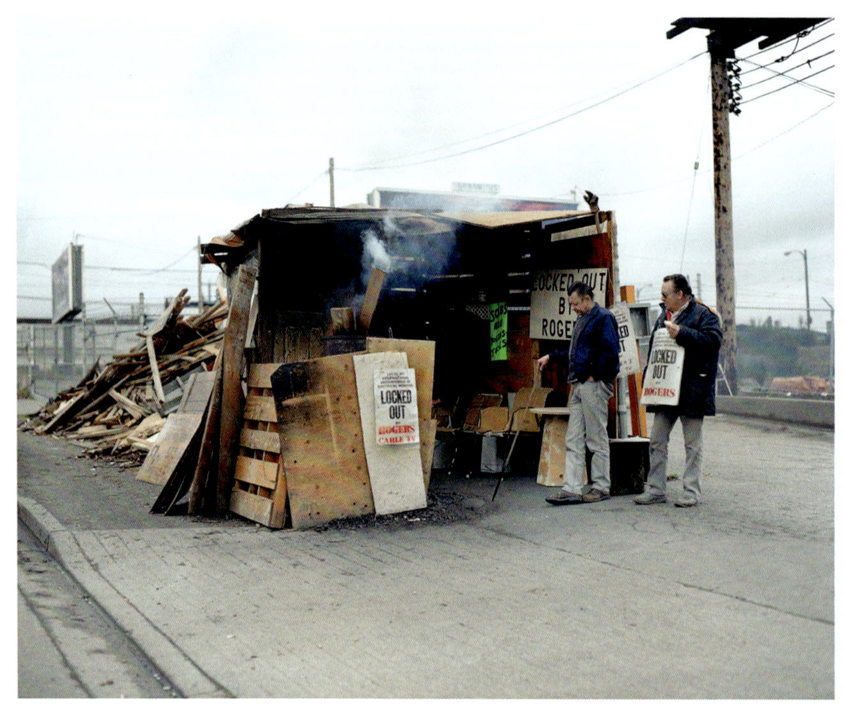

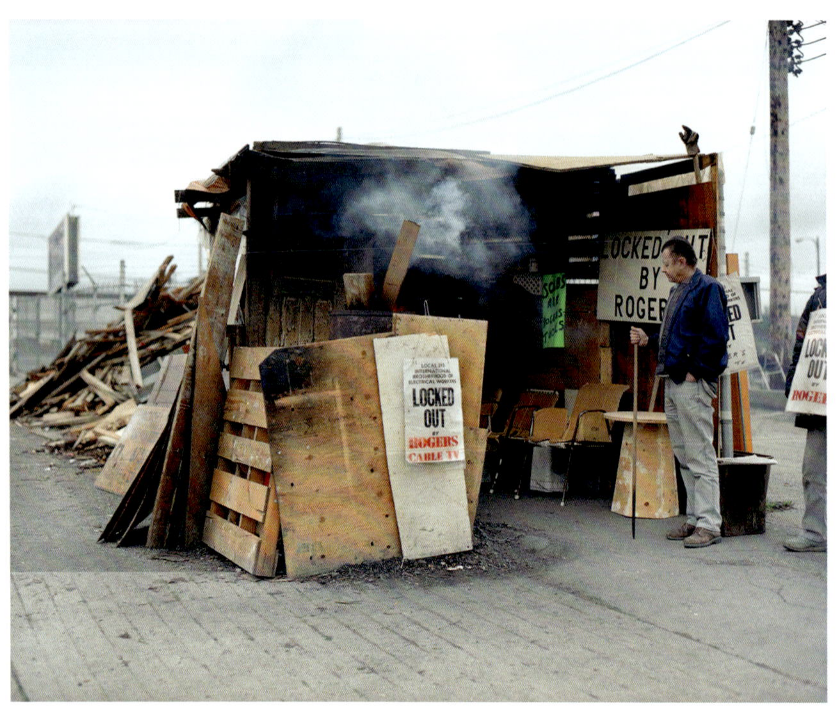

Roy Arden *Locked-Out Workers, (diptych) Vancouver, BC, 1994*

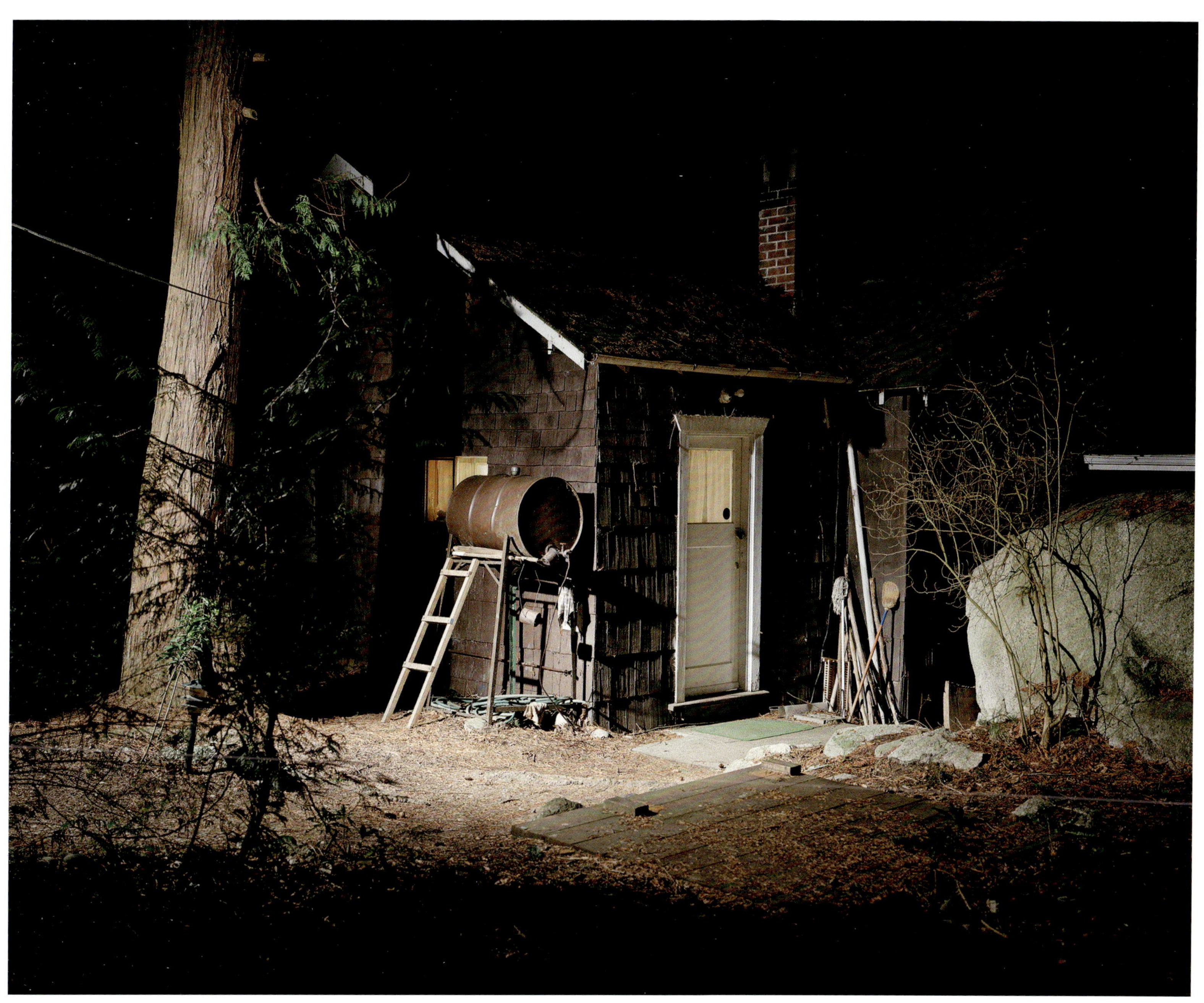

Scott McFarland *Cabin with Motion Light*, 2001

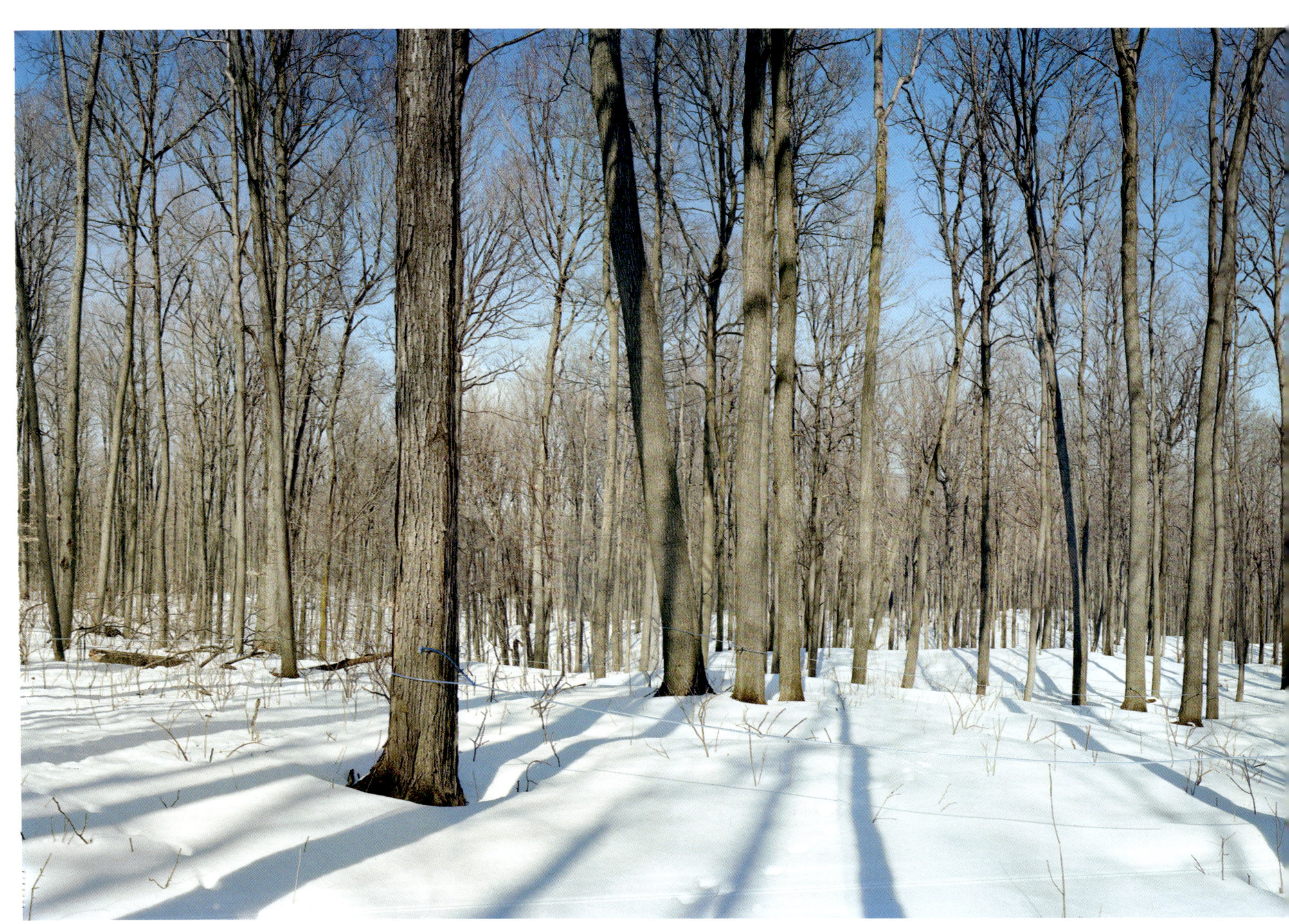

Scott McFarland *Sugar Bush, Caledon Ontario (study)*, 2009

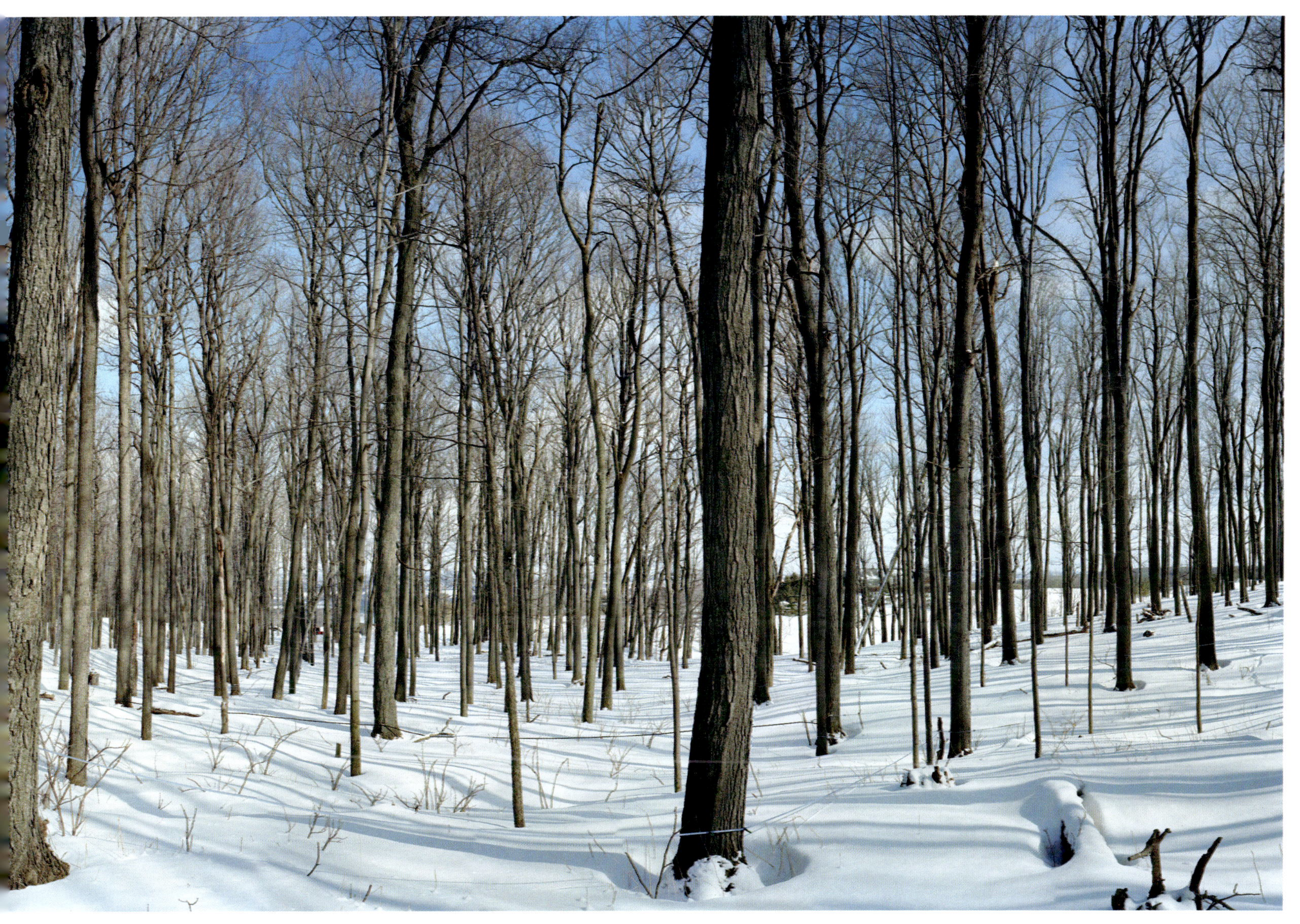

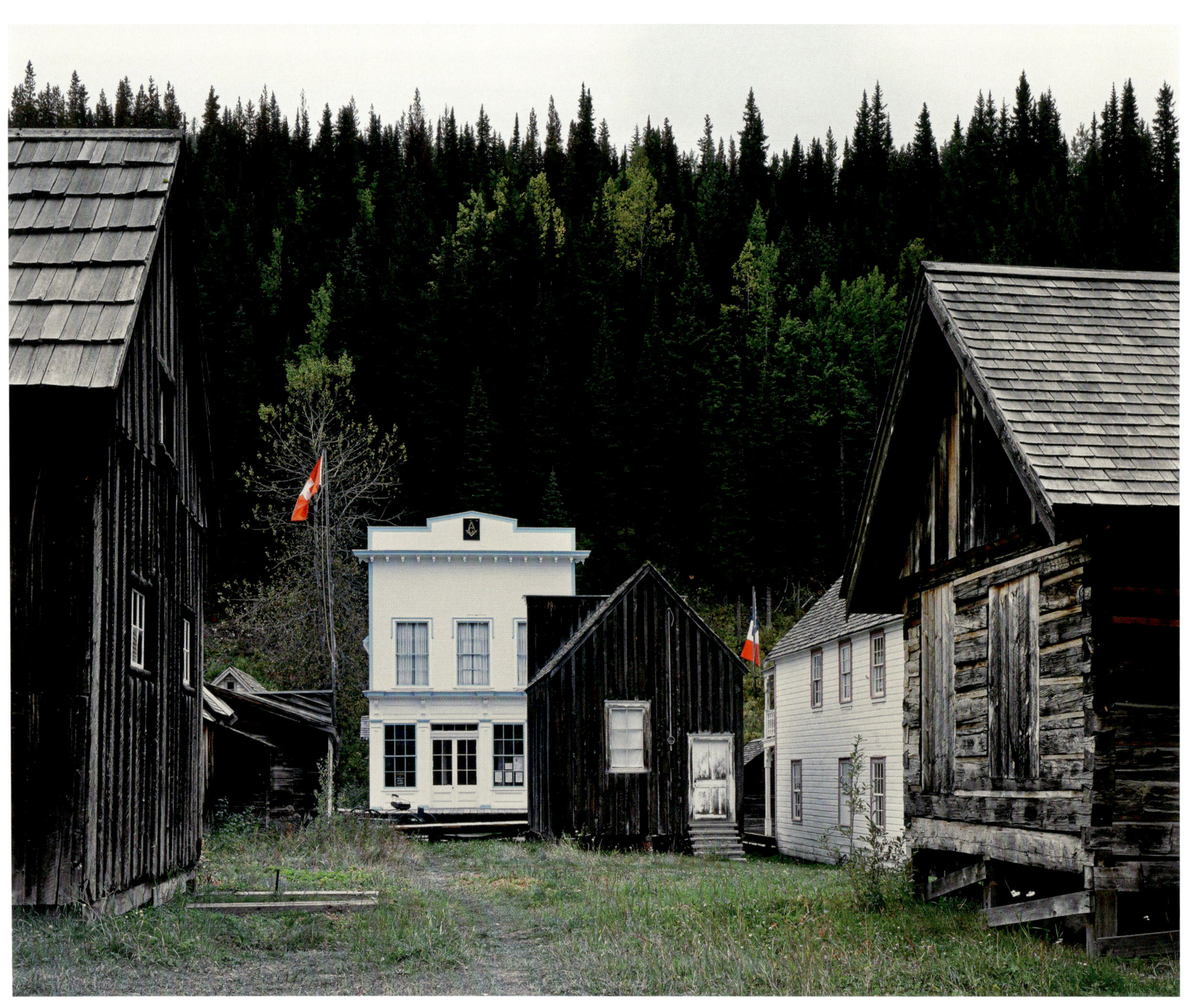

Stan Douglas *Masonic Lodge, Barkerville,* 2006

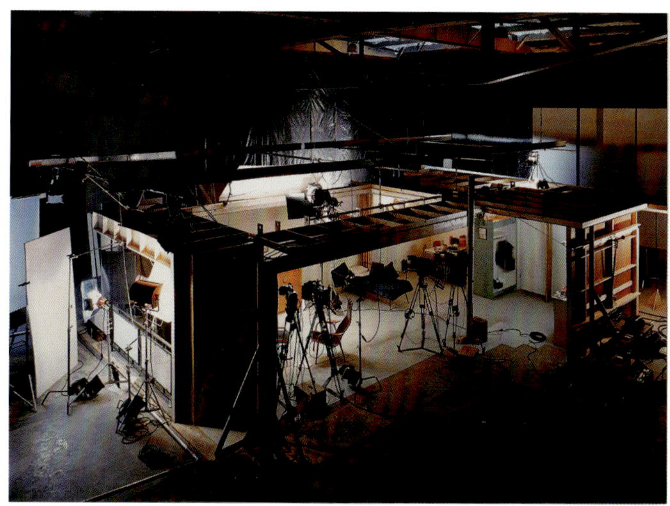

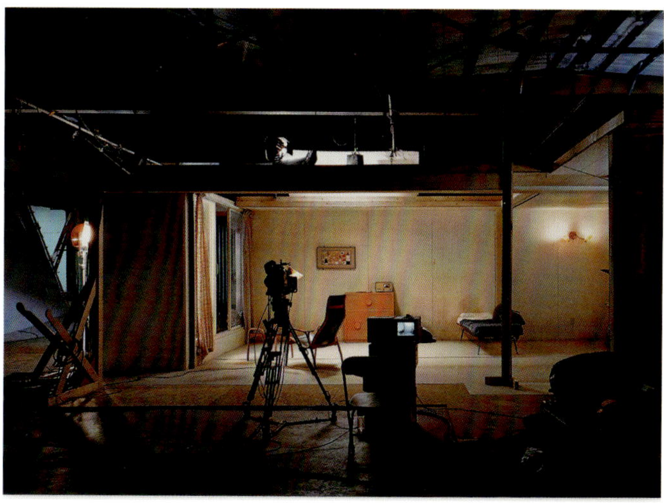

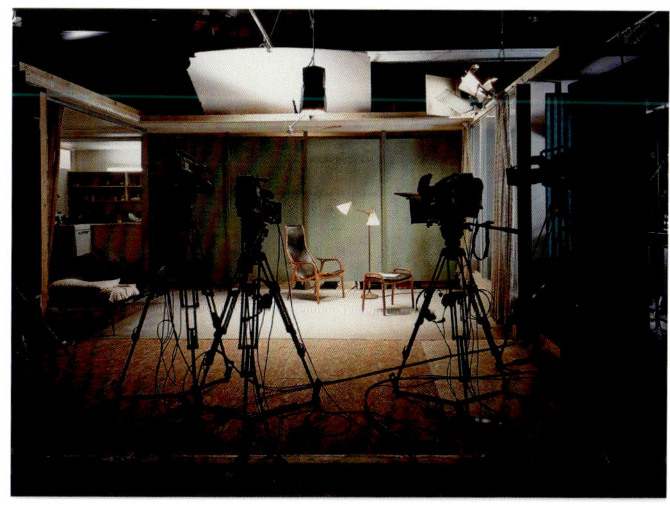

Stan Douglas *Set for Win, Place or Show (East View, West View, Overview)*, 1998

A pioneer of film and video installations, Vancouver-born artist Stan Douglas (b. 1960) combines cinematic, historical, and literary references in his practice. Douglas has long maintained a studio in Vancouver's Downtown Eastside, whose history provided the origin of *Abbott & Cordova, 7 August 1971* (2008). The image was commissioned as a photographic mural for the lobby of the Woodward's Building—a former department store developed as a condominium. Through careful historical reconstruction, a life-sized stage set, and over one hundred actors, Douglas constructed an image that restaged a peaceful demonstration, or "be-in," by residents of the neighbourhood against excessive policing. When the authorities called for the crowd to disperse, violence erupted, an episode later known as the Gastown Riot.

Unlike Douglas's careful staging in *Abbott & Cordova*, another work—*MacLeod's Books, Vancouver* (2006)—was conceived in a documentary mode. Tens of thousands of books were arranged in the two-thousand-square-foot antiquarian bookstore on West Pender Street owned by Don Stewart. Book titles and hand-written signs are legible in the resulting large-scale photograph. *Masonic Lodge, Barkerville* (2006) similarly depicts a ready-made scene: a cluster of buildings in Cariboo, British Columbia. Barkerville was the centre of the Cariboo Gold Rush in the 1860s and is now an open-air museum. Toward the end of the nineteenth century, over half of the region's population was made up of Chinese immigrants, and the town became home to the first order of the Chee Kung Tong, also known as Hongmen or the Chinese Freemasons.

Stan Douglas *Abbott & Cordova, 7 August 1971*, 2008

FOLLOWING PAGE
Stan Douglas *MacLeod's Books, Vancouver*, 2006

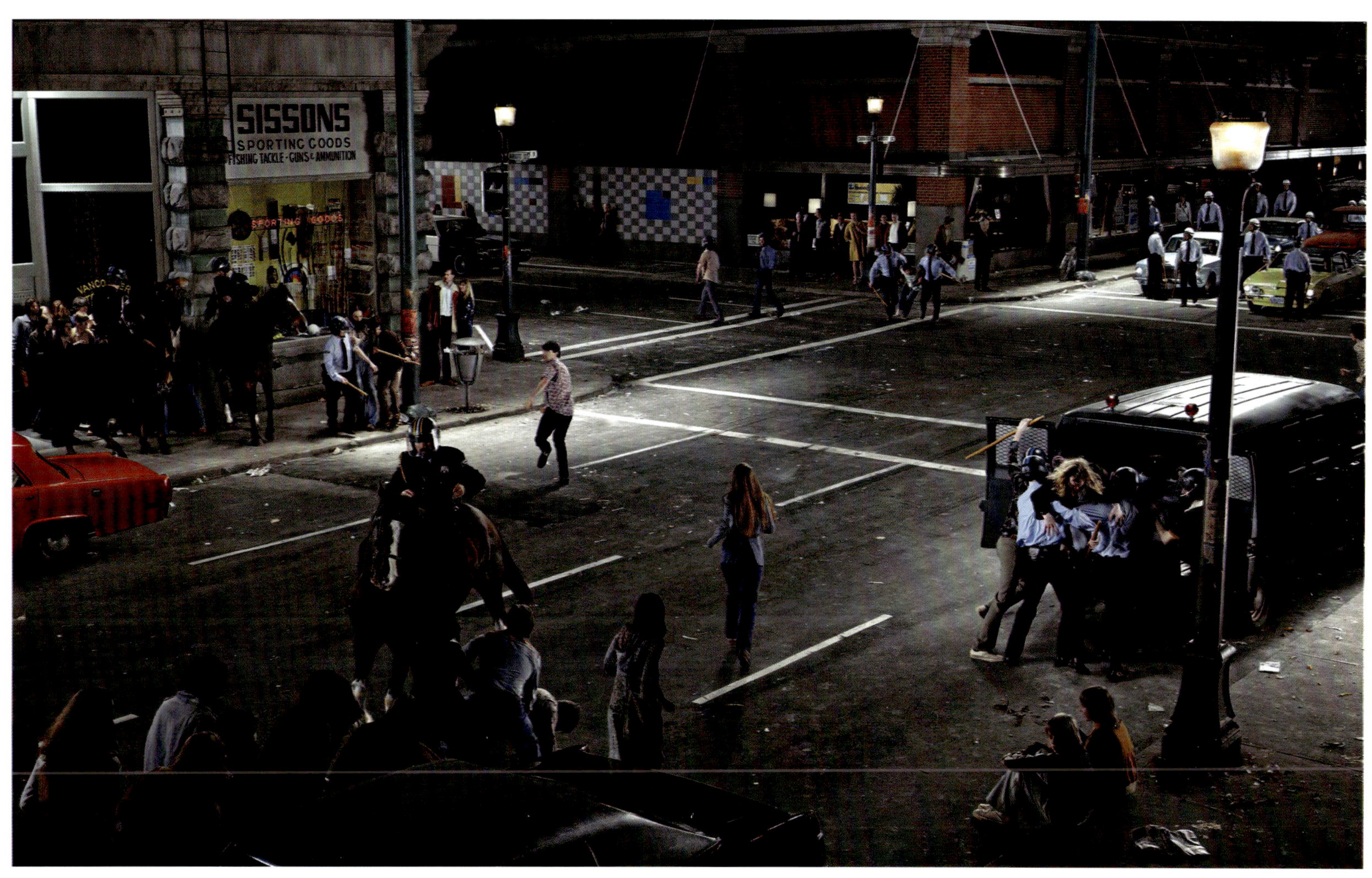
SISSONS
SPORTING GOODS
FISHING TACKLE - GUNS & AMMUNITION
SPORTING GOODS

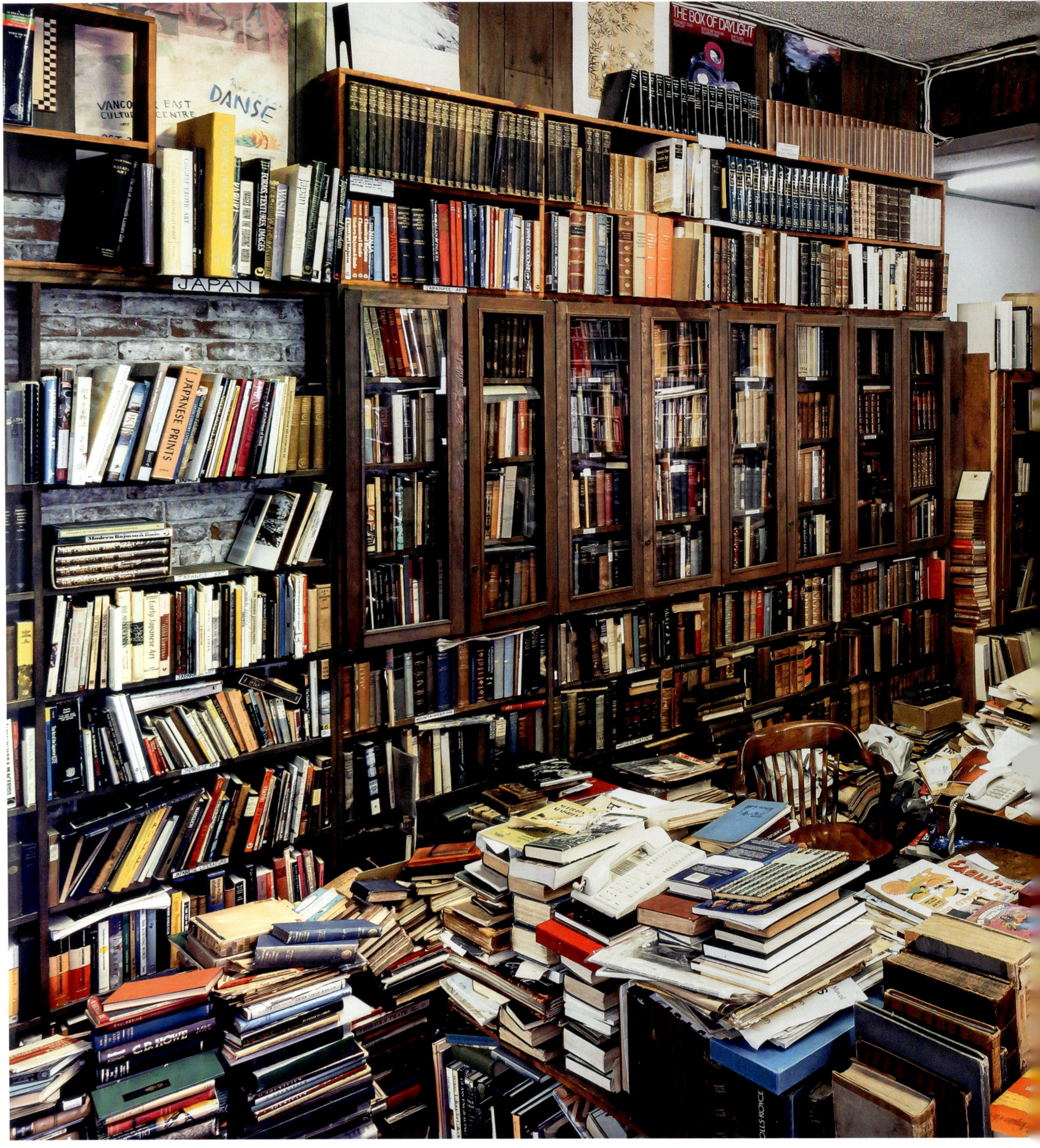
THE BOX OF DAYLIGHT
DANSE
JAPAN
JAPANESE PRINTS
Early Japanese Art
C.D. HOWE

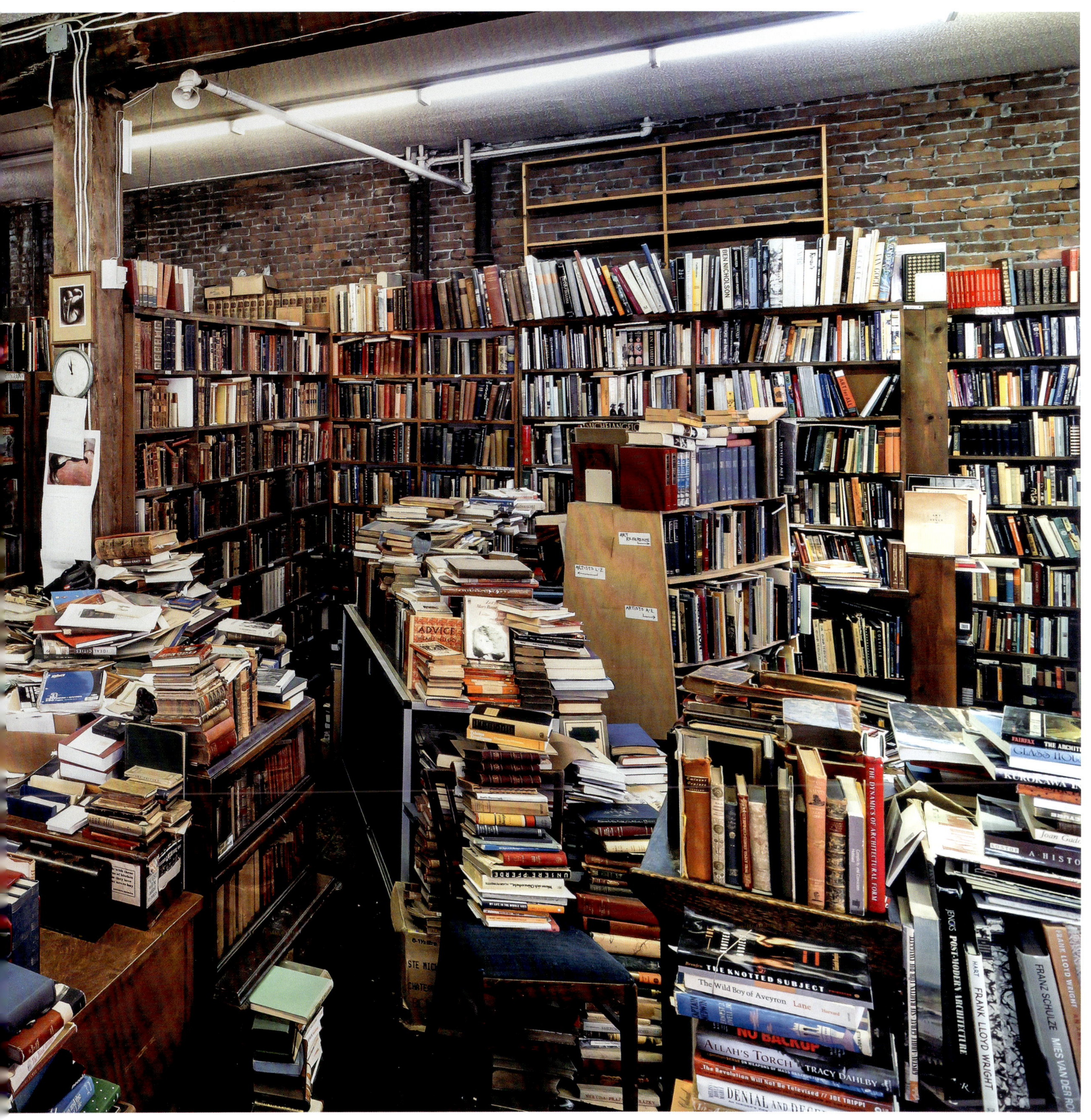

BEN NICHOLSON
VAN GOGH
MICHELANGELO
ADVICE
ARTISTS A-L
THE DYNAMICS OF ARCHITECTURAL FORM
FAIRFAX
THE KNOTTED SUBJECT
The Wild Boy of Aveyron
Lane
NO BACKUP
ALLAH'S TORCH
TRACY DAHLBY
The Revolution Will Not Be Televised // JOE TRIPPI
JENCKS
POST-MODERN ARCHITECTURE
HART
FRANK LLOYD WRIGHT
FRANZ SCHULZE

Vancouver-born Jeff Wall (b. 1946) studied at the University of British Columbia before starting a doctorate at the Courtauld Institute in London in 1970. After returning to Vancouver in 1974, he began to make photographs as colour transparencies mounted in lightboxes, works inflected by his deep knowledge of art history. Highly constructed and carefully arranged, his images channelled the history of painting, as with his explicit reference to the structure of Édouard Manet's *A Bar at the Folies-Bergère* (1882) in his *Picture for Women* (1979).

Wall's interest in past pictorial modes is evidenced by the earliest of his so-called documentary landscapes: *Steves Farm, Steveston* (1980; printed 1988). With minimal human presence, the photograph shows farmland bordered by suburban development. (Today, Steveston is part of Richmond, BC, itself a suburb of Vancouver.) While the image broaches the threat of ever-expanding housing tracts, it equally engages with Dutch and English landscape traditions in painting. *Steves Farm* has an obvious cinematographic quality: a diffuse light and painterly palette of ochres and greens seems somehow appropriate for the horses in the foreground and almost picturesque, dilapidated outbuildings. *River Road* (1994; printed 1997), an image also taken in Richmond, similarly shows a house and cluster of buildings on a lot bordering the Fraser River. Taken in the winter of 1994, the scale and illumination of the transparency draws the viewer's attention to an otherwise unremarkable scene of everyday life. Just as mundane, *Concrete Ball* (2002) depicts a concrete plinth and sphere, beyond which are the tennis courts and soccer pitches of Vancouver's Andy Livingstone Park.

Jeff Wall *Concrete Ball*, 2002

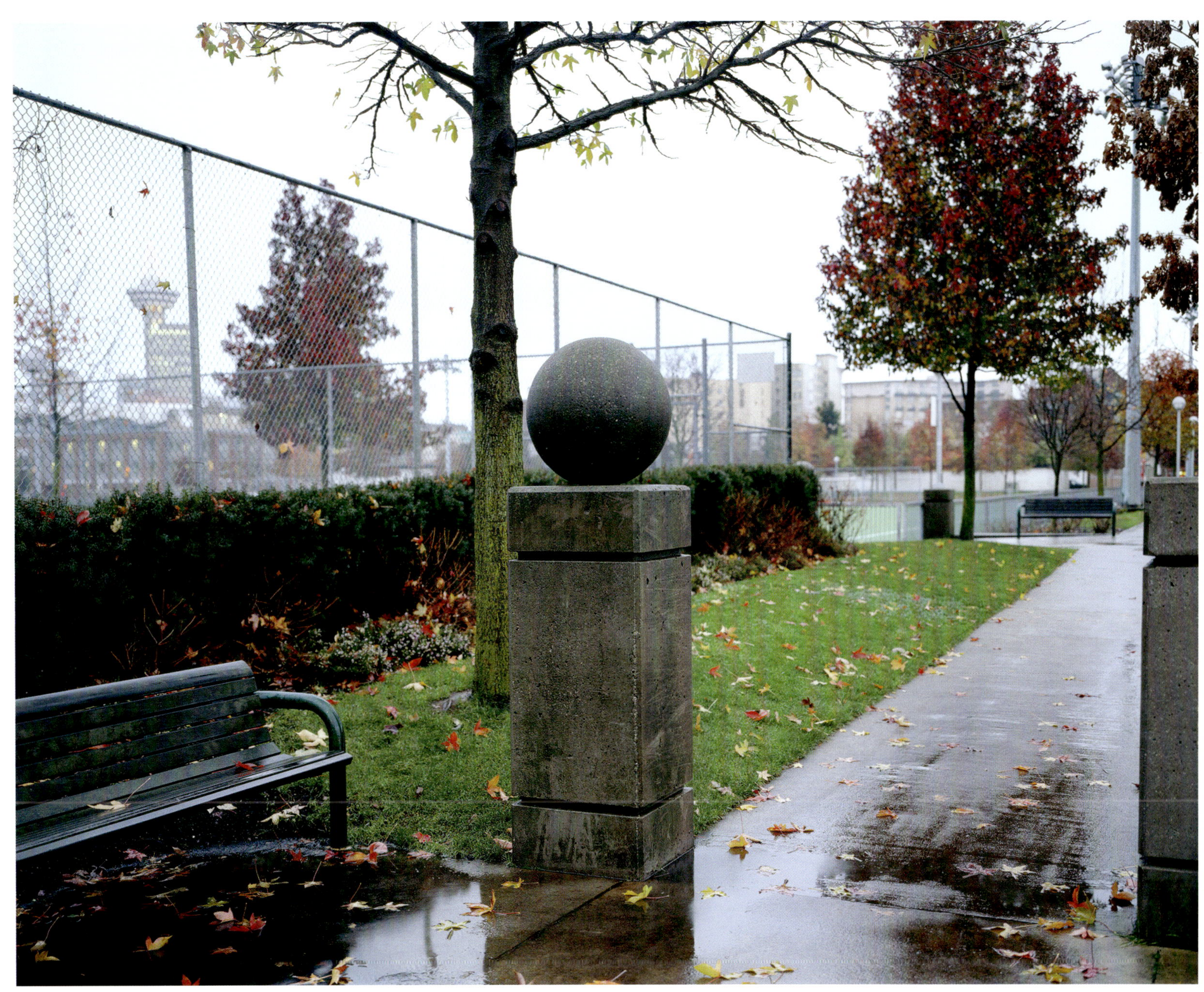

Jeff Wall   *Double Self-Portrait*, 1979; printed 2012

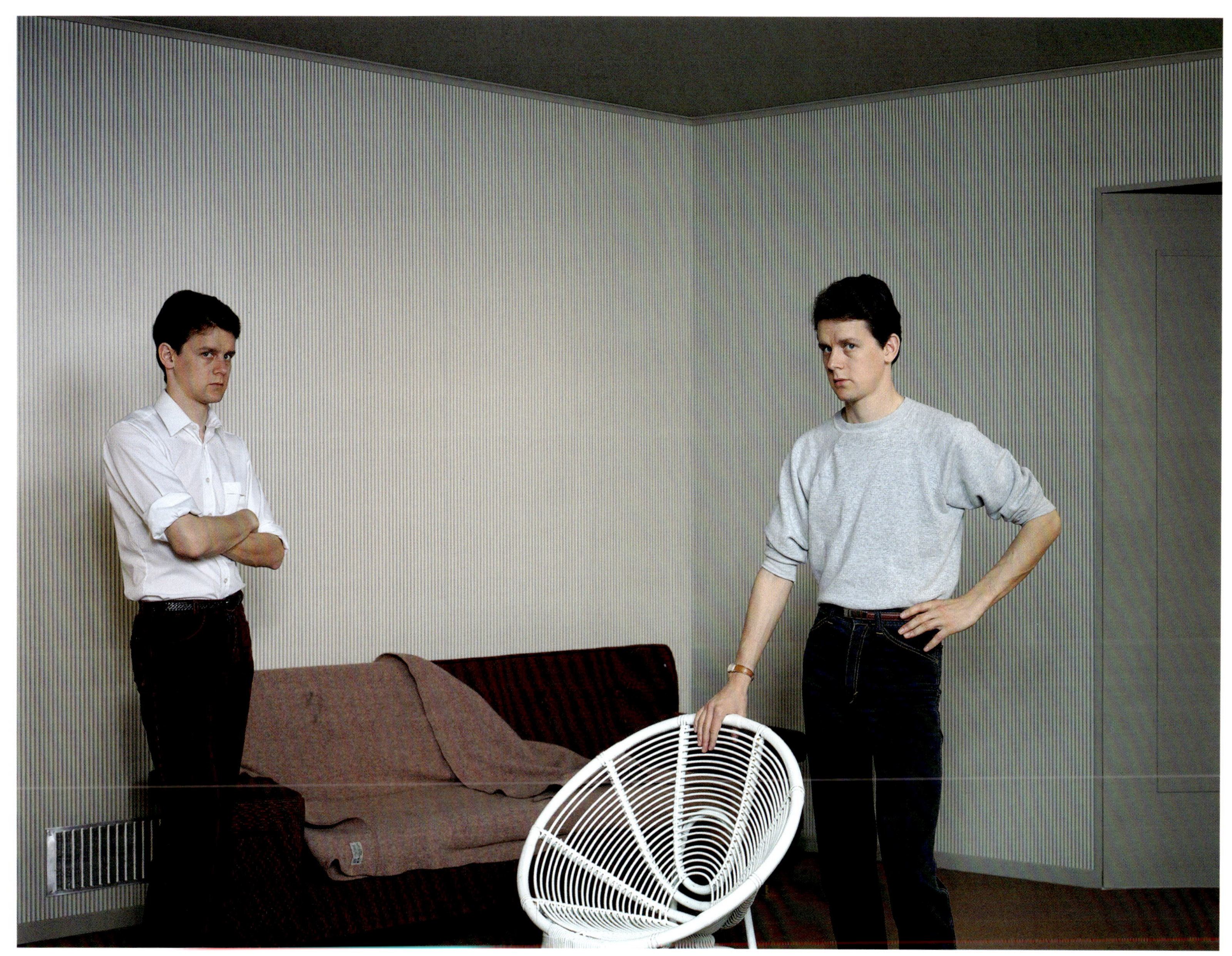

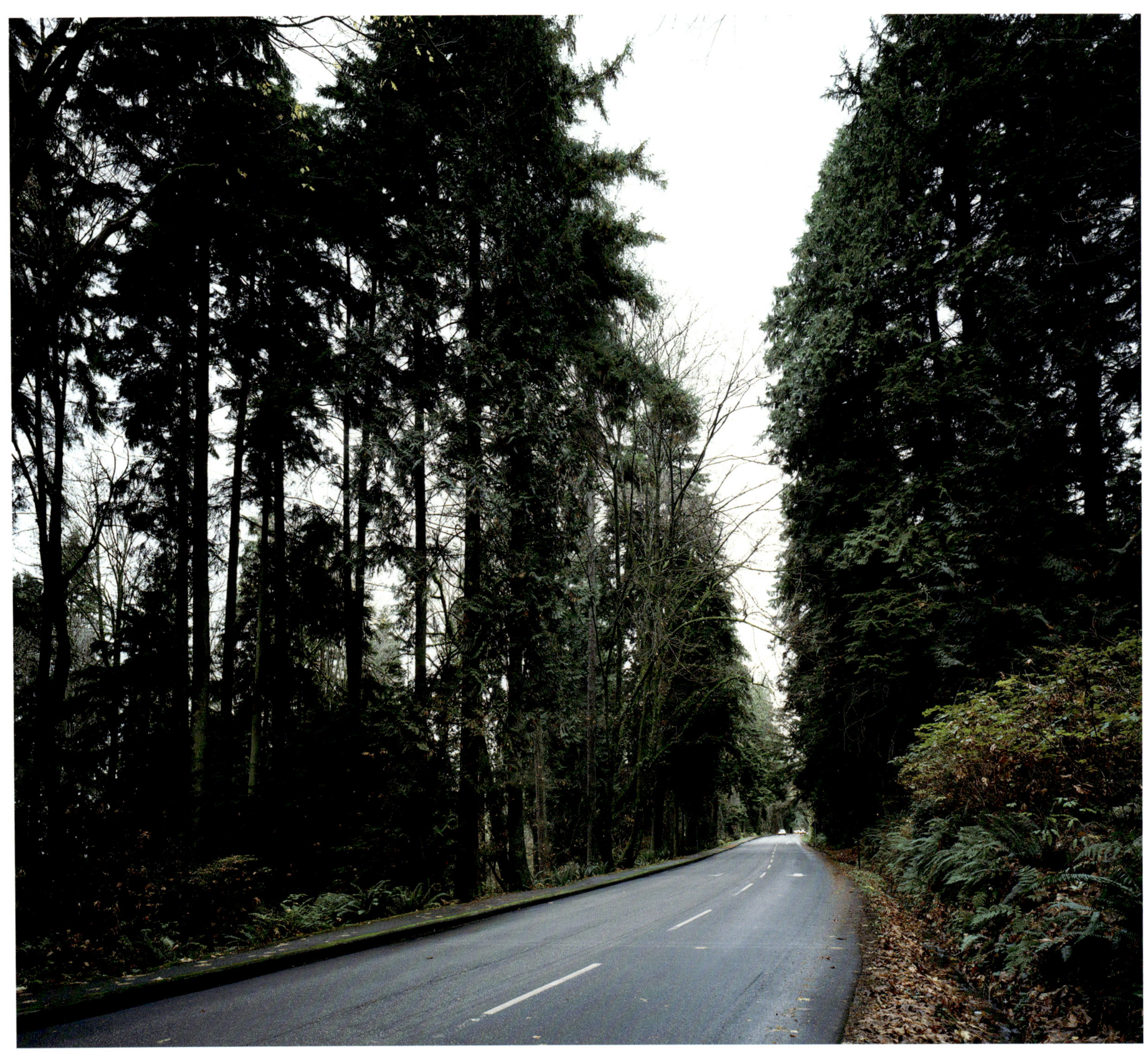

Jeff Wall *Park Drive,* 1994; printed 2014

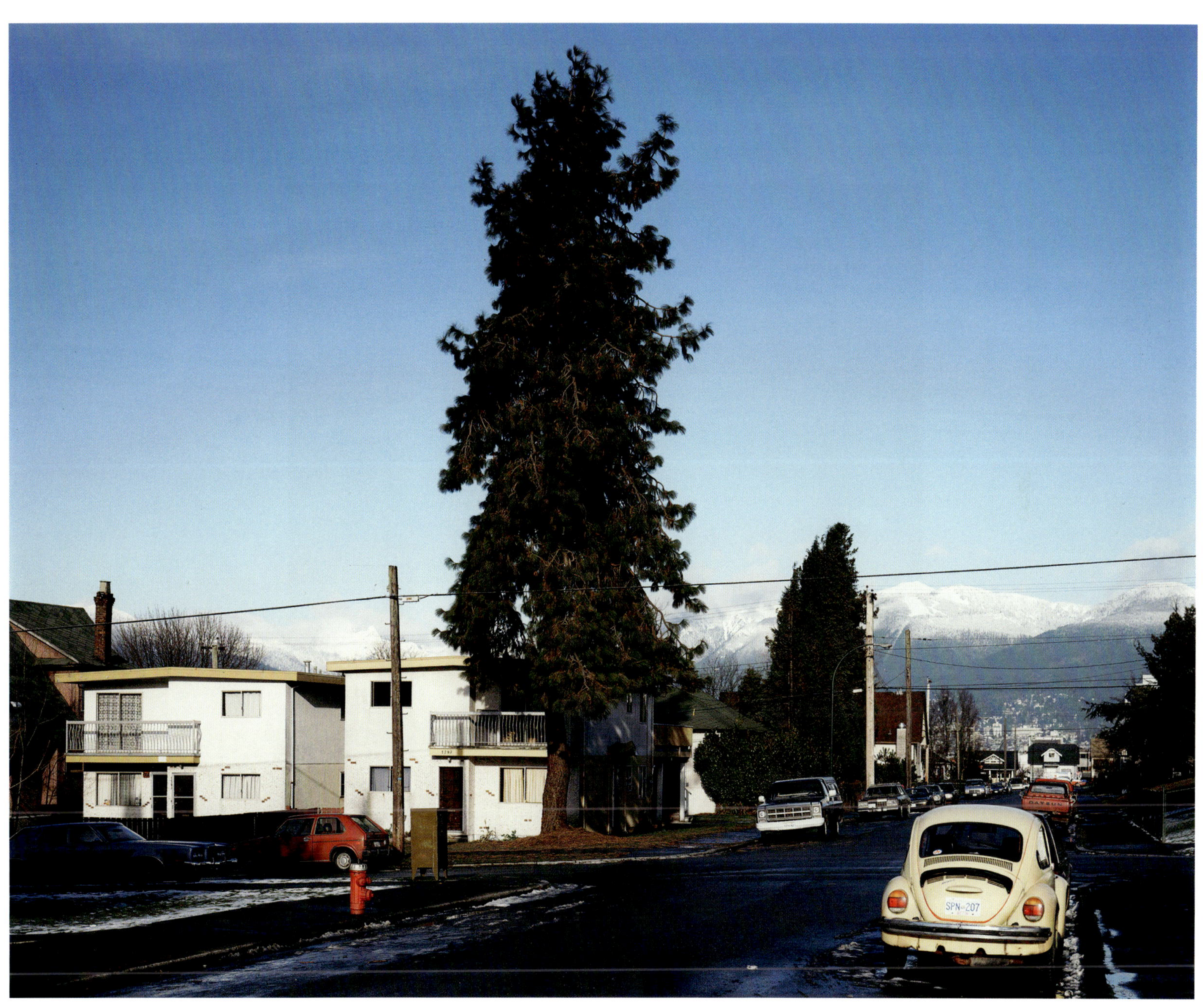

Jeff Wall *The Pine on the Corner,* 1990; printed 2016

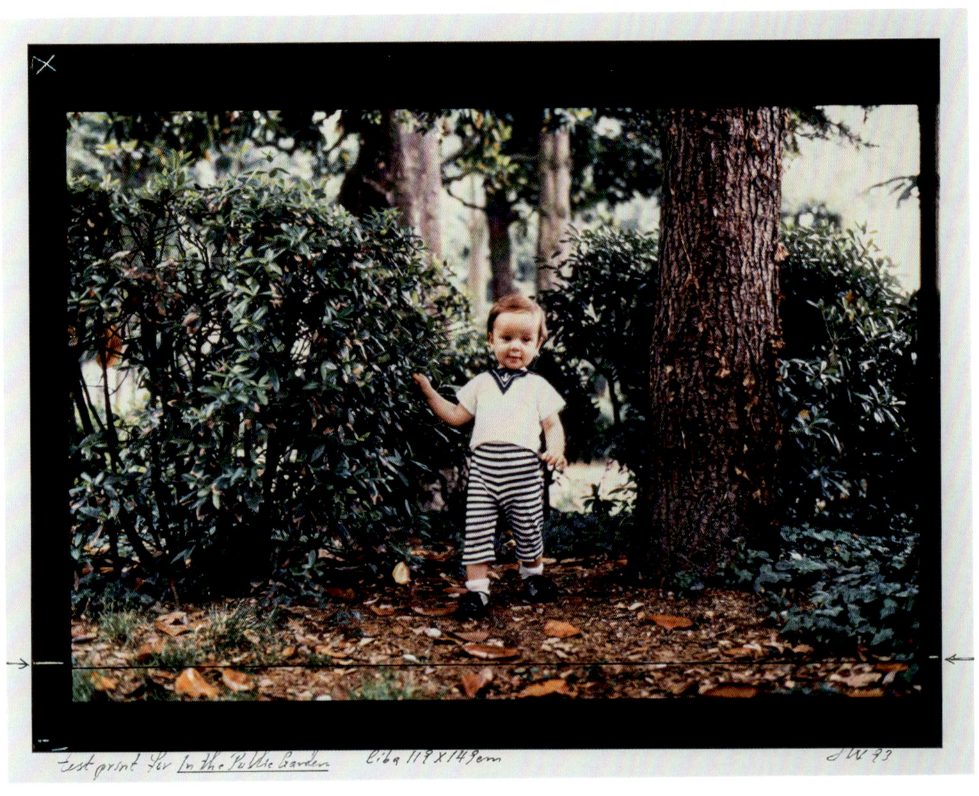

Jeff Wall   Test print for *In the Public Garden,* 1993

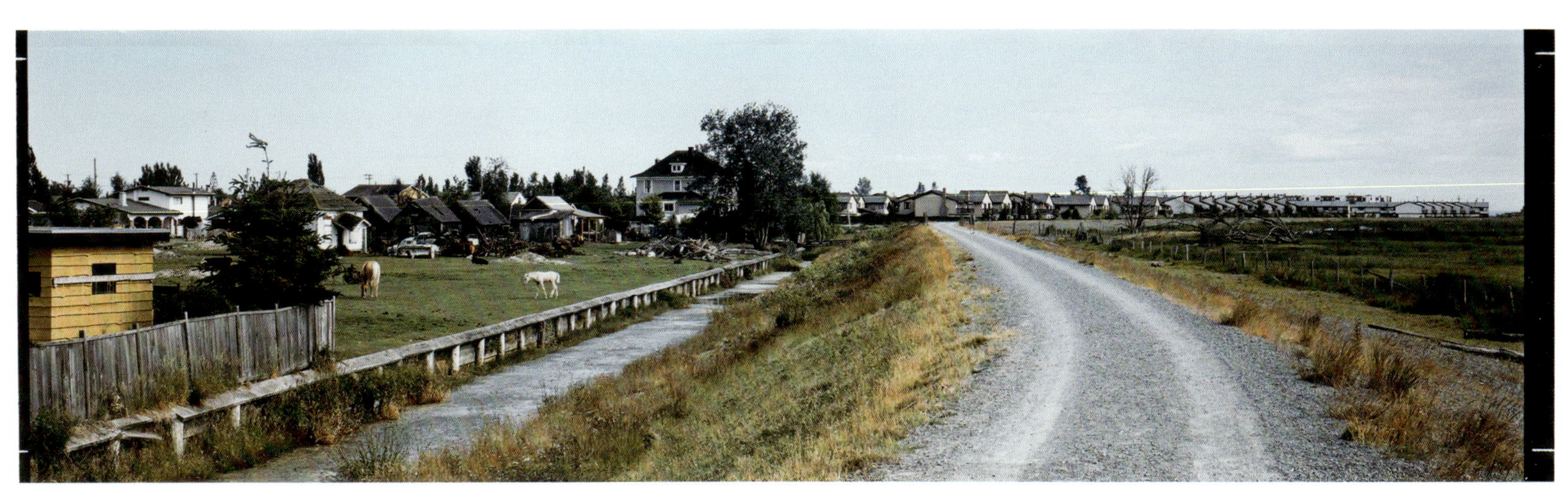

Jeff Wall *Steves Farm, Steveston,* 1980; printed 1988

Rodney Graham *Cedars, Stanley Park, #7*, 1991–1993

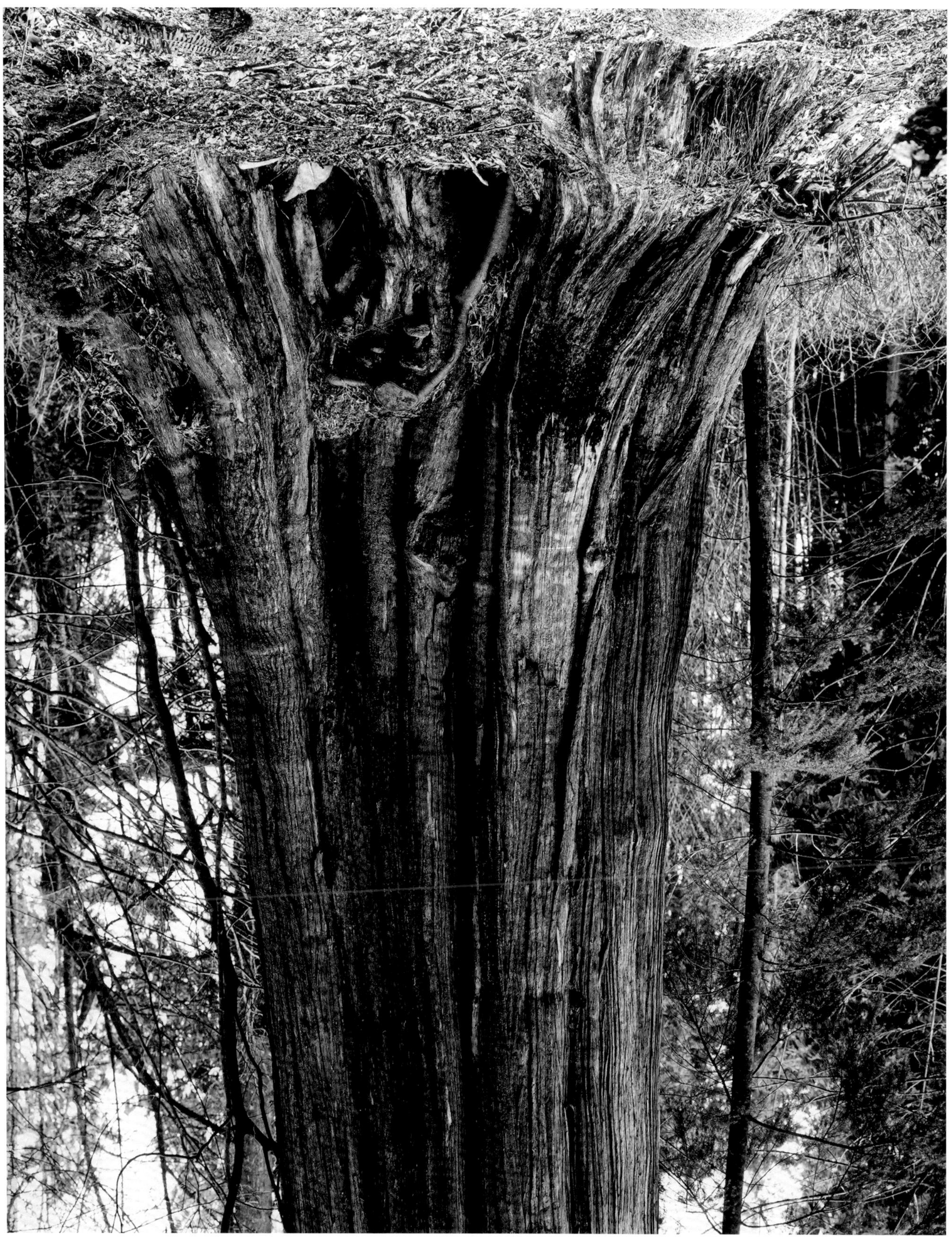

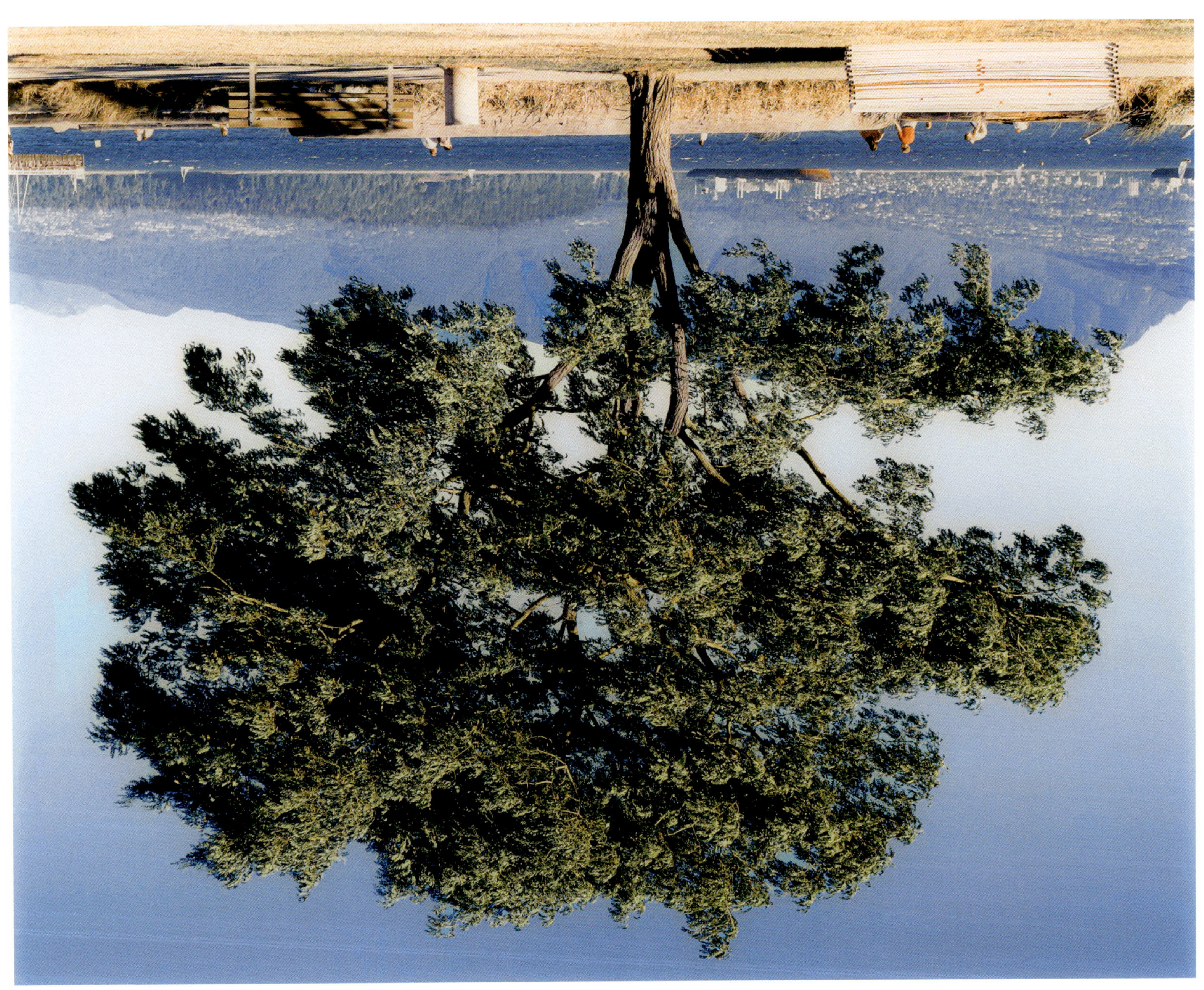

Rodney Graham *Tree with Bench, Vancouver, B.C., 1996*

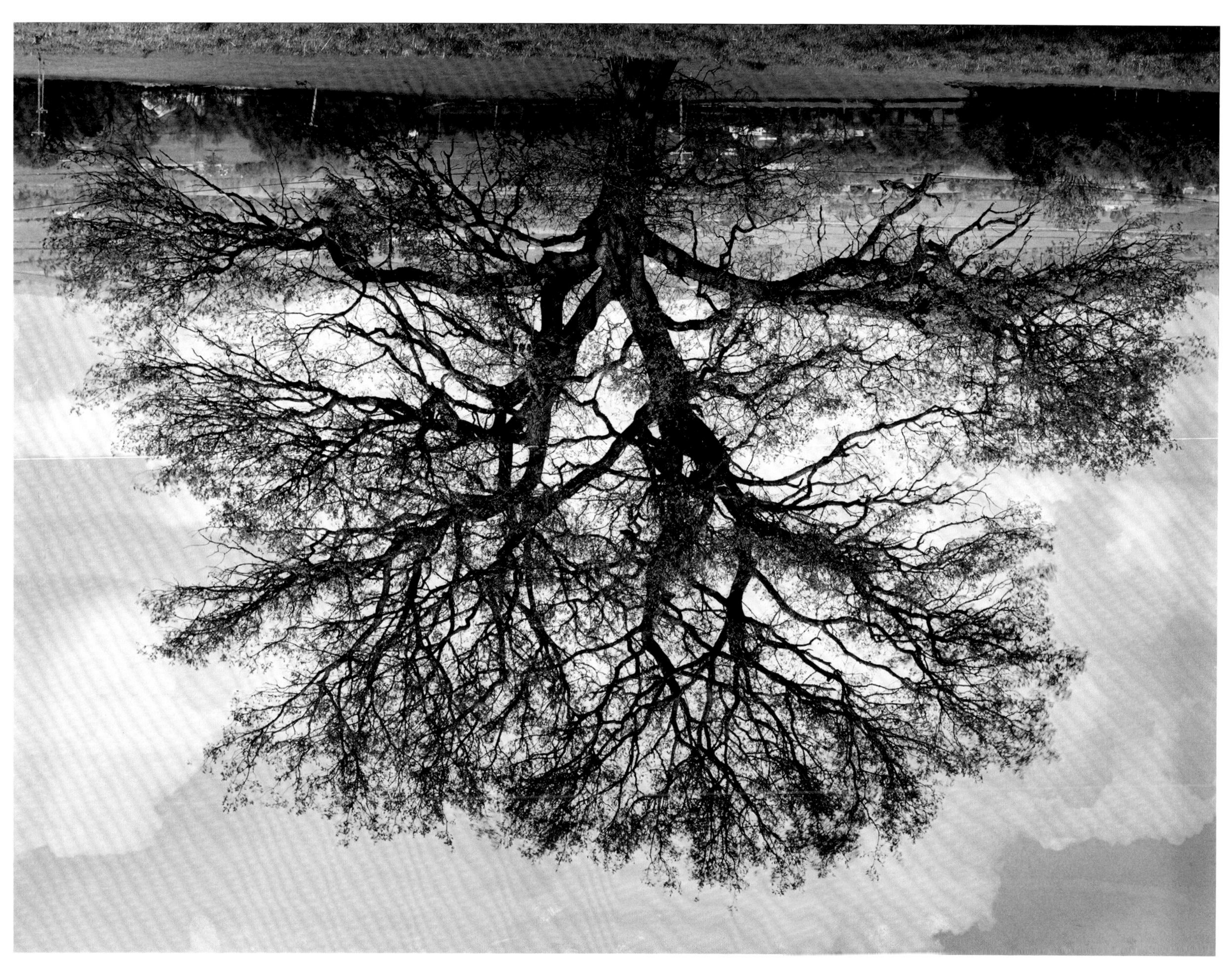

Rodney Graham *Welsh Oaks #5*, 1998

When Rodney Graham (1949–2022) first started making photographs in the 1970s, he approached the task with a keen sense of the medium's history. Born in Vancouver, he studied at the University of British Columbia from 1968 to 1971 without taking a degree, but he remained a student of history, philosophy, and literature throughout his life. In 1979 Graham built a room-sized structure on his uncle's farm in Abbotsford, British Columbia. *Camera Obscura* (1979) functioned as a viewing chamber for an oak tree on the property. Graham's photographs of inverted trees—*Cedars, Stanley Park, #7* (1991–1993), *Tree with Bench, Vancouver, B.C.* (1996), and *Welsh Oaks #5* (1998) are all examples—allude to the inversion that takes place in these chambers.

Beginning in the late 1990s, and especially toward the end of his life, a playful irreverence entered his work—namely in his constructed photographs where he performed as an invented persona. *Fishing on a Jetty* (2000) restages a crucial scene from Alfred Hitchcock's *To Catch a Thief* (1955), with Graham standing in as John Robie (played by Cary Grant) and Vancouver for Nice, France. Grant plays a burglar eluding police by disguising himself as a fisherman. "The shot is a typical Hitchcock joke," Graham said. "Taken out of context it appears as if Robie is facing the wrong way, because the water is behind him."[1] Conceived as a pendant to this photograph, Graham's *Can of Worms* (2000) is the artist's first lightbox. It serves as a mischievous allusion to the lightbox format used by fellow Vancouver artist Jeff Wall since 1977. In Graham's work, the modest image is made absurd by the unnecessarily long, coiled electric cord—itself a reference to a fishing line or coil of rope seen on a dock. Excised from the diptych, the rusted-out paint can becomes a still life.

Rodney Graham *Can of Worms*, 2000

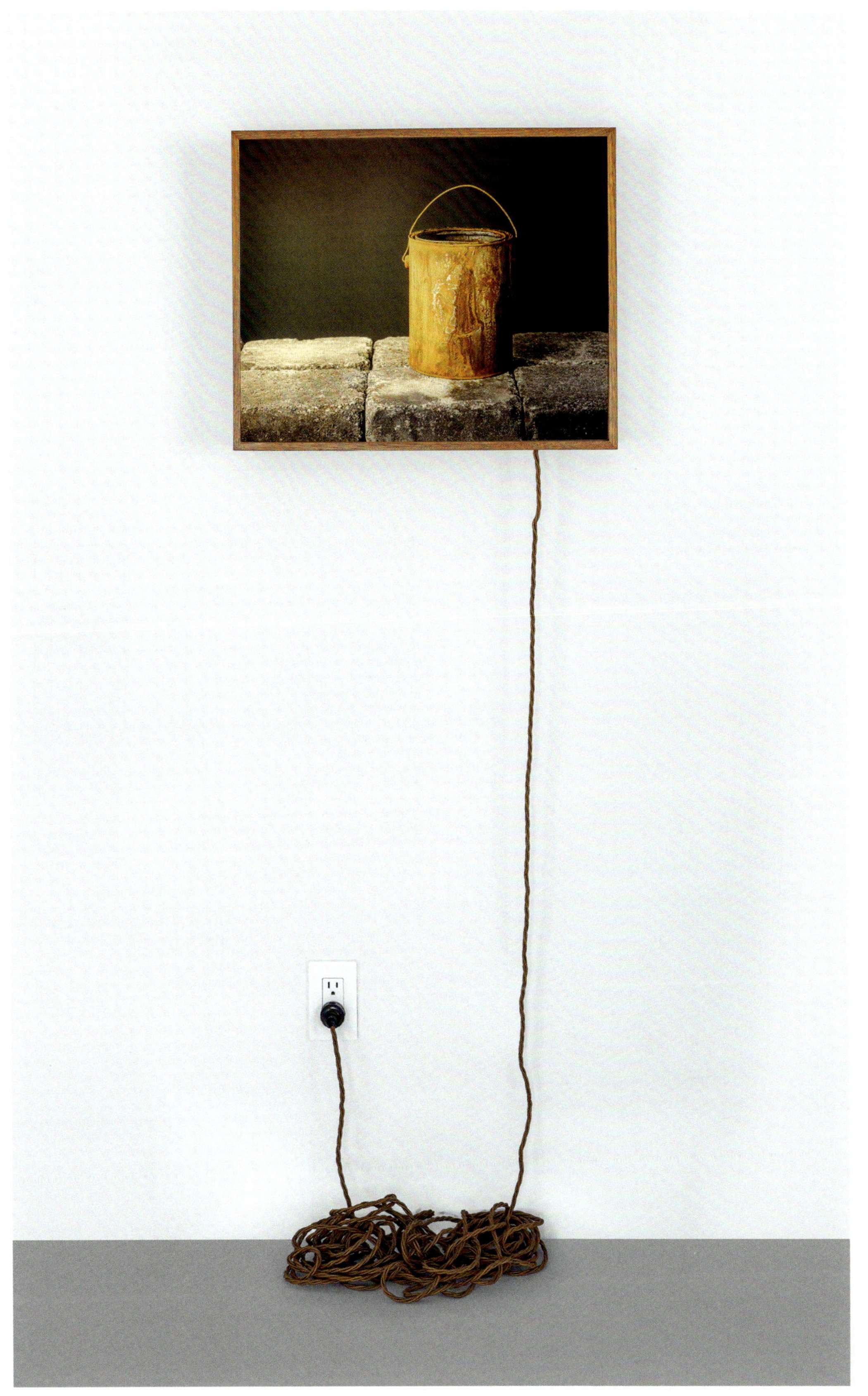

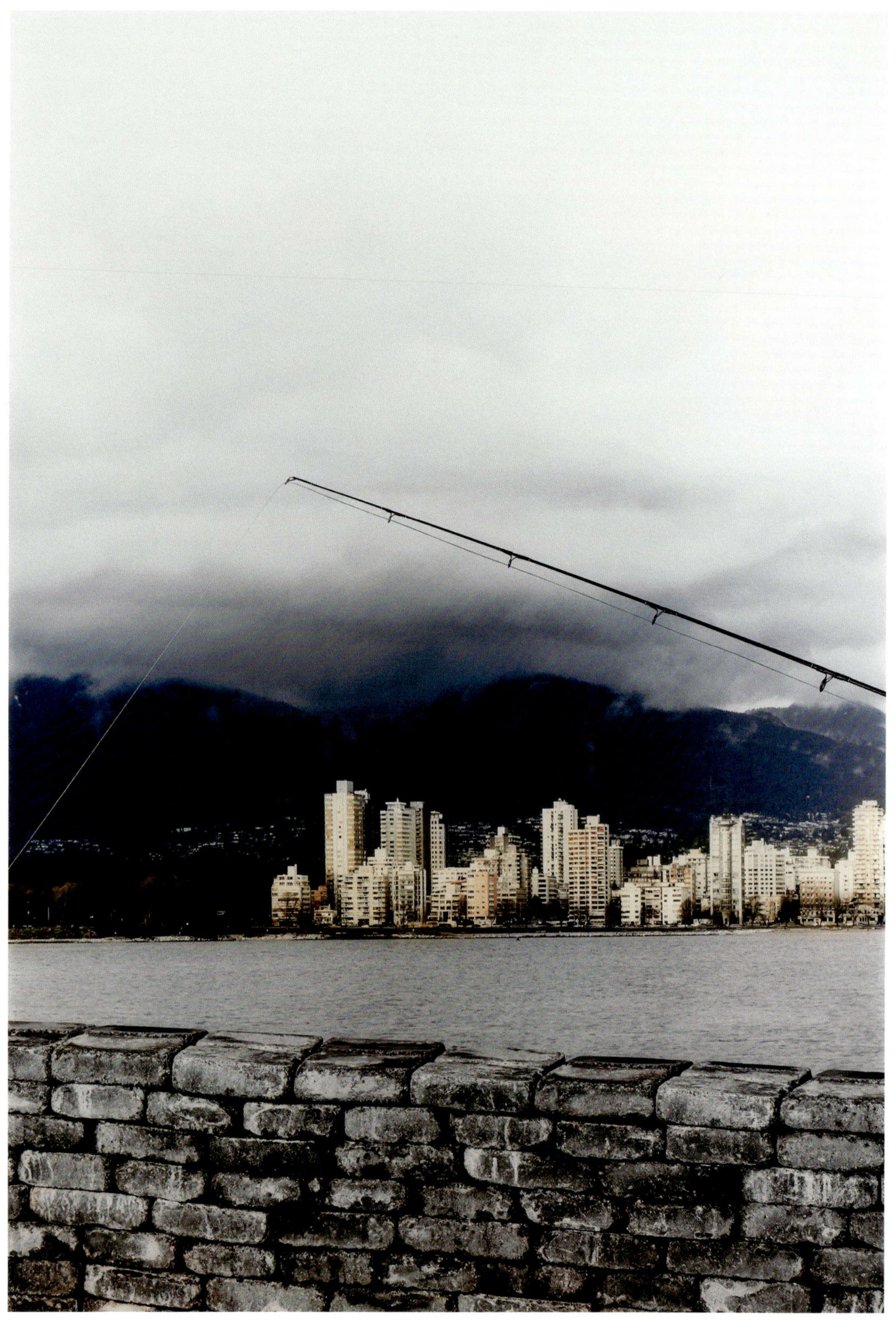

Rodney Graham *Fishing on a Jetty,* 2000

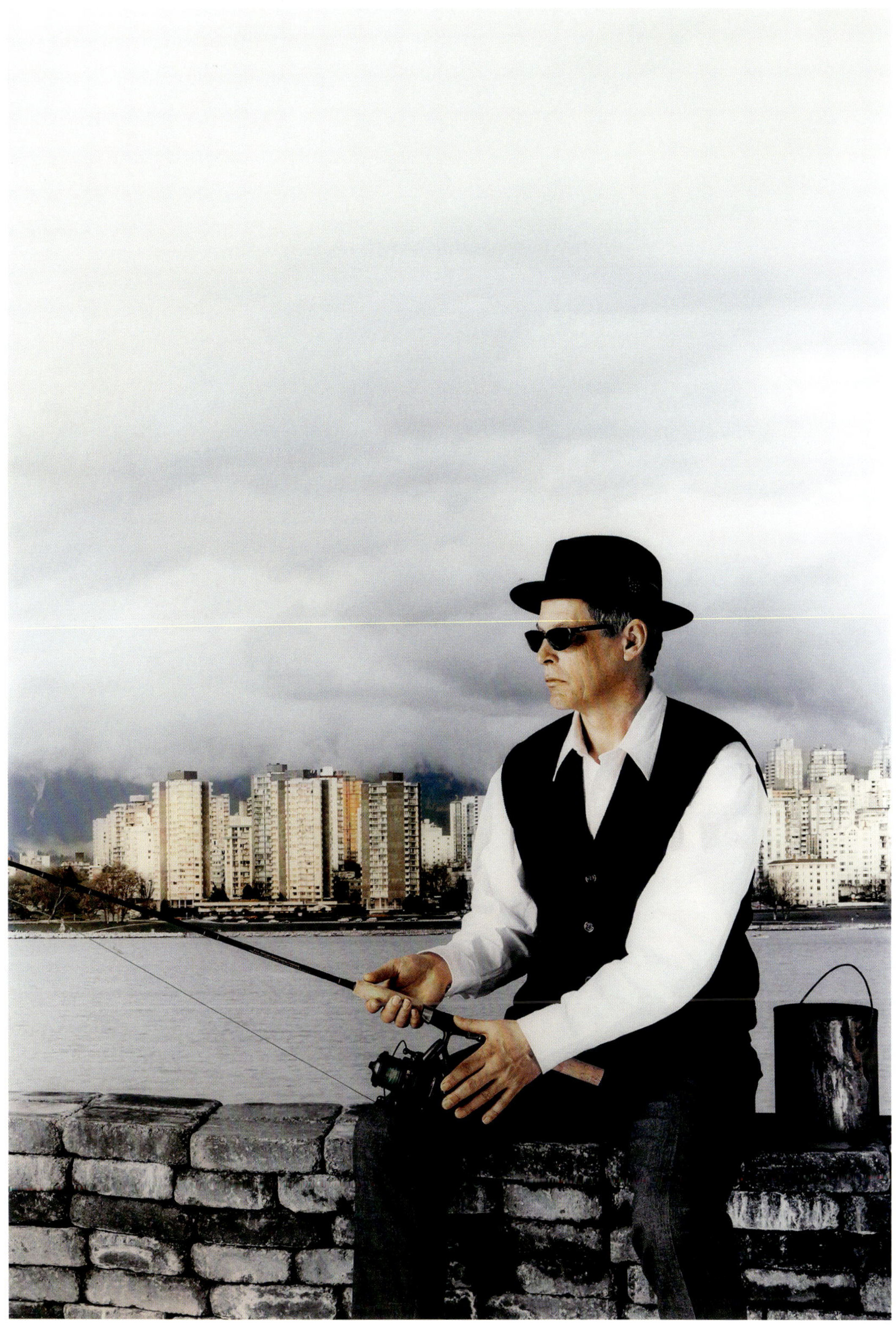

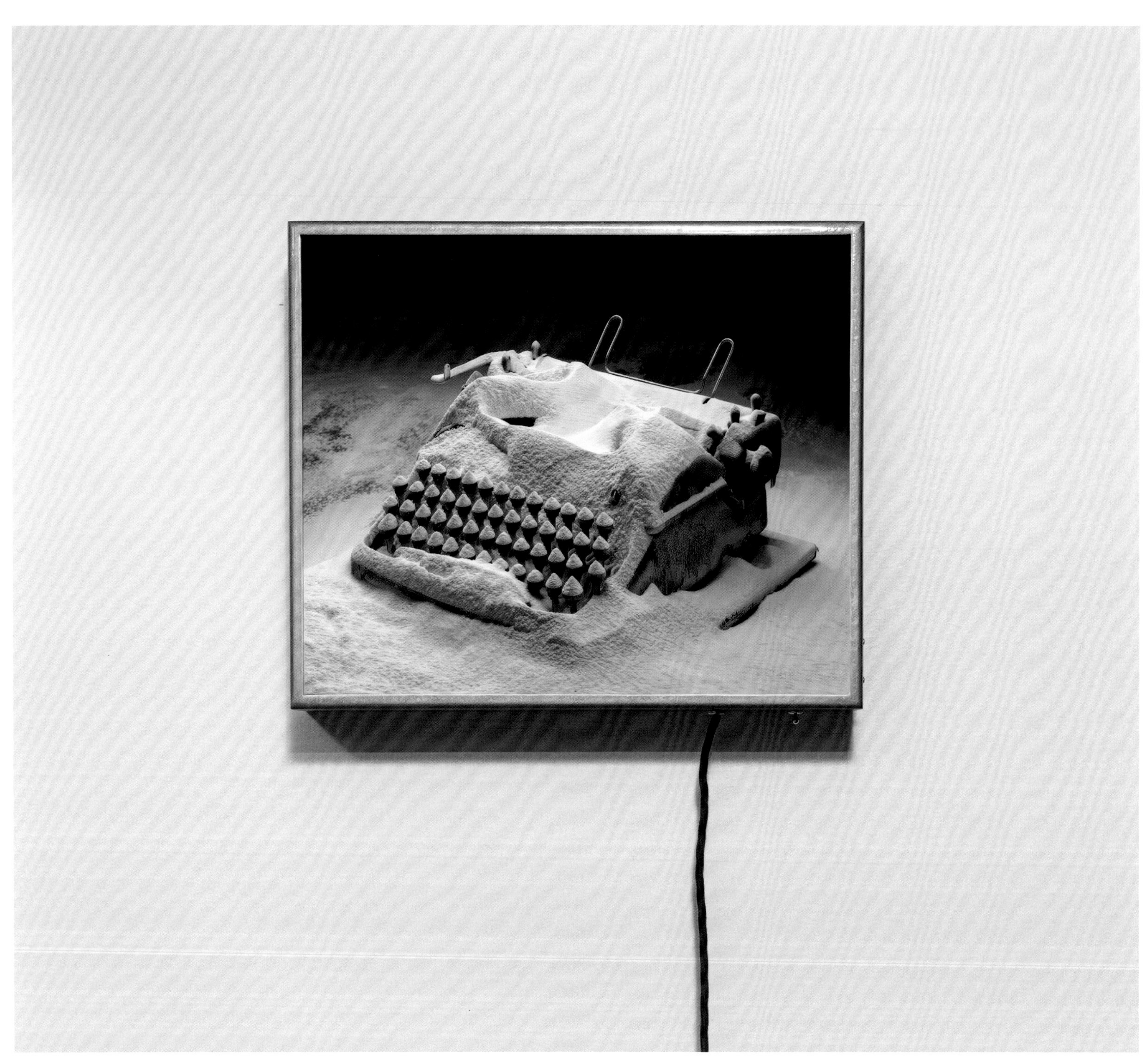

Rodney Graham *Typewriter with Flour,* 2003

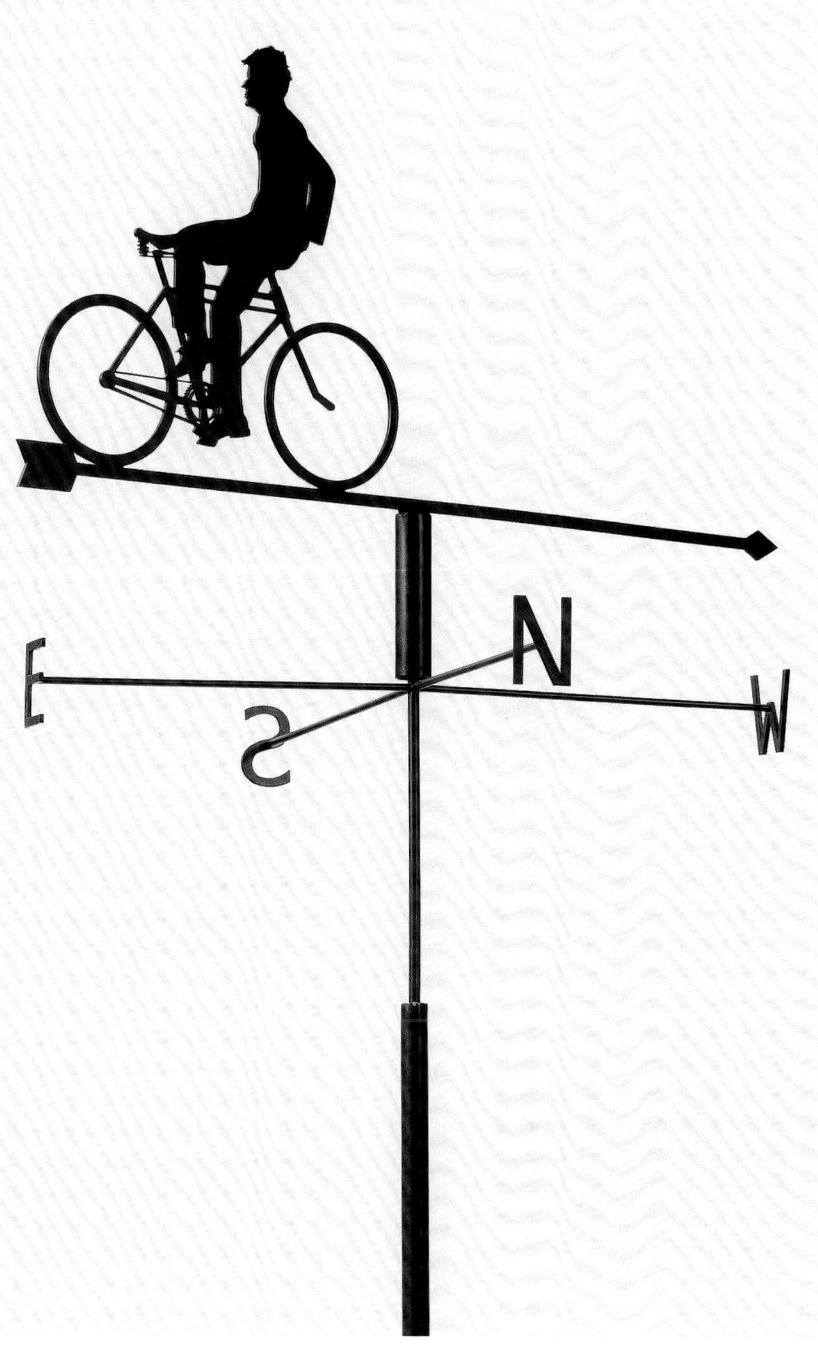

Rodney Graham *Weathervane*, 2002

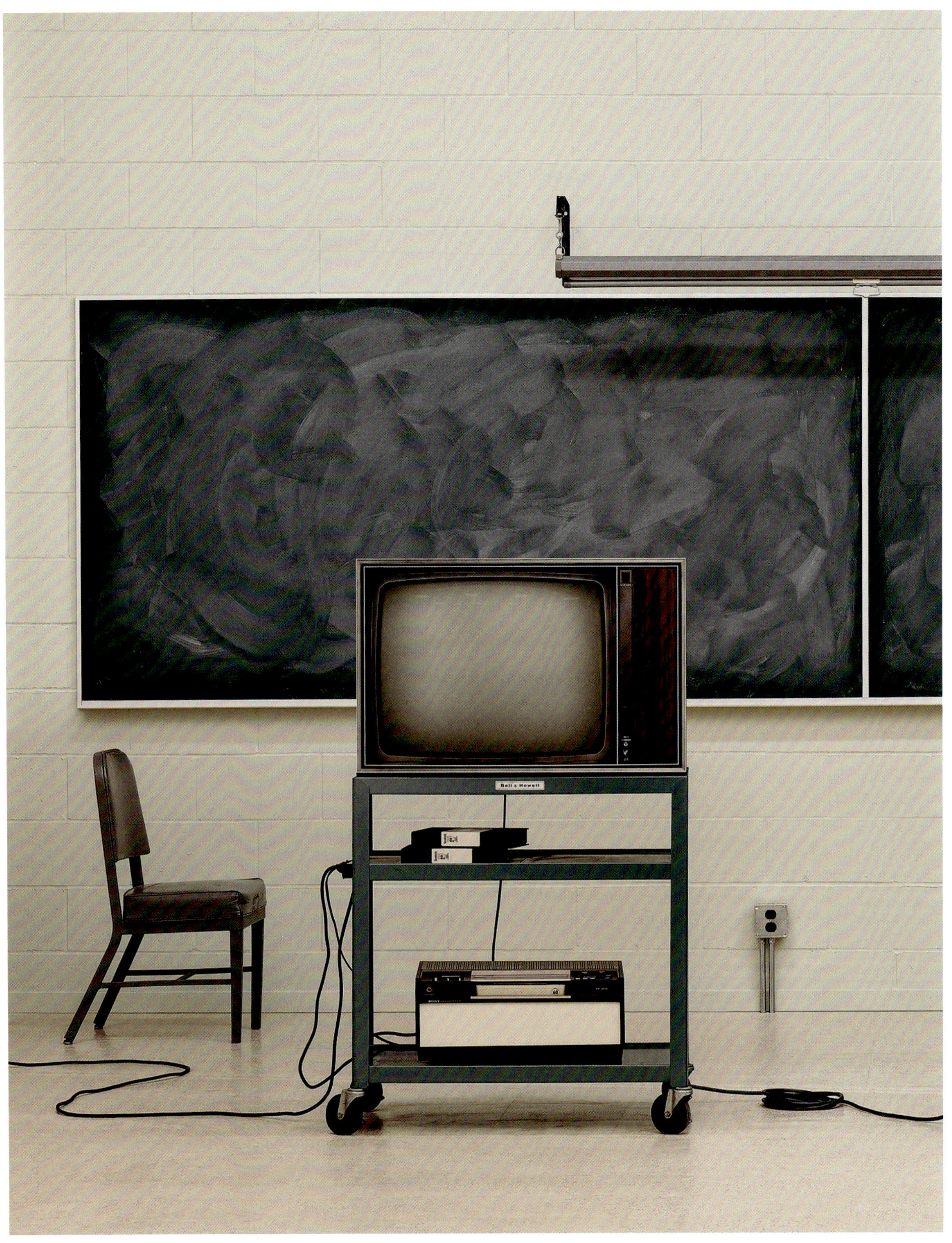

Rodney Graham *Media Studies '77*, 2016

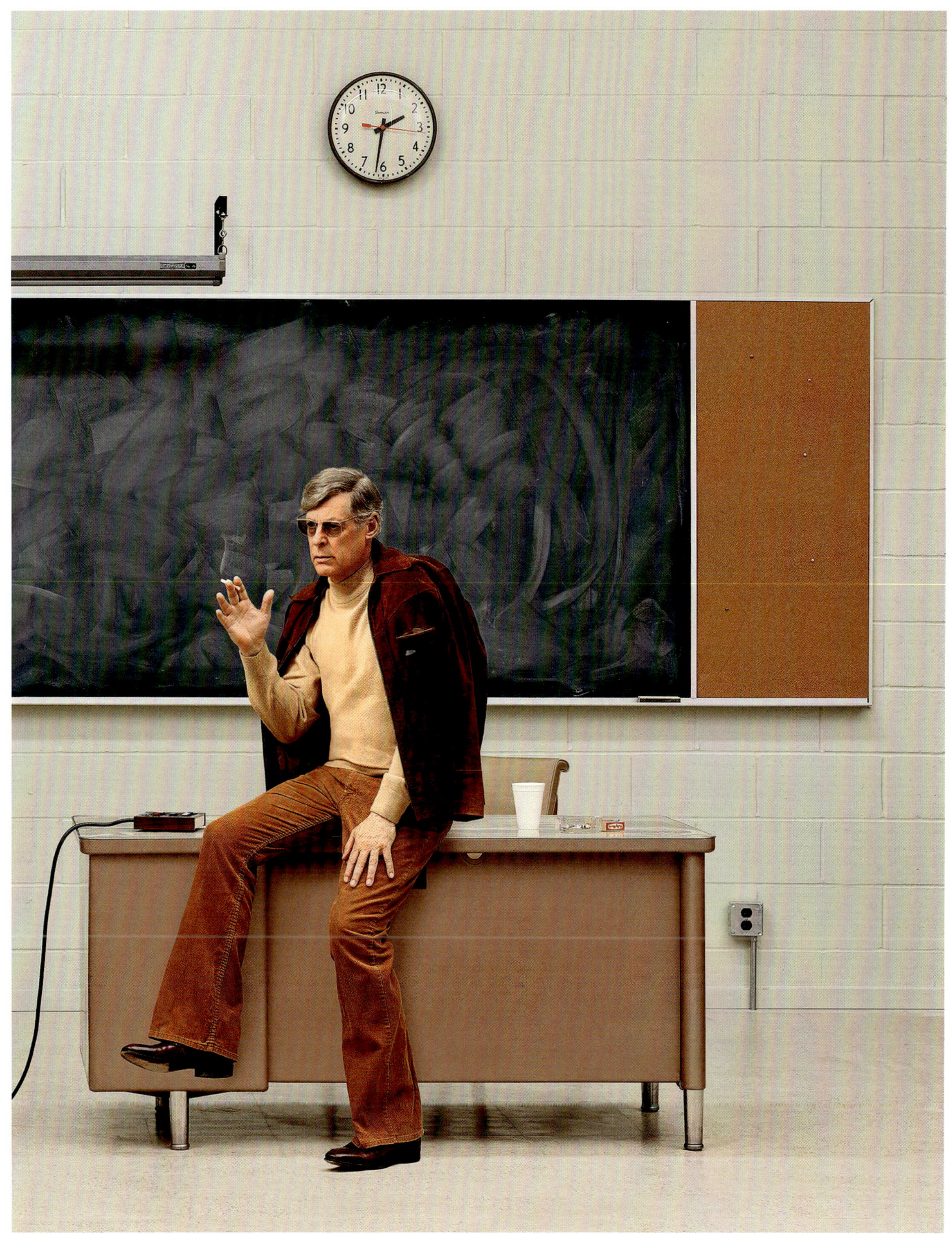

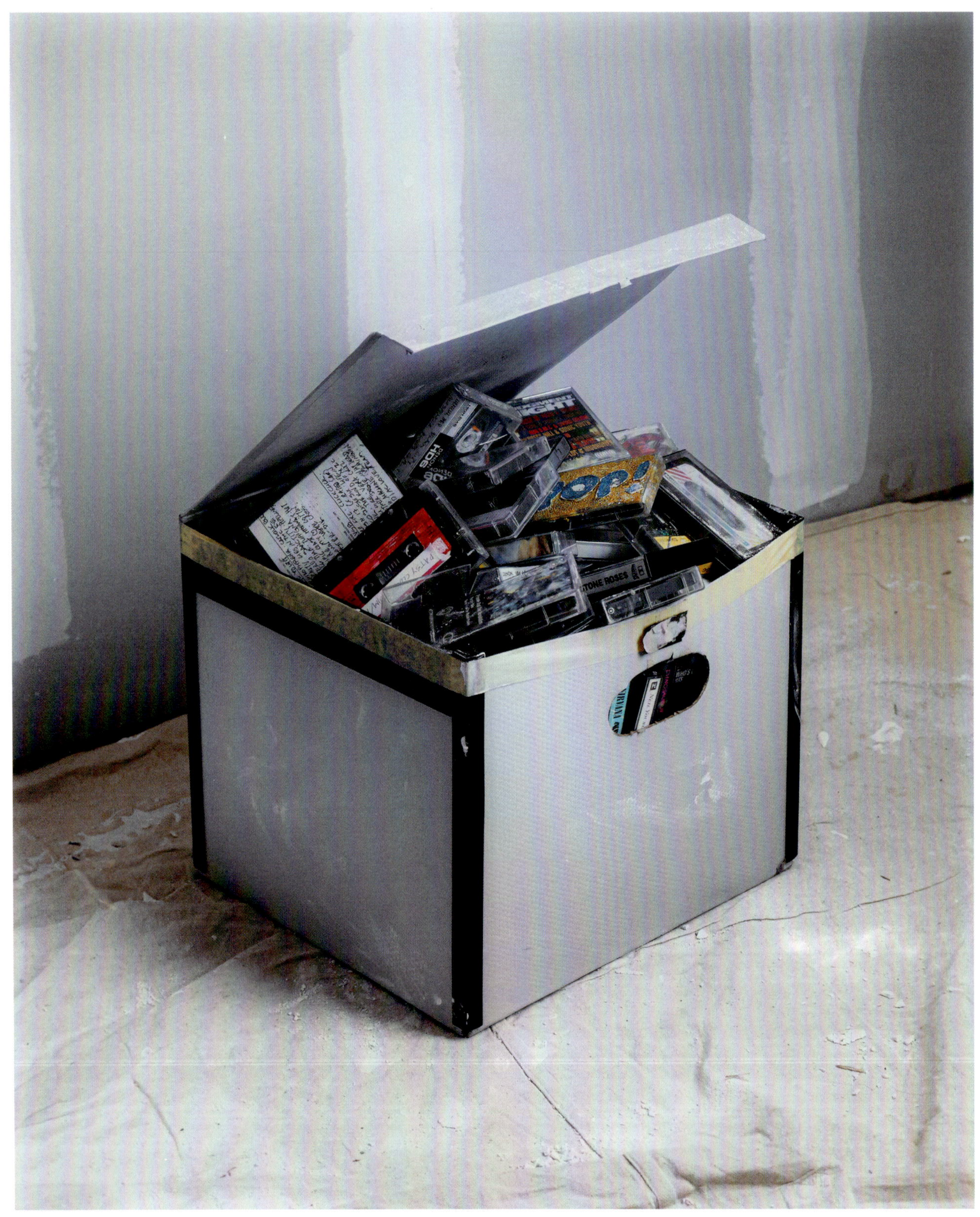

Rodney Graham *Studies for Smoke Break 2 (Plaster): Box of Tapes*, 2012

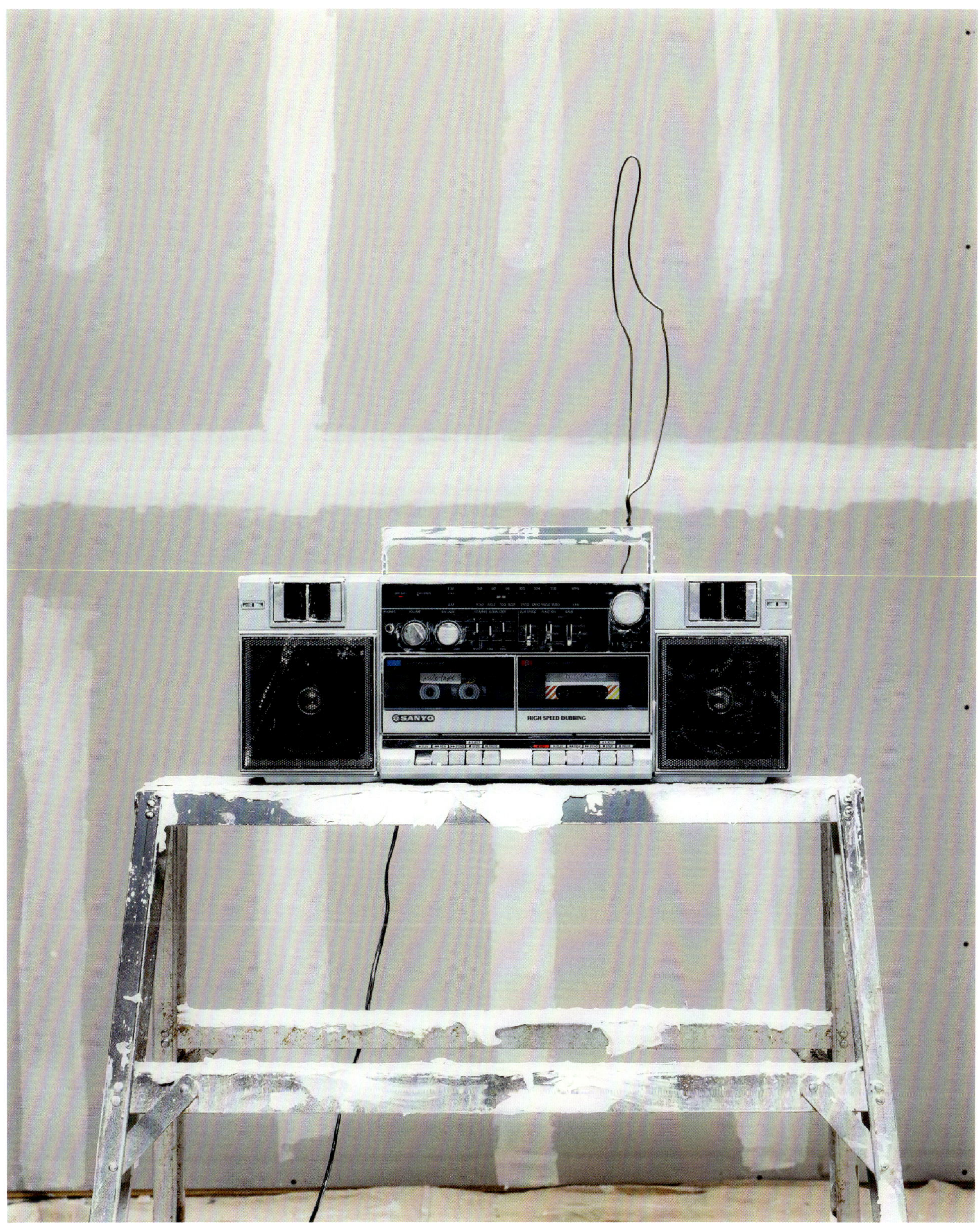

Rodney Graham *Studies for Smoke Break 2 (Plaster): Boombox*, 2012

Christopher Williams
180HR15 Michelin XAS
Manufactured by: Tigar Tyres d.o.o., Pirot, Serbia, Est. 1935
Parent Company: SCA Compagnie Générale des
Établissements Michelin, Clermont-Ferrand, France, Est. 1889
Studio Rhein Verlag, Düsseldorf February 22, 2016, 2016

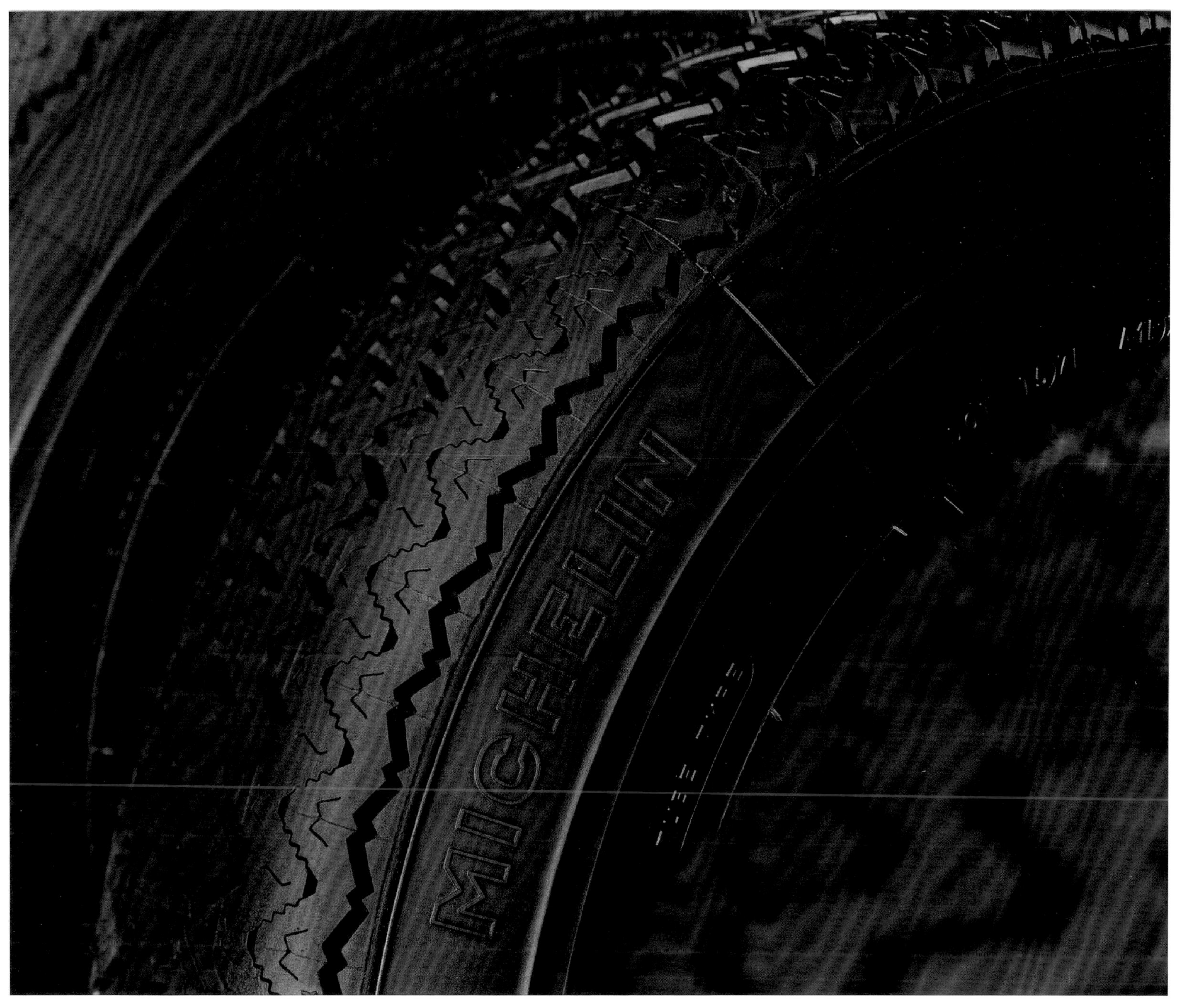
MICHELIN

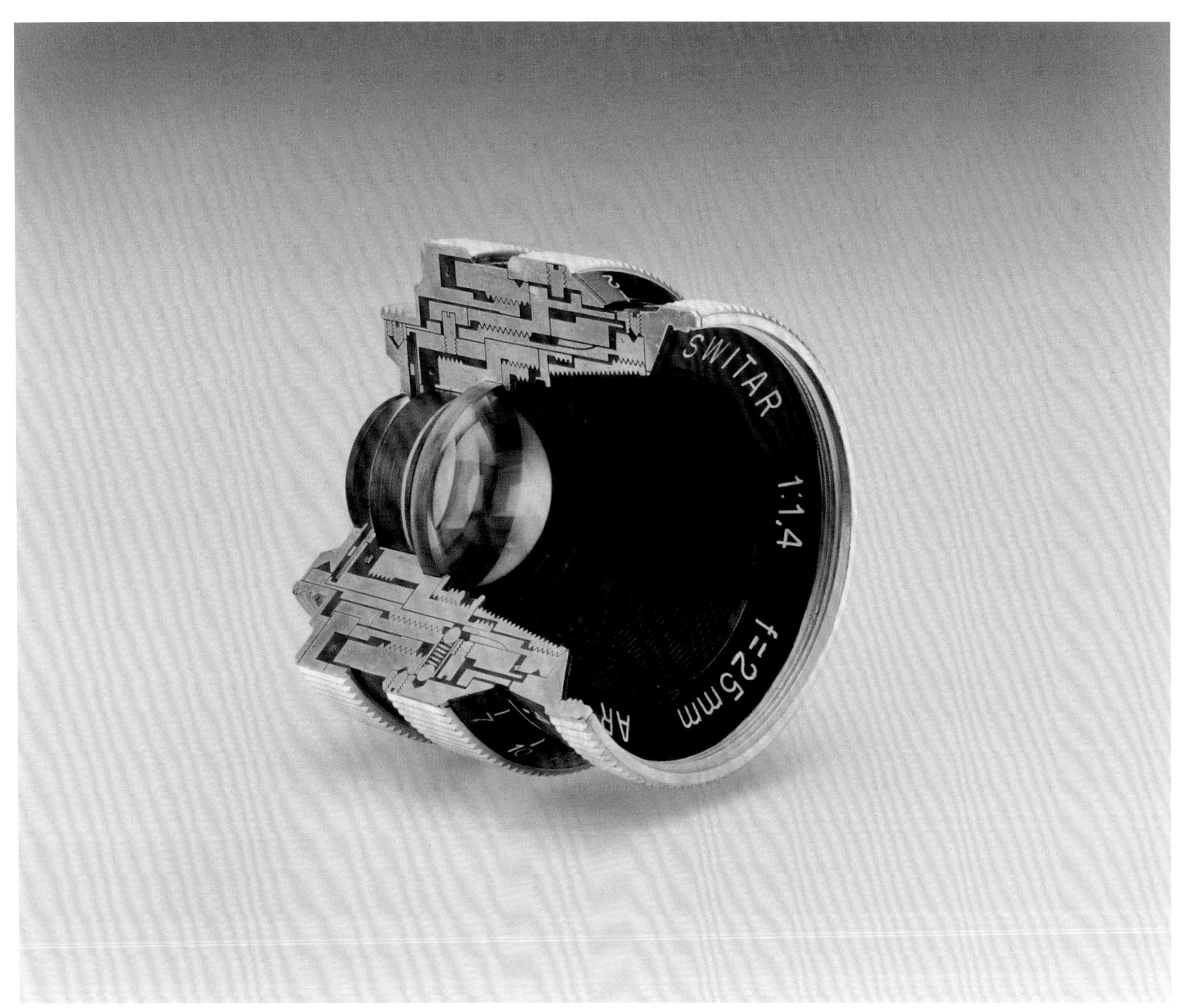

Christopher Williams
Cutaway model Switar 25mm f1.4 AR.
Glass, wood and brass.
Photography by the Douglas M. Parker Studio, Glendale, California,
November 17, 2007–November 30, 2007, 2008

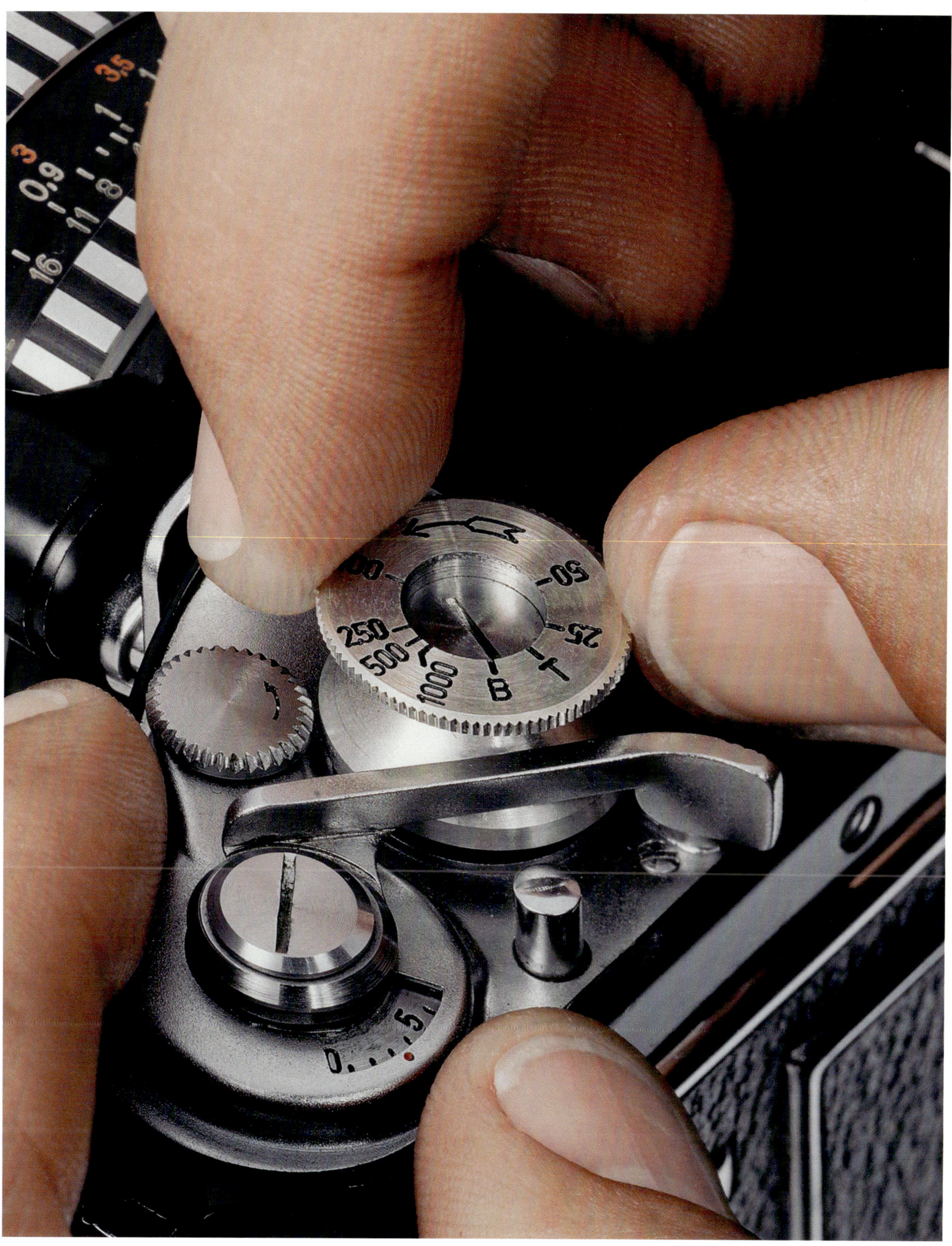
3,5
3
0,9
1
16
11
8
250
500
1000
B
T
25
50

PREVIOUS PAGE

Christopher Williams

Fig. 4: Changing the shutter speed Exakta Varex IIa 35 mm film SLR camera
Manufactured by Ihagee Kamerawerk Steenbergen & Co, Dresden, German Democratic Republic Body serial no. 979625 (Production period: 1960–1963)
Carl Zeiss Jena Tessar 50mm f/2.8 lens Manufactured by VEB Carl Zeiss Jena, Jena, German Democratic Republic Serial no. 8034351 (Production period: 1967–1970)
Model: Christoph Boland Studio Thomas Borho, Oberkasseler Str. 39, Düsseldorf, Germany June 19, 2012, 2012

Thomas Ruff *jpeg gs02, 2007*

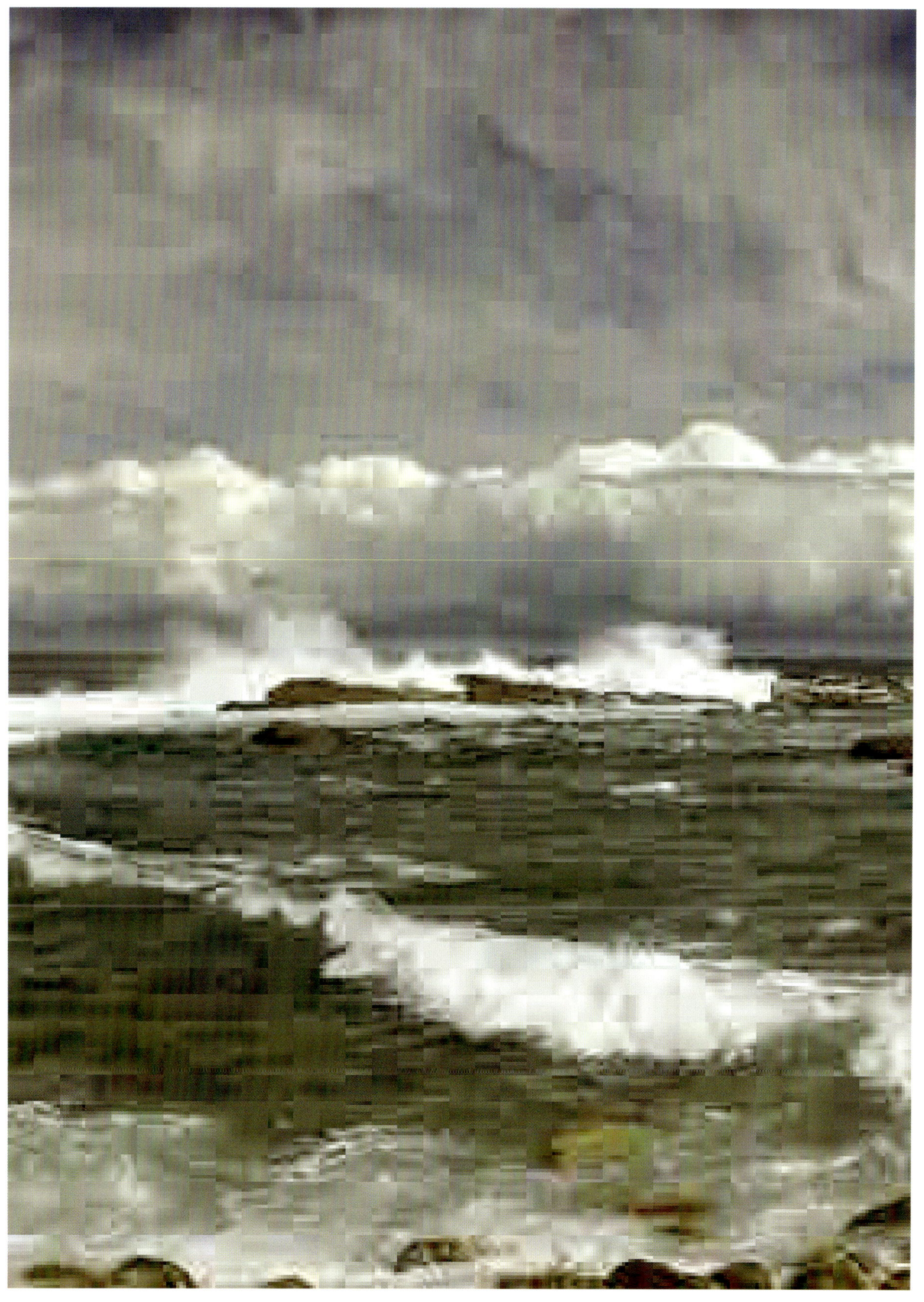

Andrew Dadson *White Tree*, 2017

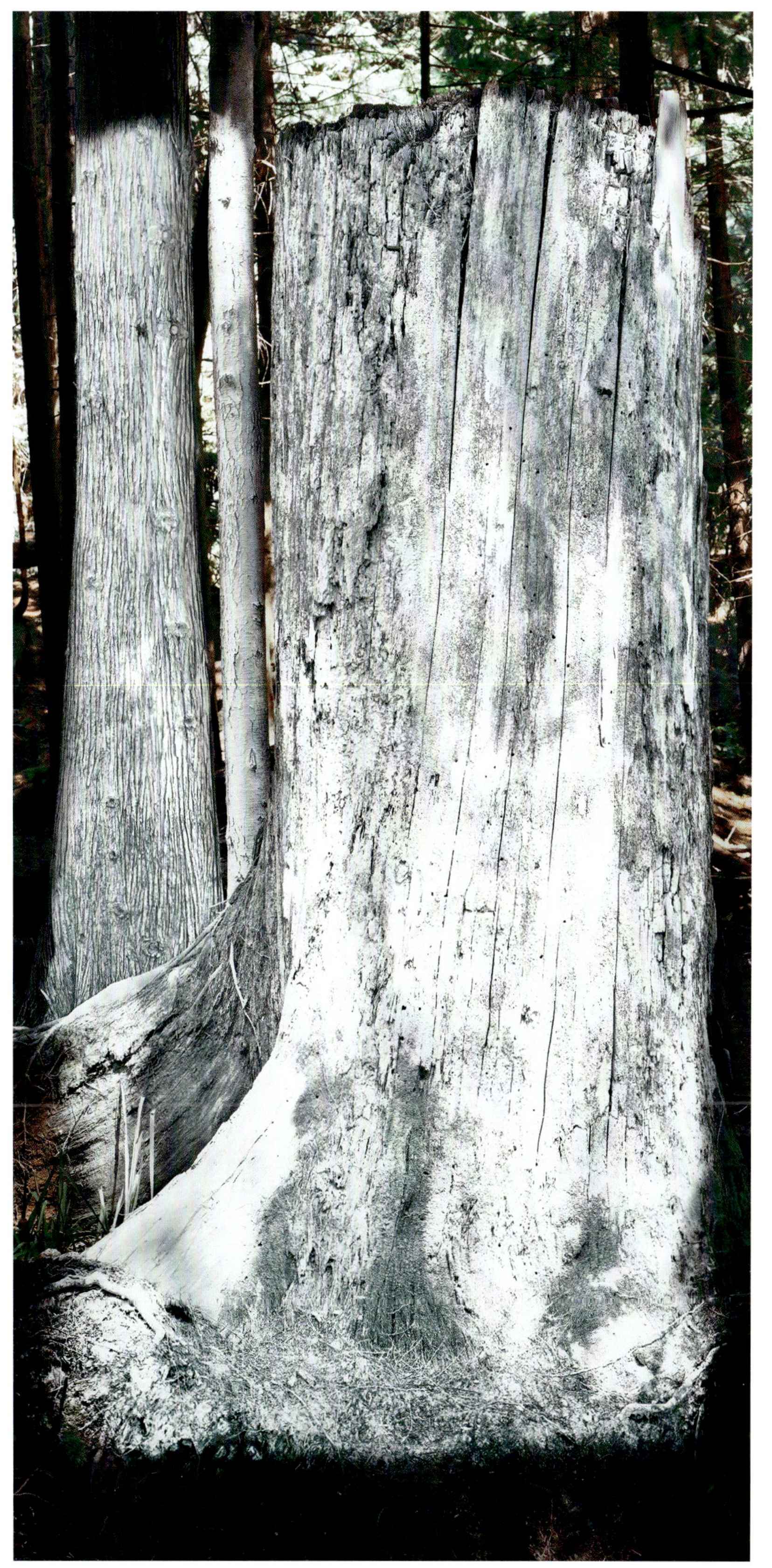

Born in Berkeley, California, John McCracken (1934–2011) first came to art-world prominence through the 1966 *Primary Structures* exhibition at the Jewish Museum in New York, organized by Kynaston McShine. His sculptures might be understood as a conflation of so-called minimal art associated with New York and what has been called the "finish fetish" of the West Coast. The latter was characterized by aerodynamic forms, pristine surfaces, and new materials—in part influenced by the local surfboard production and car customization scenes flourishing in Los Angeles at the time. McCracken made his sculptures by applying liquid layers of coloured polyester resin to hollow wooden forms. After each layer, he would sand and buff to achieve the illusion of a single colour permeating the surface of the form. "My works are minimal and reductive, but also maximal," McCracken suggested. "I try to make them concise, clear statements in three-dimensional form, and also to take them to a breathtaking level of beauty."[2]

McCracken was predisposed to what he called "single things": columns, blocks, and planks. These simple forms are coated in highly polished, saturated colour. Planks, such as *Hyko-Ra* (1987), are positioned so that they lean against the wall and rest on the floor at once, engaging with a signal preoccupation of so-called minimal sculptors of the period: the relationship of an object to an existing architectural space. McCracken's first solo exhibition at a museum was held at the AGO in 1969.

John McCracken *Hyko-Ra*, 1987

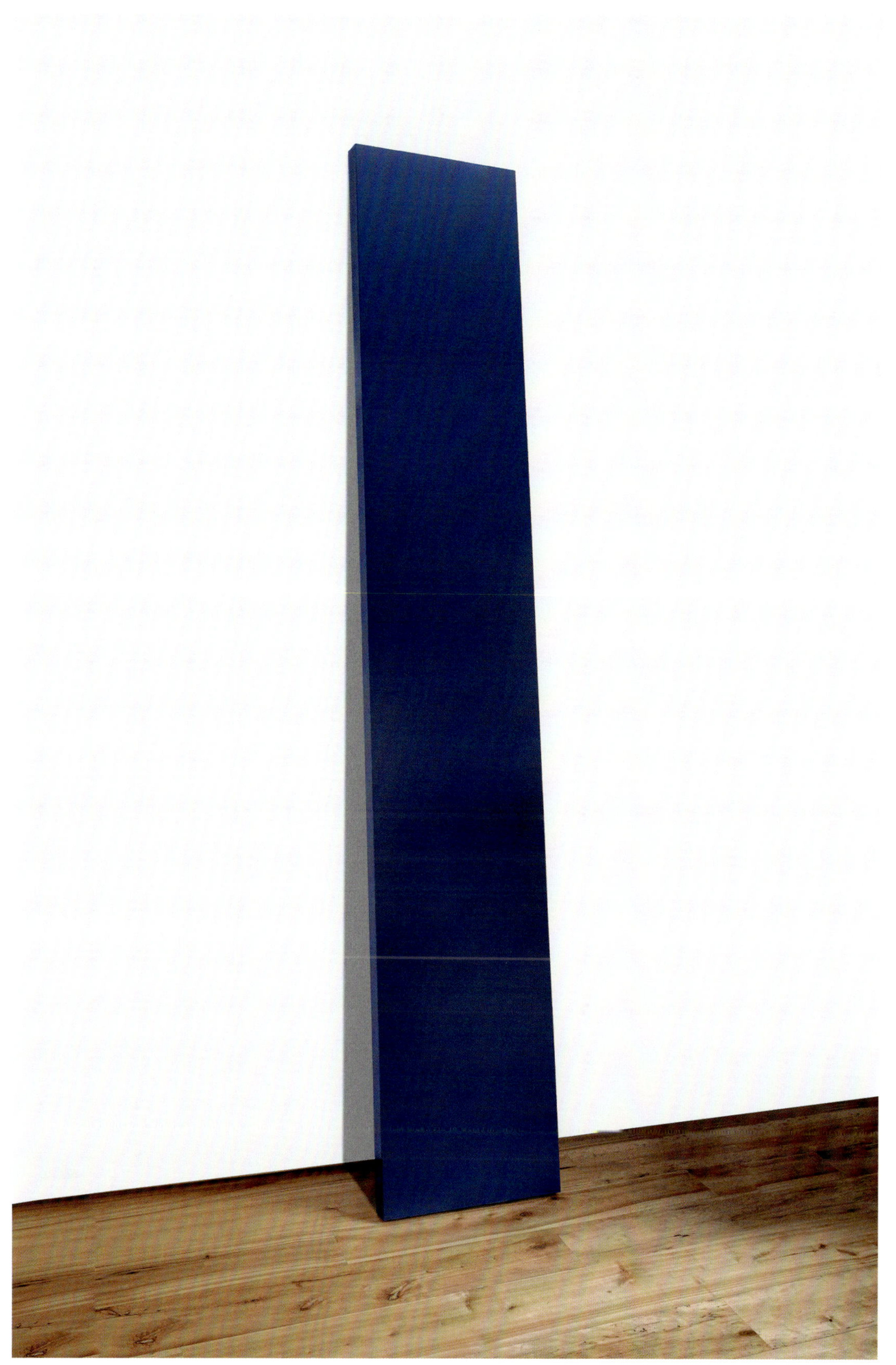

Thomas Demand *Brennerautobahn,* 1994; reprinted 2024

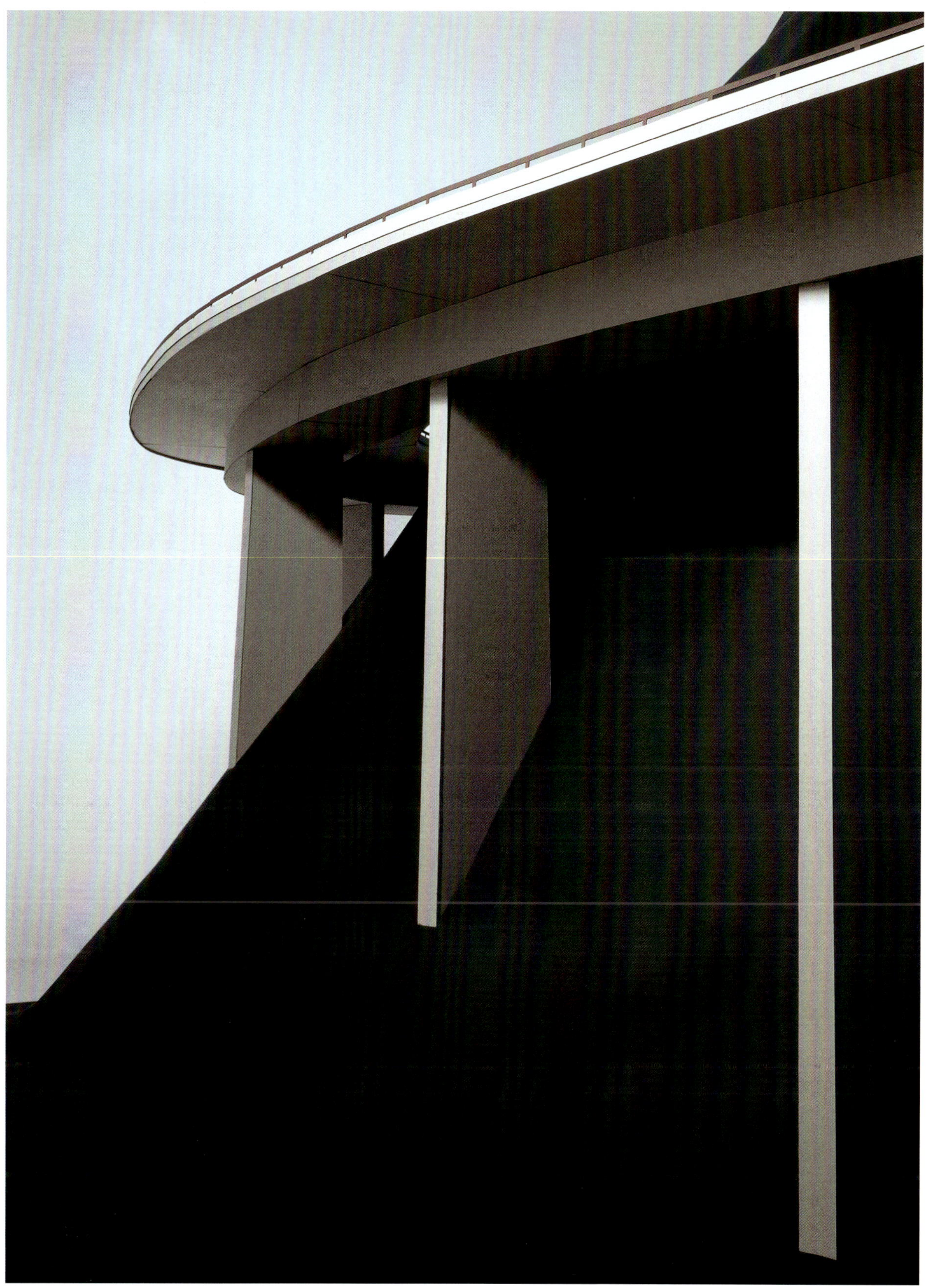

General Idea *2-024: Pan Over Drafting Table, Scattered with Precision Instruments and Occasional Sketches*, October 18, 1975

THE 1984 MISS GENERAL IDEA PAGEANT PAVILLION

DEPARTMENT 2. THE 1984 MISS GENERAL IDEA PAGEANT

PAGE | PAGE

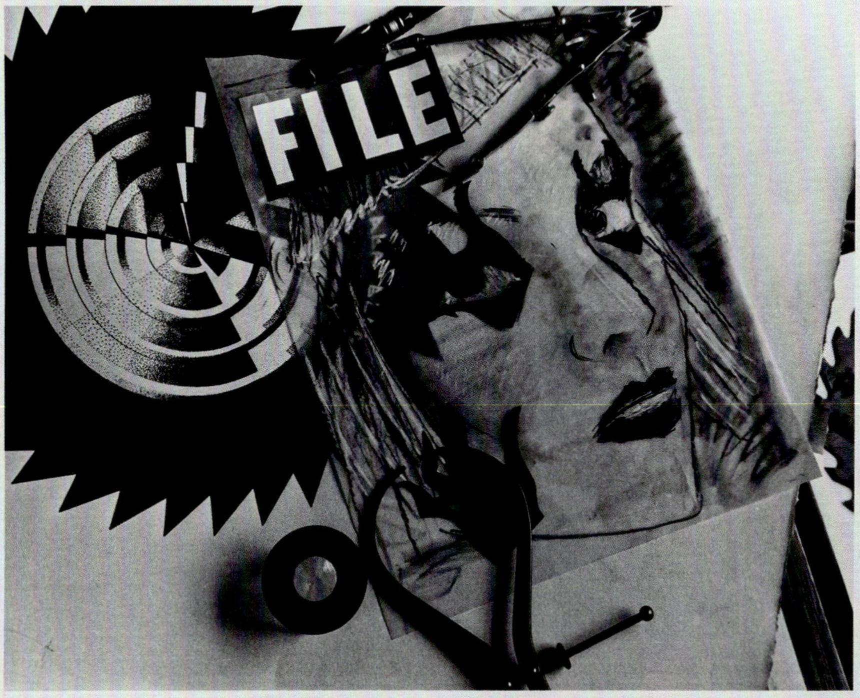

headline

text

PAN OVER DRAFTING TABLE, SCATTERED WITH PRECISION INSTRUMENTS & OCCASSIONAL SKETCHES.

VOICE OVER: My Hand of the Spirit Makeup was captured in this fashion sketch by General Idea. As soon as I saw it, new forms for the future grappled to my aesthetic — This season, my mind responded, uncage the animal in you. Abandon originality for the aboriginal vision.

ADDENDA

PHOTO: General Idea of a drawing by General Idea.

COPY NUMBER 2/2 2-024

LAYOUT DATE

SIGNATURE GENERAL IDEA

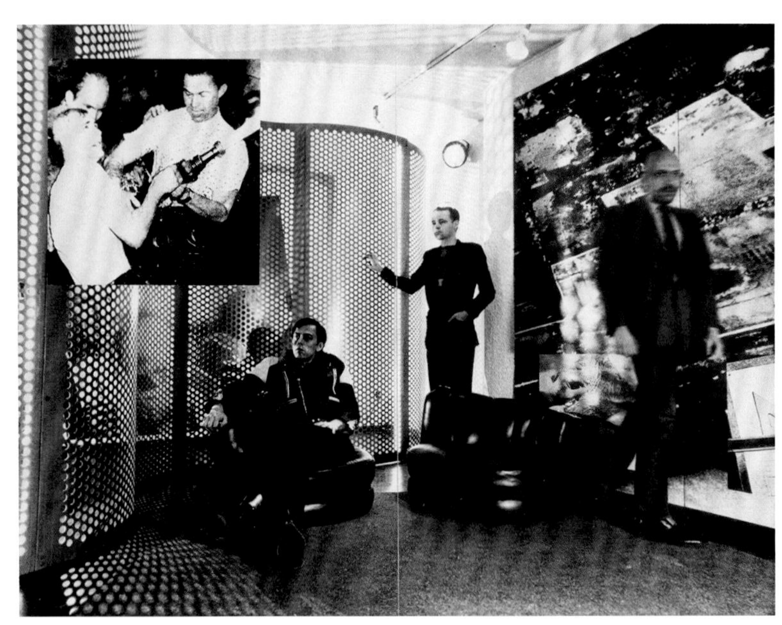

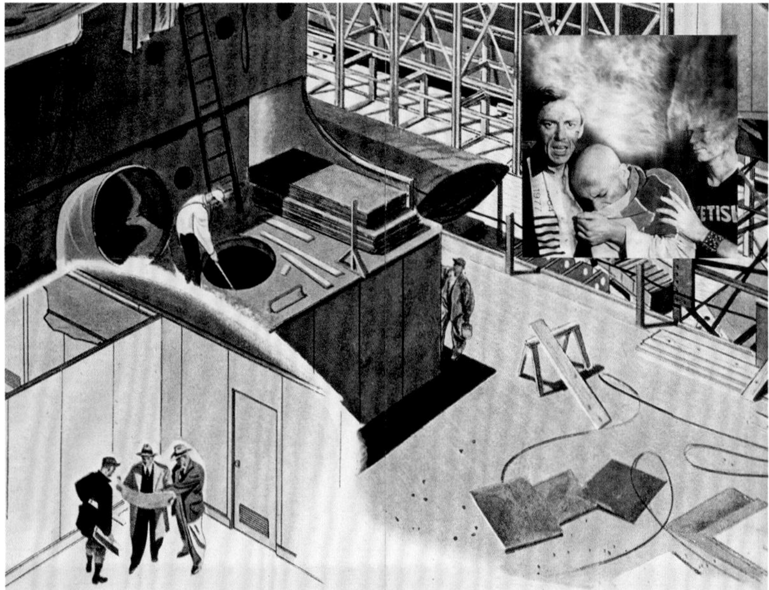

General Idea *Three Men #1–#4*, 1977

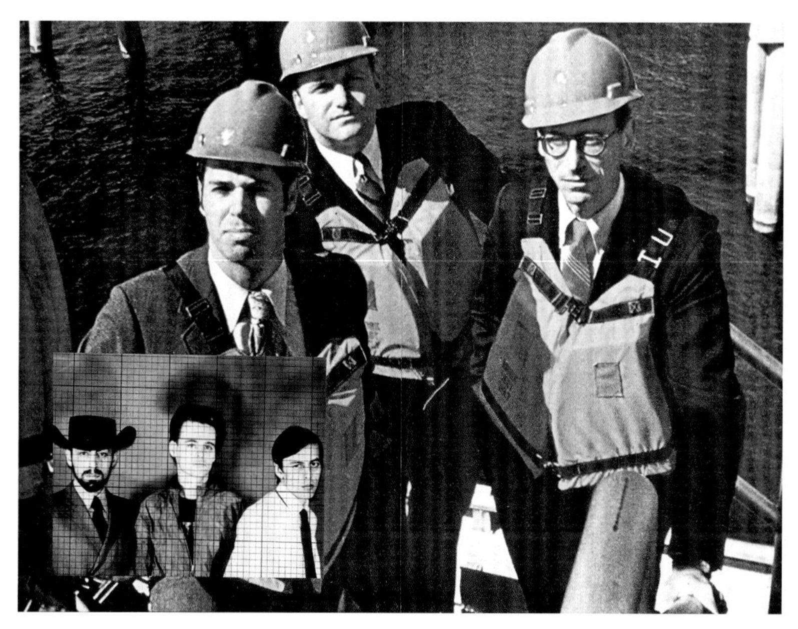

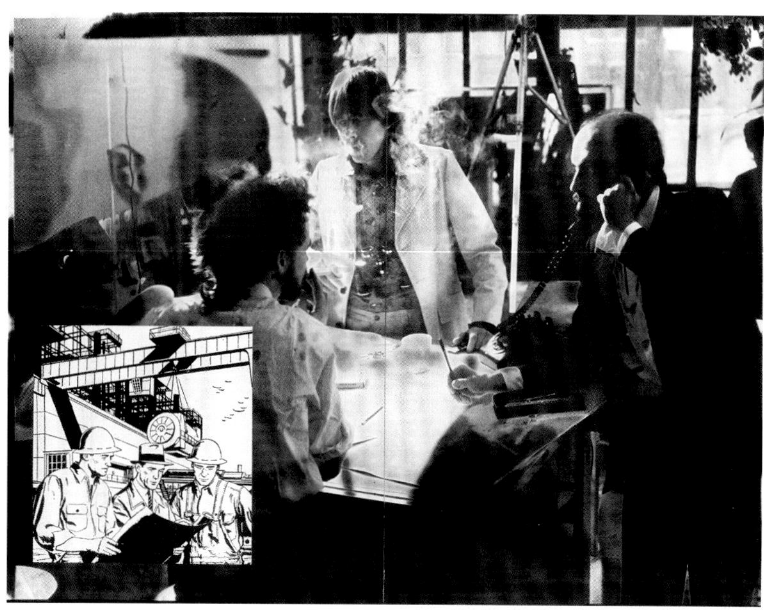

Although today General Idea is known as an artist group made up of Felix Partz, Jorge Zontal, and AA Bronson, when they started working together in 1969 they were a much larger, and more fluid, group of collaborators. Their name arose when they submitted a work for the exhibition *Concept 70* at Toronto's Nightingale Gallery (later known as A Space). The organizers mistook the title of the work, *General Idea,* for the artist. This misattribution suited them well, evoking corporations like General Electric or General Motors, and over the following twenty-five years, they explored how their identity as a group frustrated the persistent myth of a singular artist genius. *Three Men #1–#4* (1977) was an attempt by Partz, Zontal, and Bronson to reify their identity as an artist trio. Picking up copies of *Fortune* magazine from the 1950s, they noticed that businessmen, architects, and builders often appeared in groups of three. Lifting these images from *Fortune*, in each of the four panels they pair the found image with a carefully constructed self-portrait—underscoring the corporate method of their collaboration.

Liquid Assets (1980) was first conceived by General Idea as a multiple for *The Boutique from the 1984 Miss General Idea Pavillion* (1980), a galvanized steel kiosk in the shape of a dollar sign. *The Boutique* was created as the gift shop for their imagined building to house the 1984 Miss General Idea Pageant. *Liquid Assets* was offered for sale alongside *Architectonic* and *Double Palette* (both 1980), other unconventional drinking vessels intended to serve as cocktail accessories for the *Colour Bar Lounge*—the pavilion's glamorous canteen. At the time, the group couldn't afford to complete the planned edition of fifty cocktail holders, so *Liquid Assets* existed in just ten examples. The remaining forty pieces of the edition, of which this is one, were produced by Bywater Editions in collaboration with AA Bronson. In 1998 Sandy Simpson, General Idea's former Toronto dealer, gave *The Boutique*—with its impressive array of multiples—to the AGO, which holds the collection of record for the artist group.

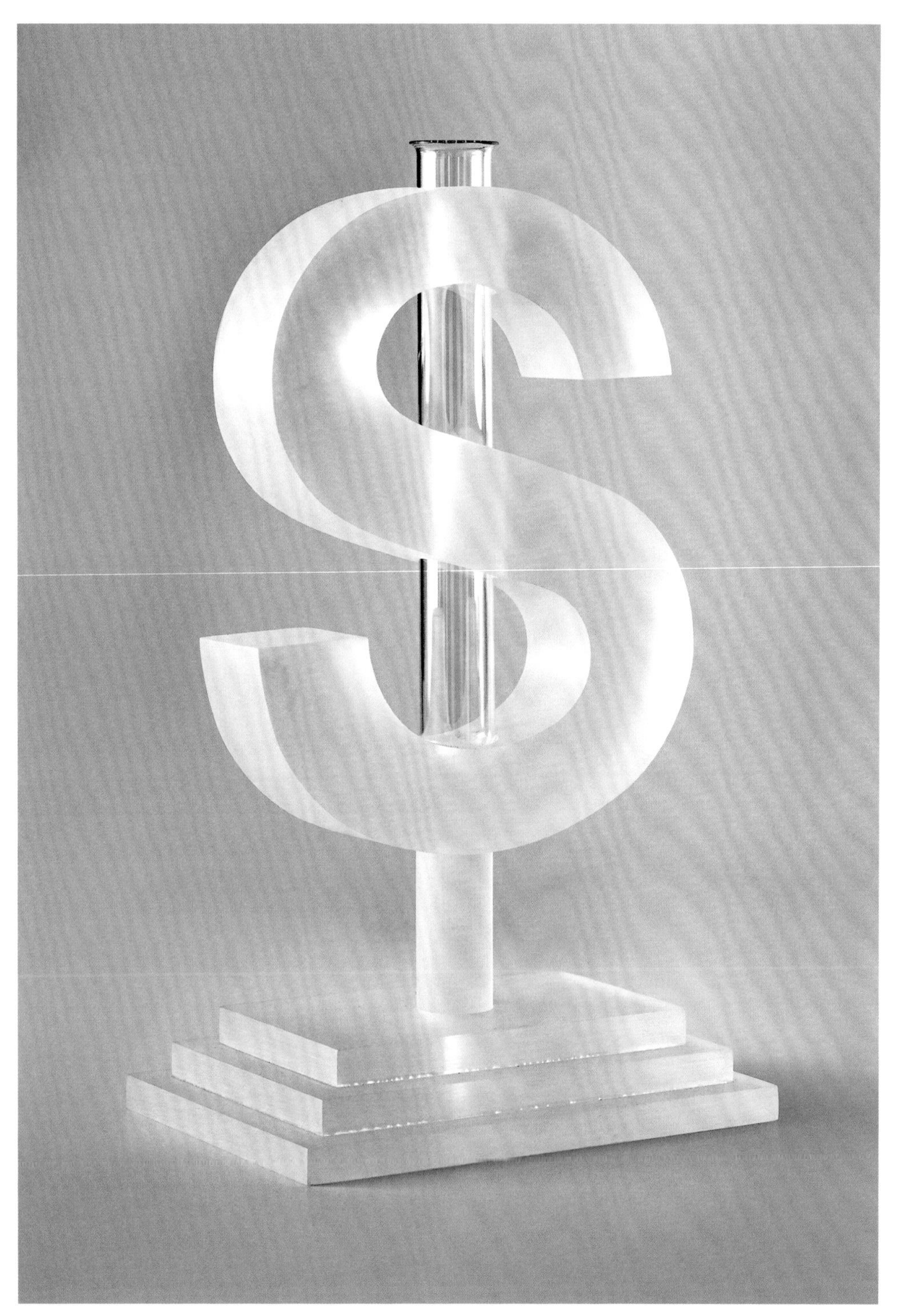

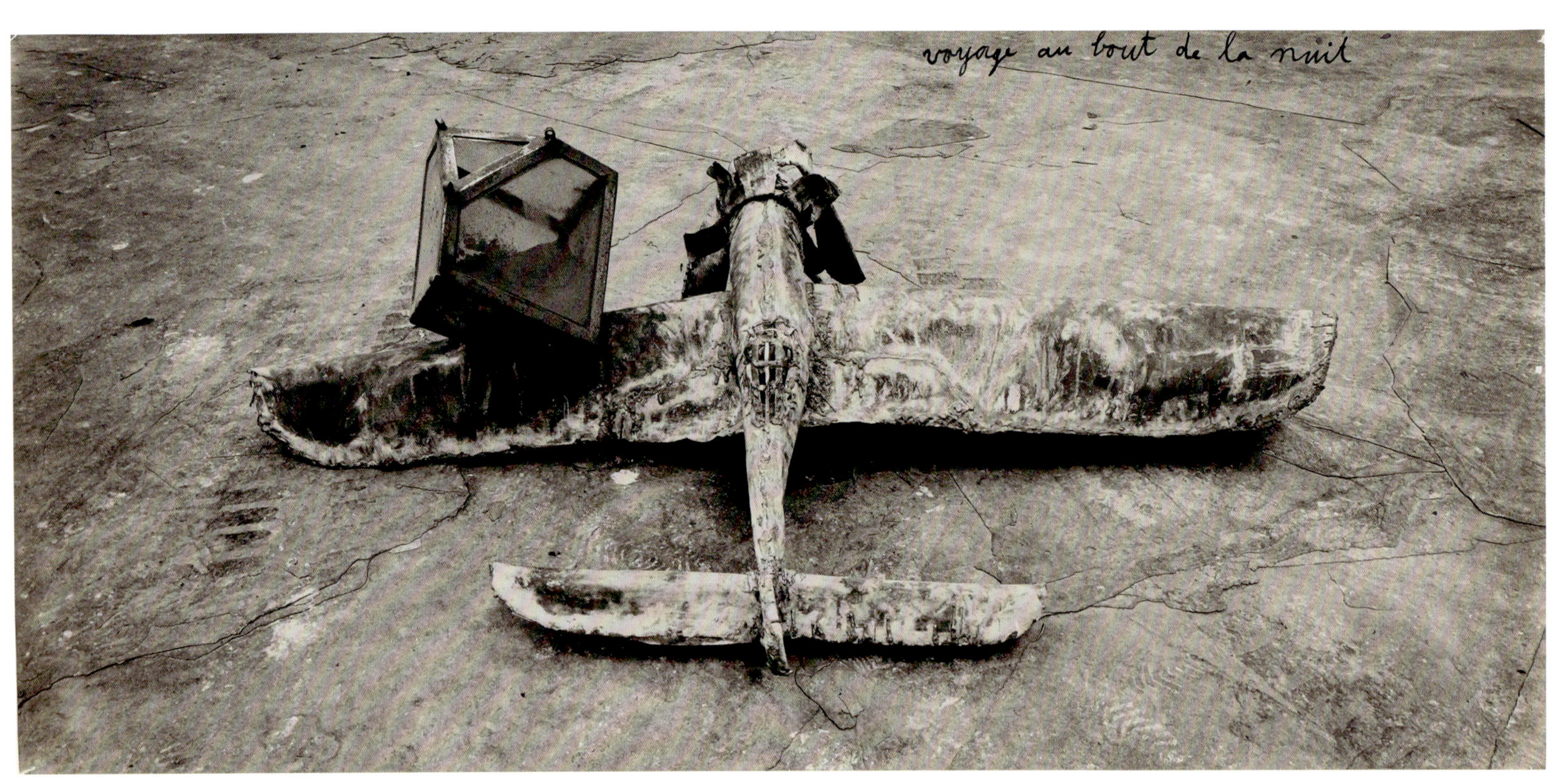

Anselm Kiefer *Voyage au bout de la nuit,* 2006

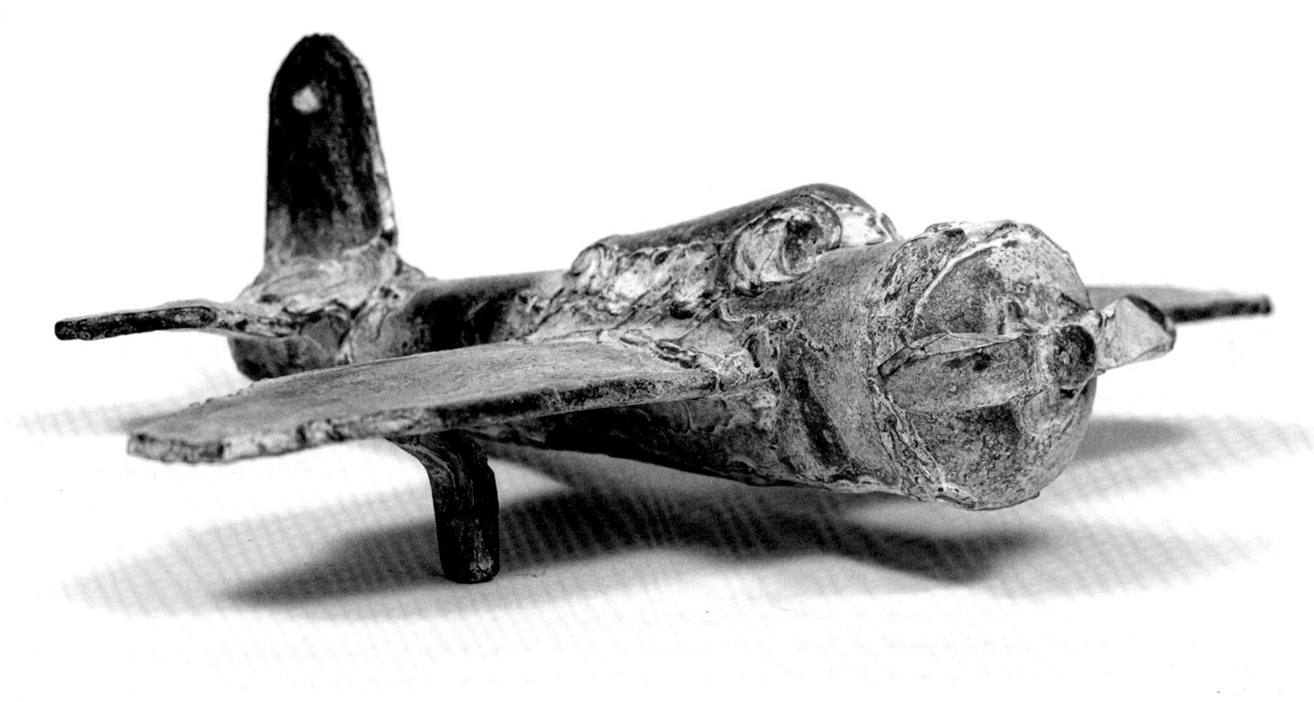

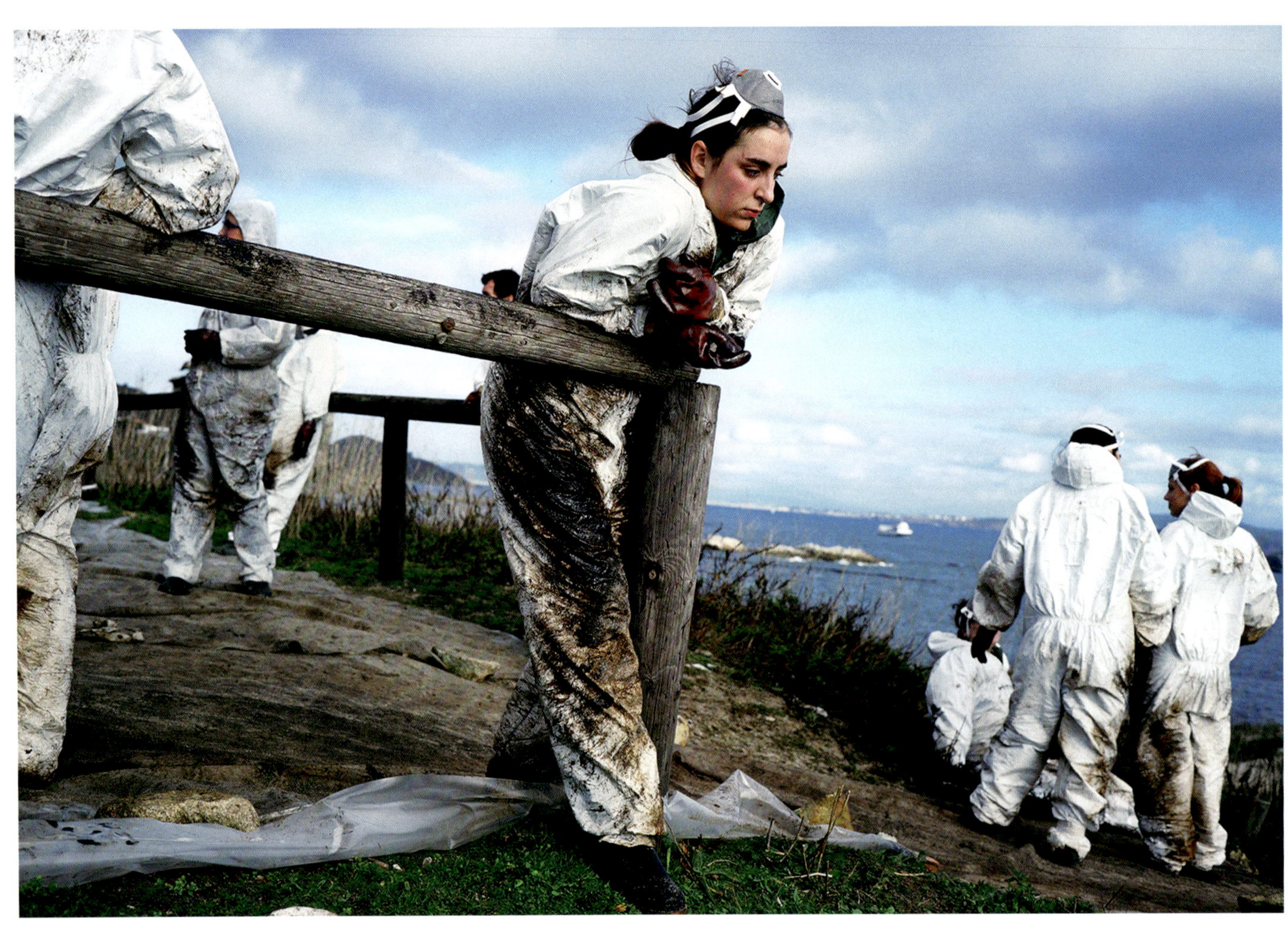

Allan Sekula *Volunteer watching, volunteer smiling (Isla de Ons, 12/19/02), 2002–2003*

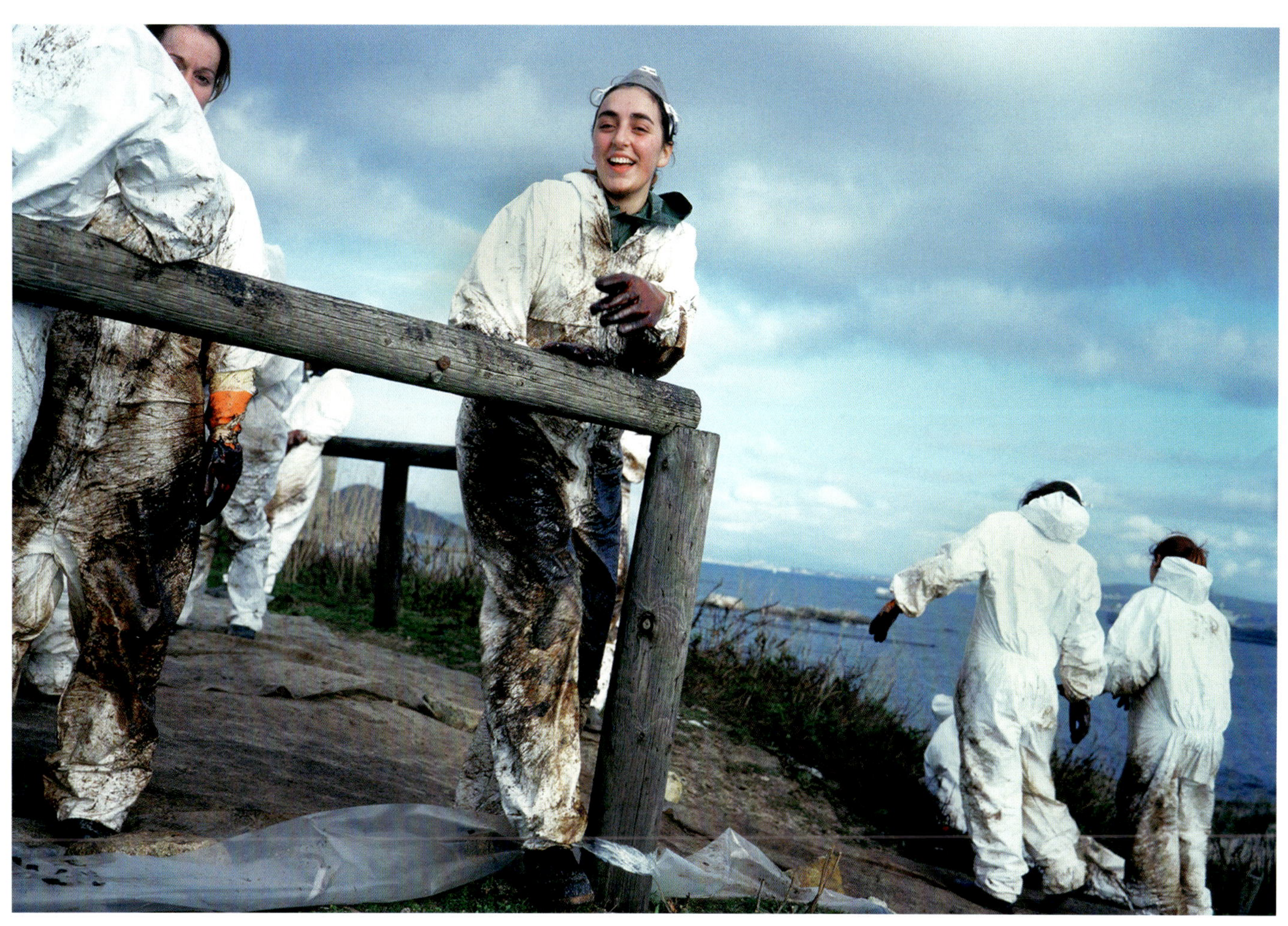

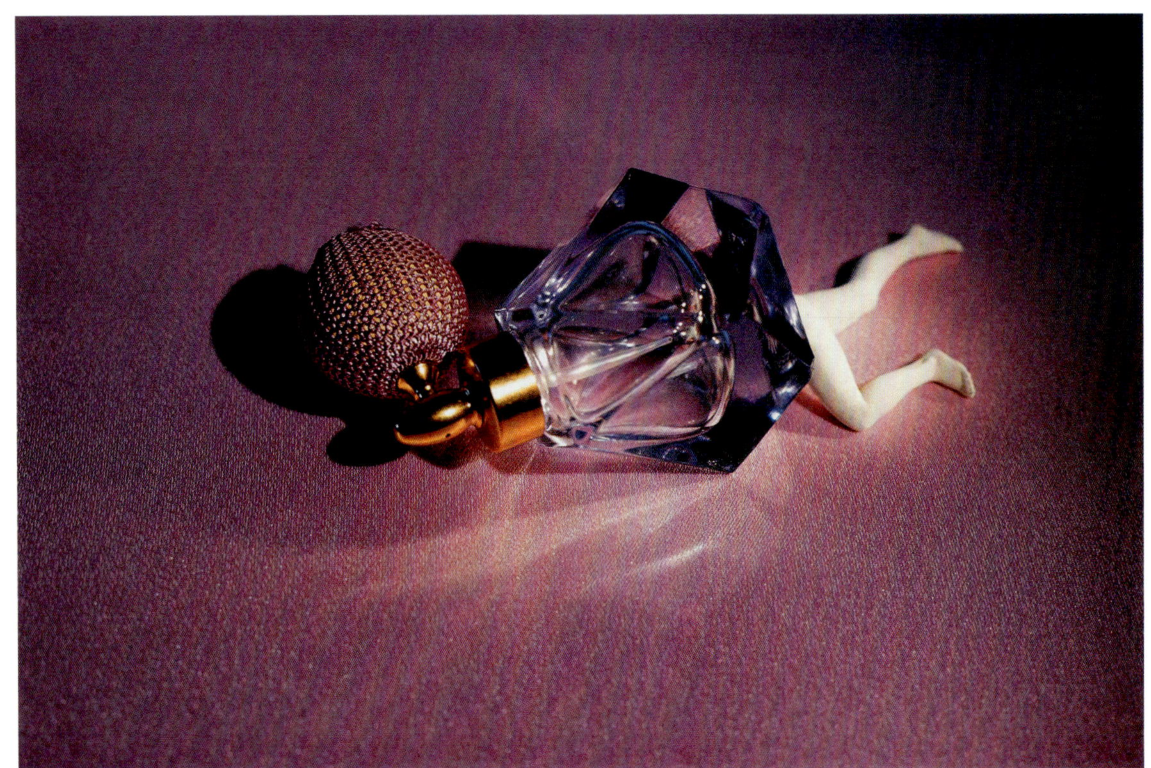

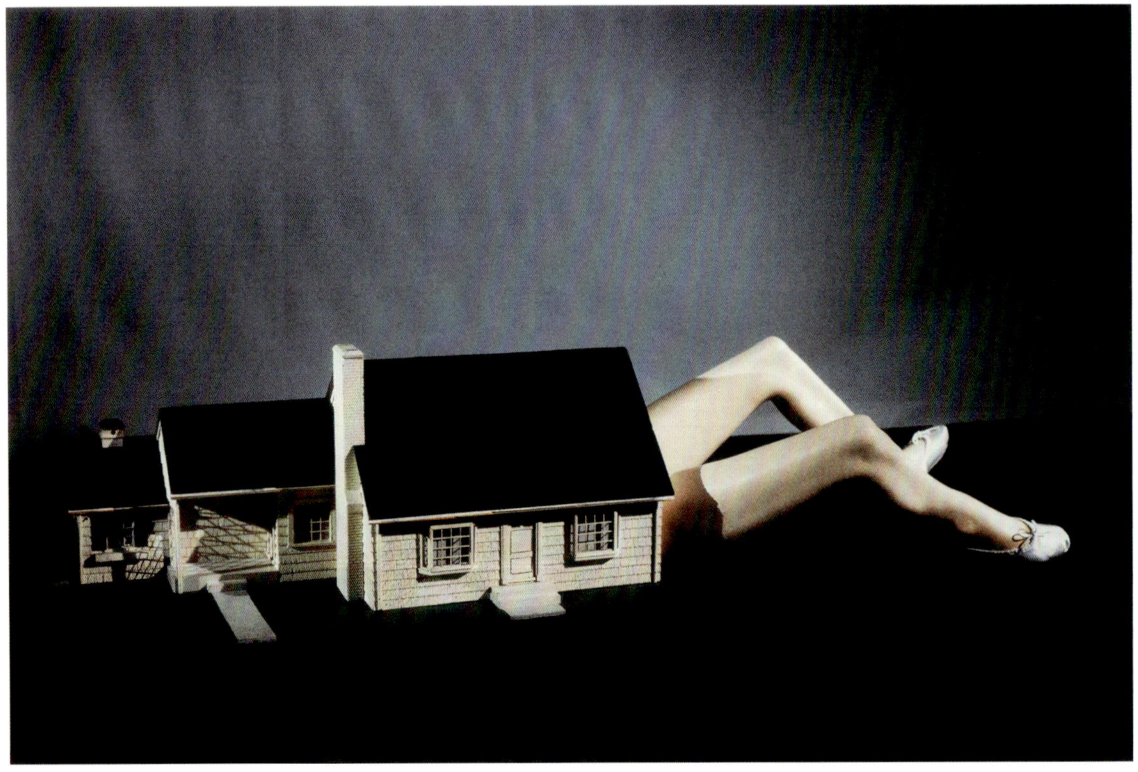

Laurie Simmons *Lying Objects (Set of Four)*, 1992

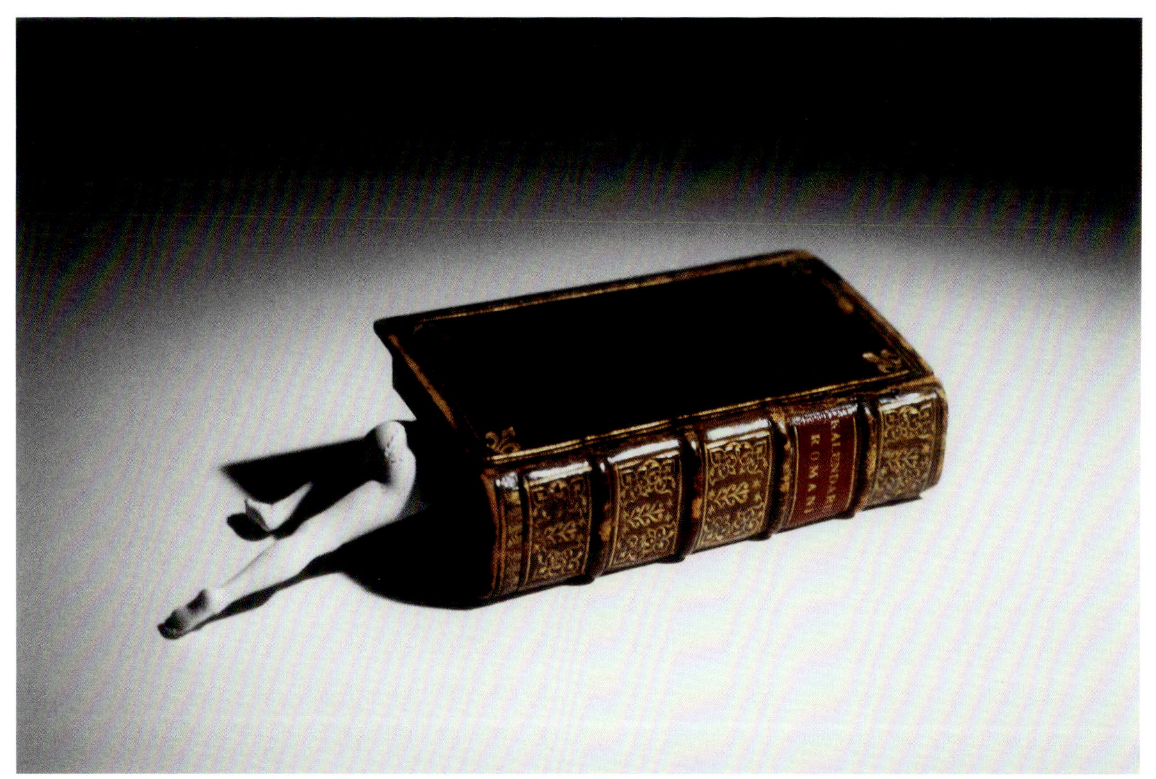
ROMANI

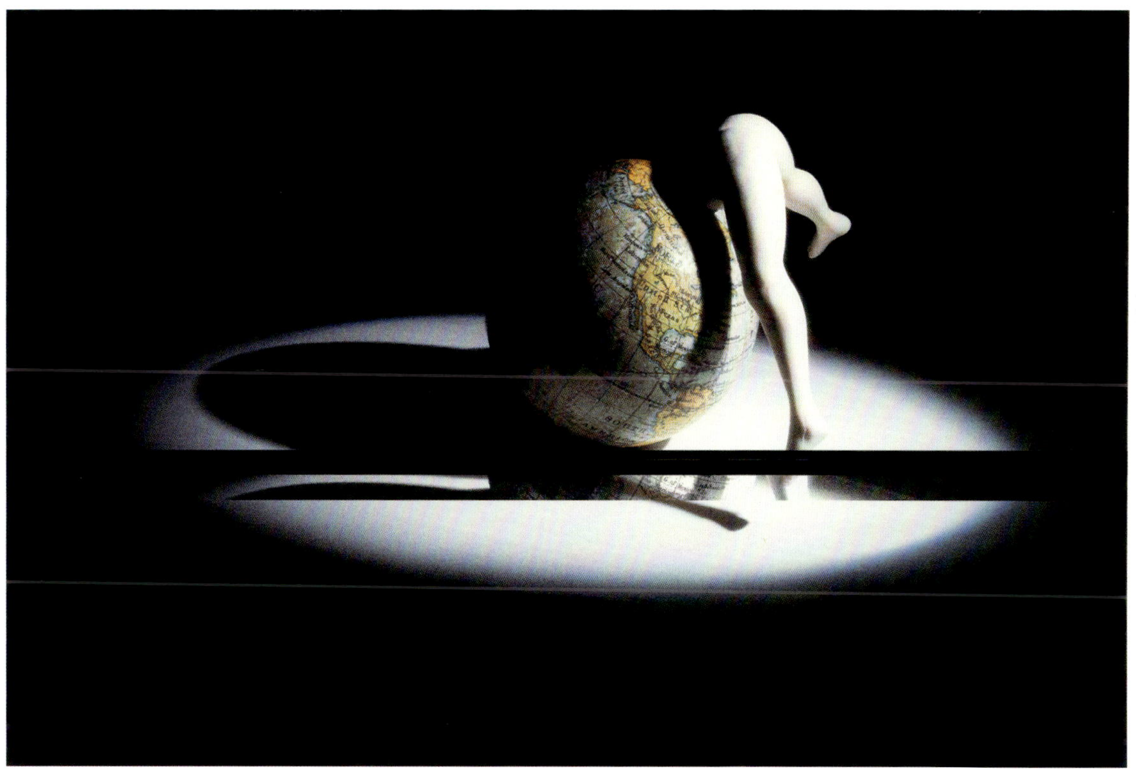

Erwin Wurm *Disobedience*, 2014

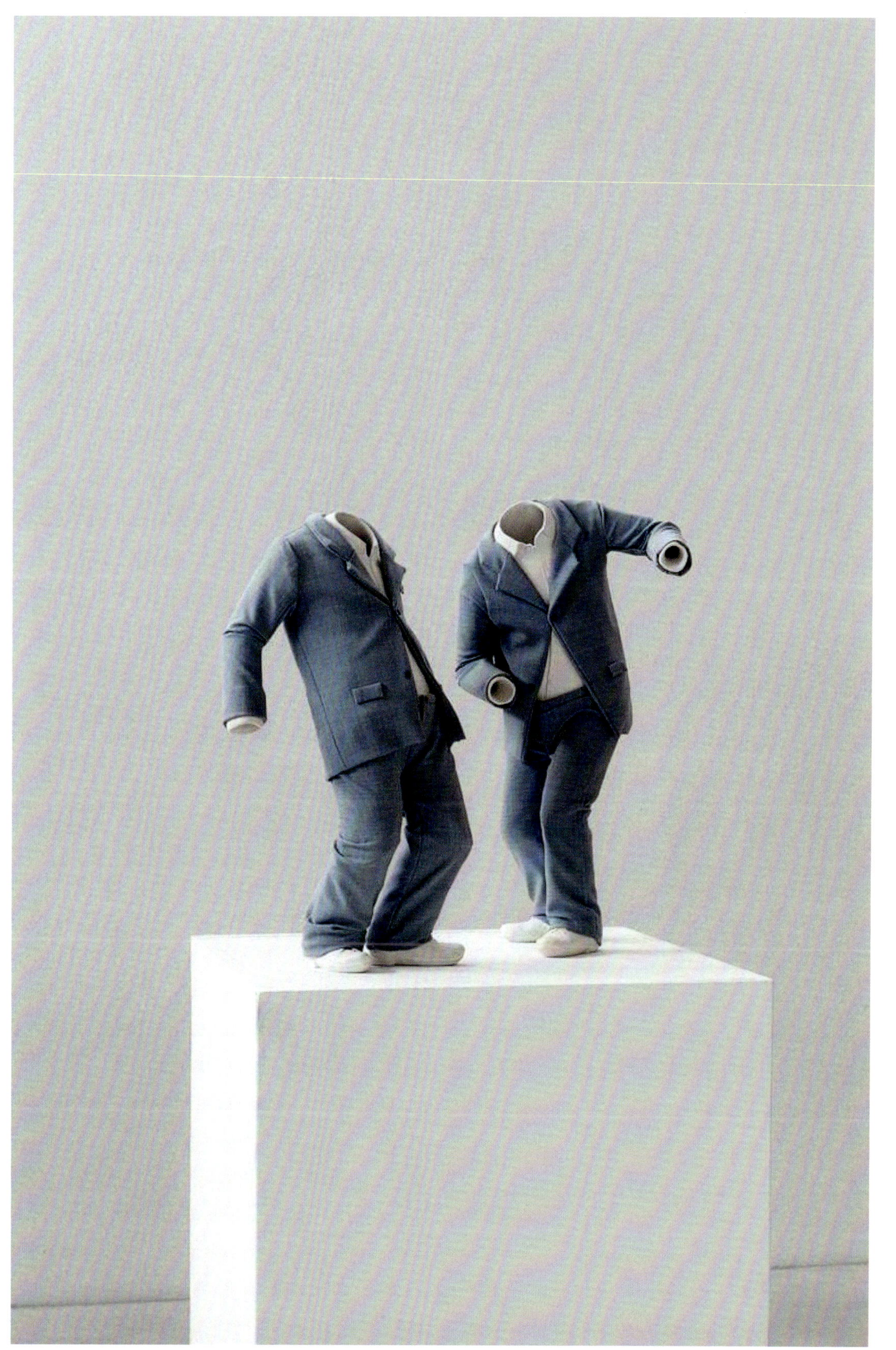

London-born Julian Opie (b. 1958) emerged onto the 1980s British art scene with large-scale, boldly painted steel sculptures of everyday objects such as chocolate bars, books, and food containers. By the time he graduated from Goldsmiths College in 1982, he was afforded enough historical distance from Pop art's colourful representations of consumer culture to take up some of its strategies. In 1997 Opie's reductive style took the form of highly recognizable, simplified portraits of his friends. By the early 2000s he turned to an engagement with digital technologies.

This is Julian walking. (2002), a continuous loop of an outlined figure walking in profile, invites varied interpretations. While the figure shows energy with his unending drive, he also appears trapped in a loop of digital purgatory. The work comprises an animation presented on an LCD monitor, testing the limits of the then-new technology. This is equally the case with Opie's outdoor, site-responsive public artworks, such as *People walking.* (2006), an animation on an LED screen located in front of Rogers Communications' main office at 333 Bloor Street East. Together with the art advisor Jeanne Parkin, Phil Lind commissioned Opie to make a work that emulated the constant stream of passersby.

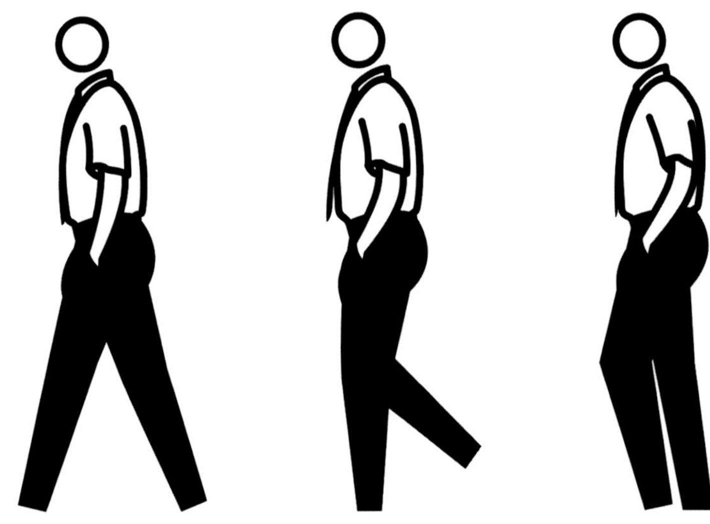

Julian Opie *This is Julian walking.*, 2002

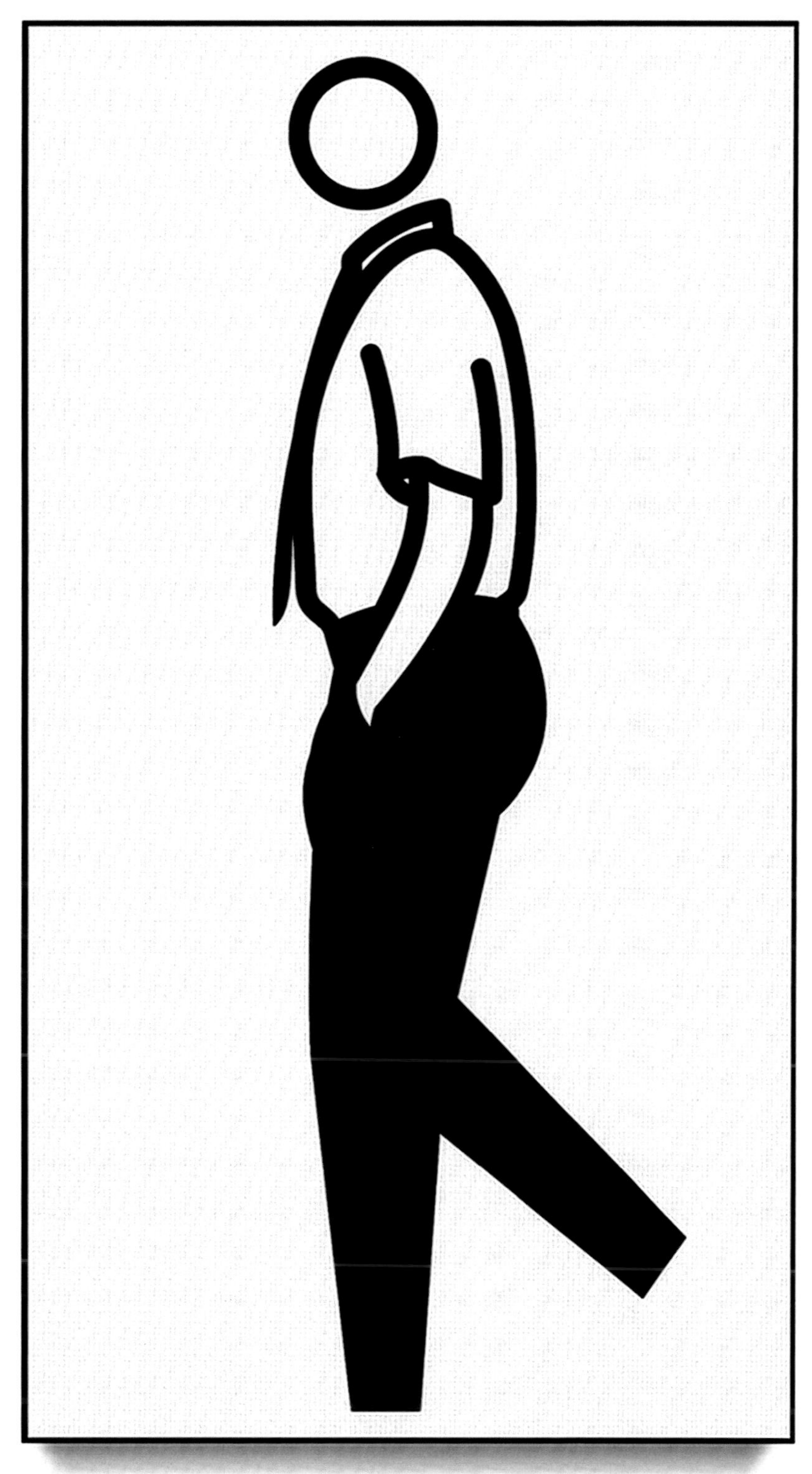

Bettina Pousttchi *Vancouver Time*, 2018

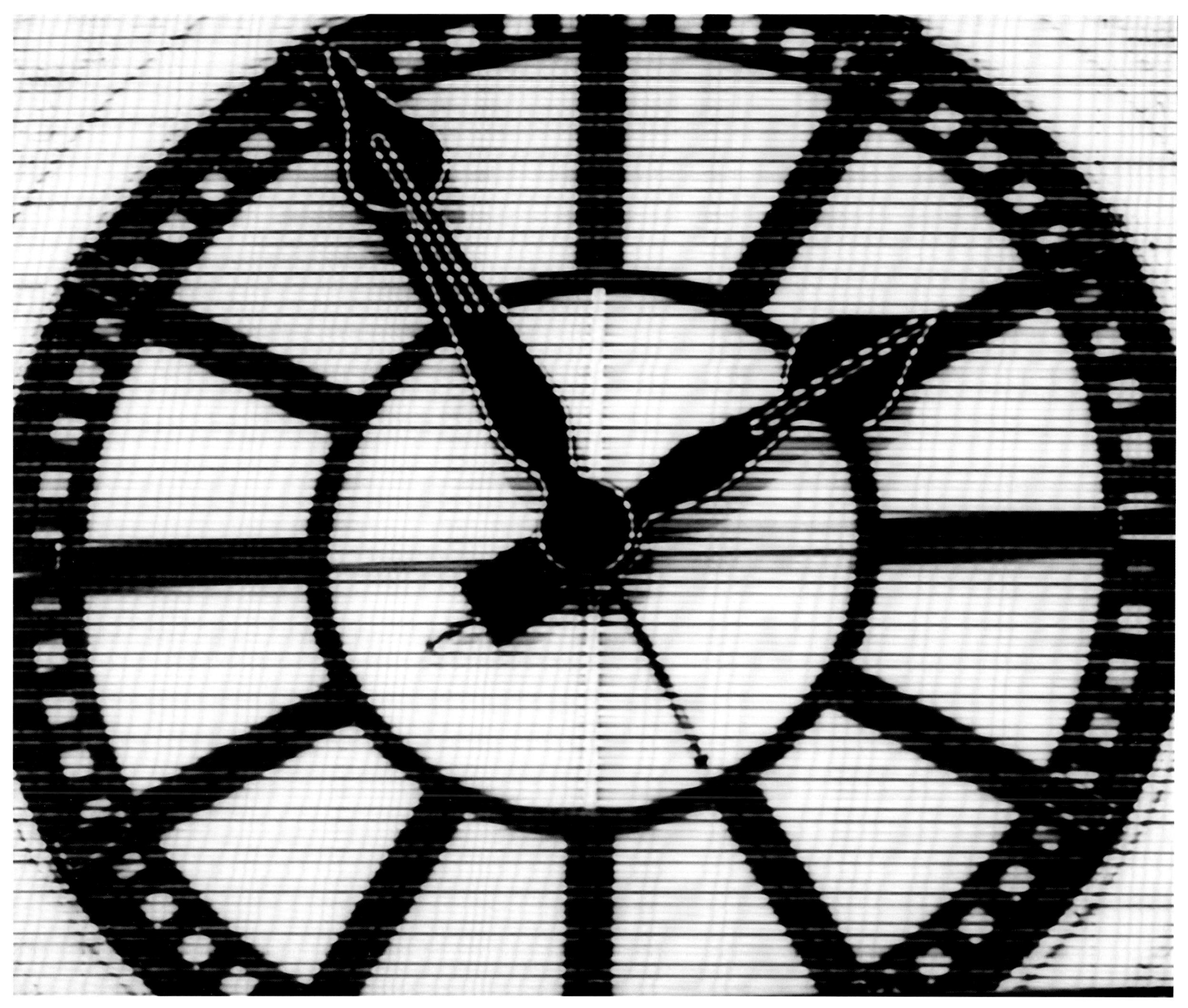

Jonathan Monk *Rew-Shay Hood Project VI*, 2008–2009

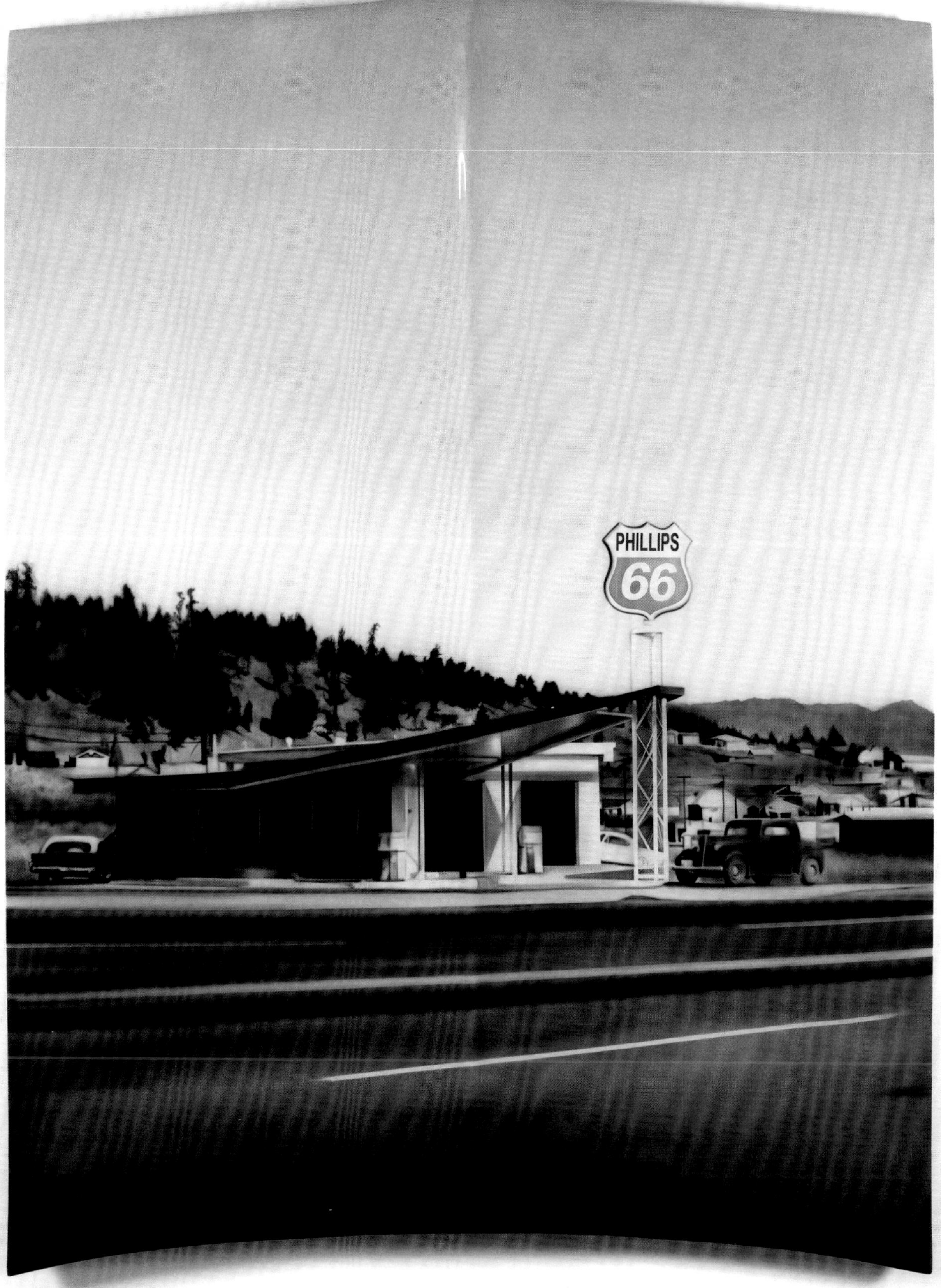
PHILLIPS
66

Chris Burden *Trapezoid Bridge,* 2003

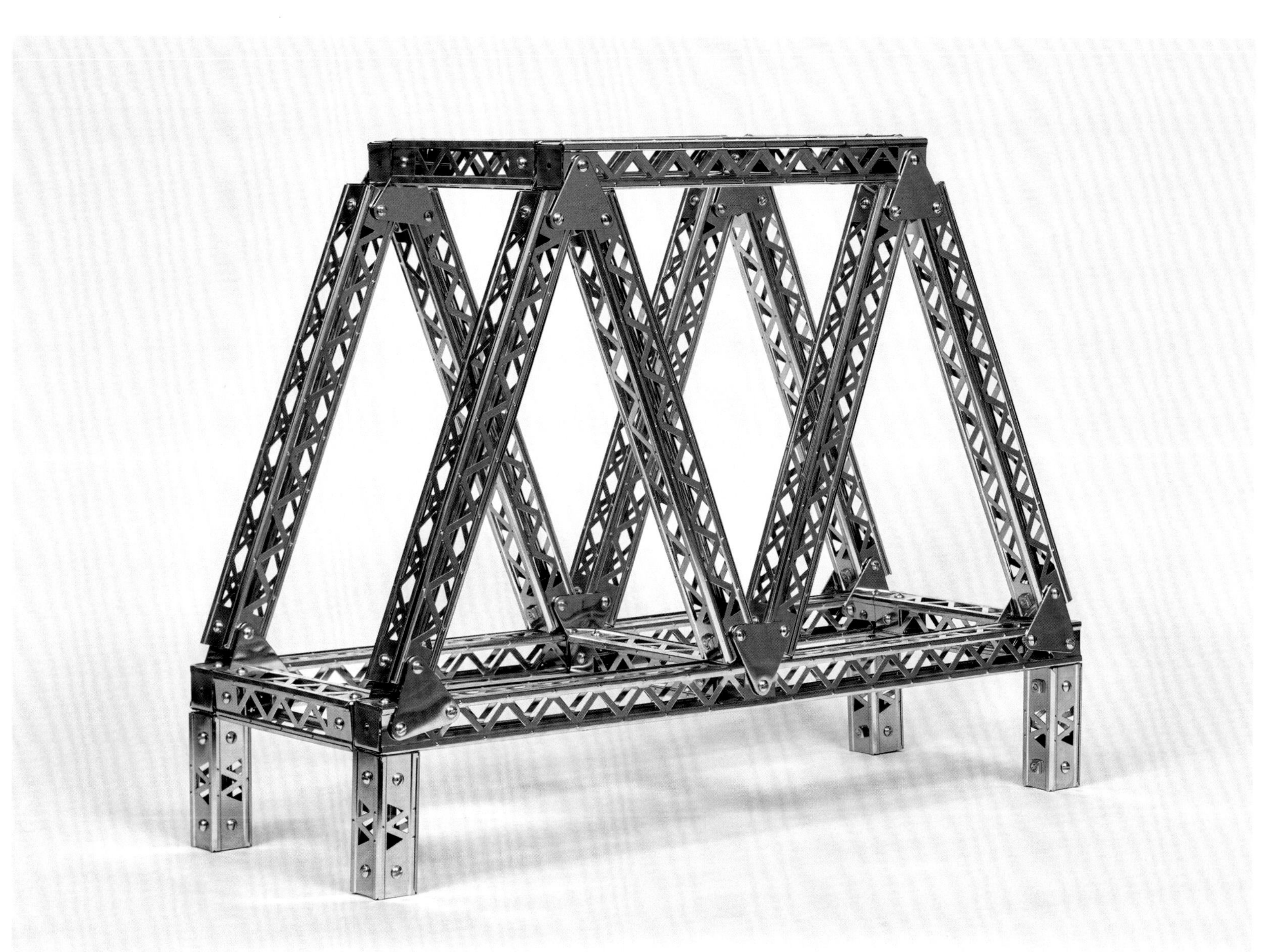

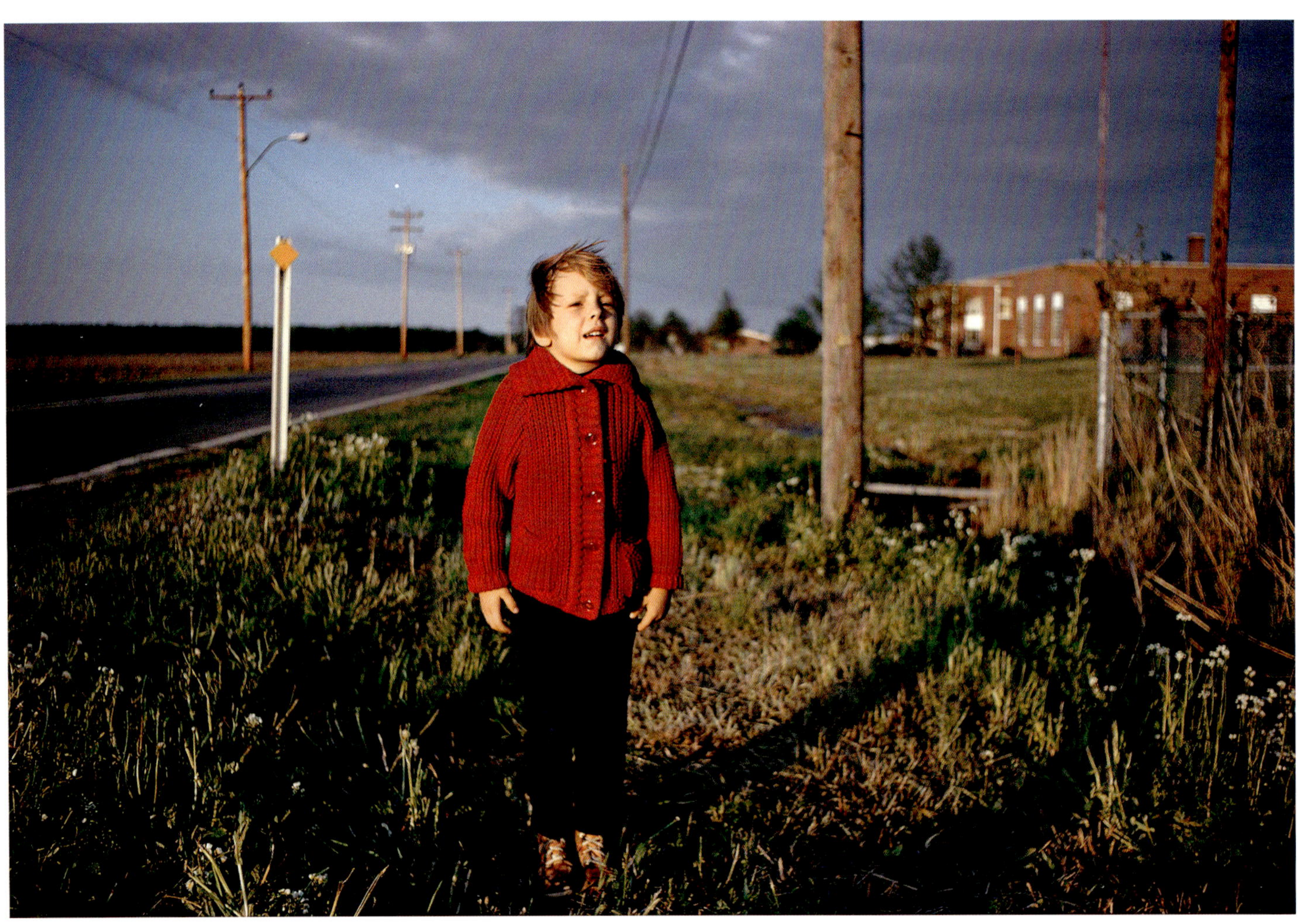

William Eggleston *Untitled,* 1971

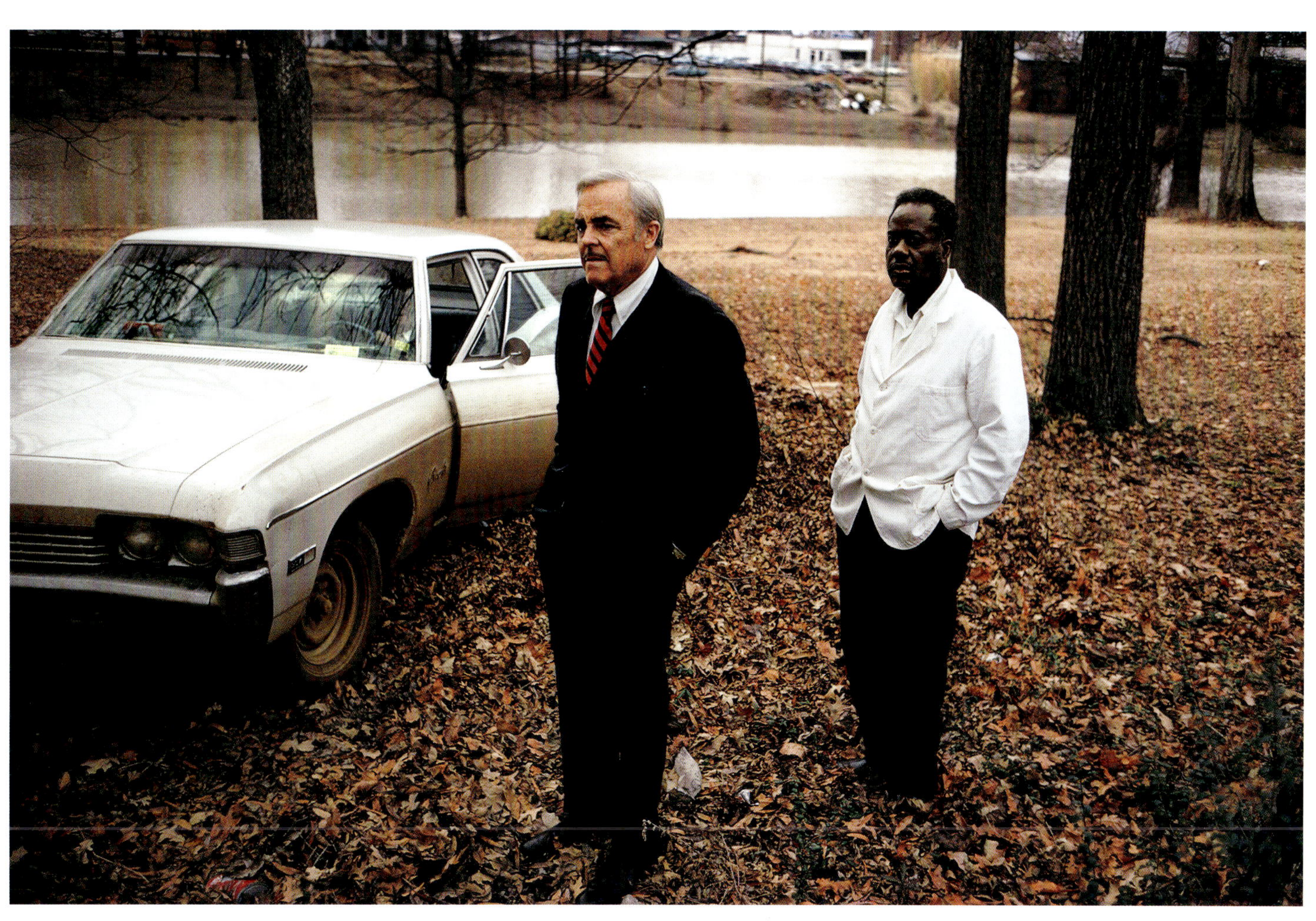

William Eggleston *Sumner, Mississippi,* c.1970

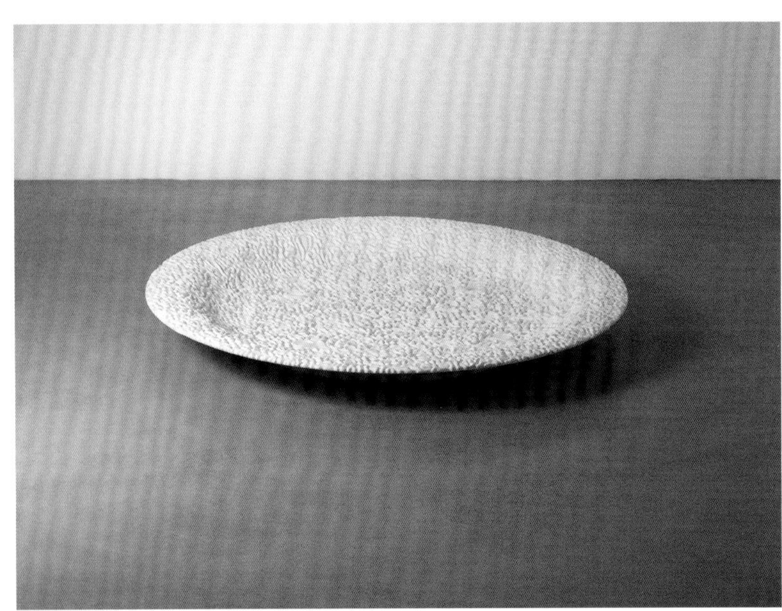

Ai Weiwei *Marble Plate*, 2010

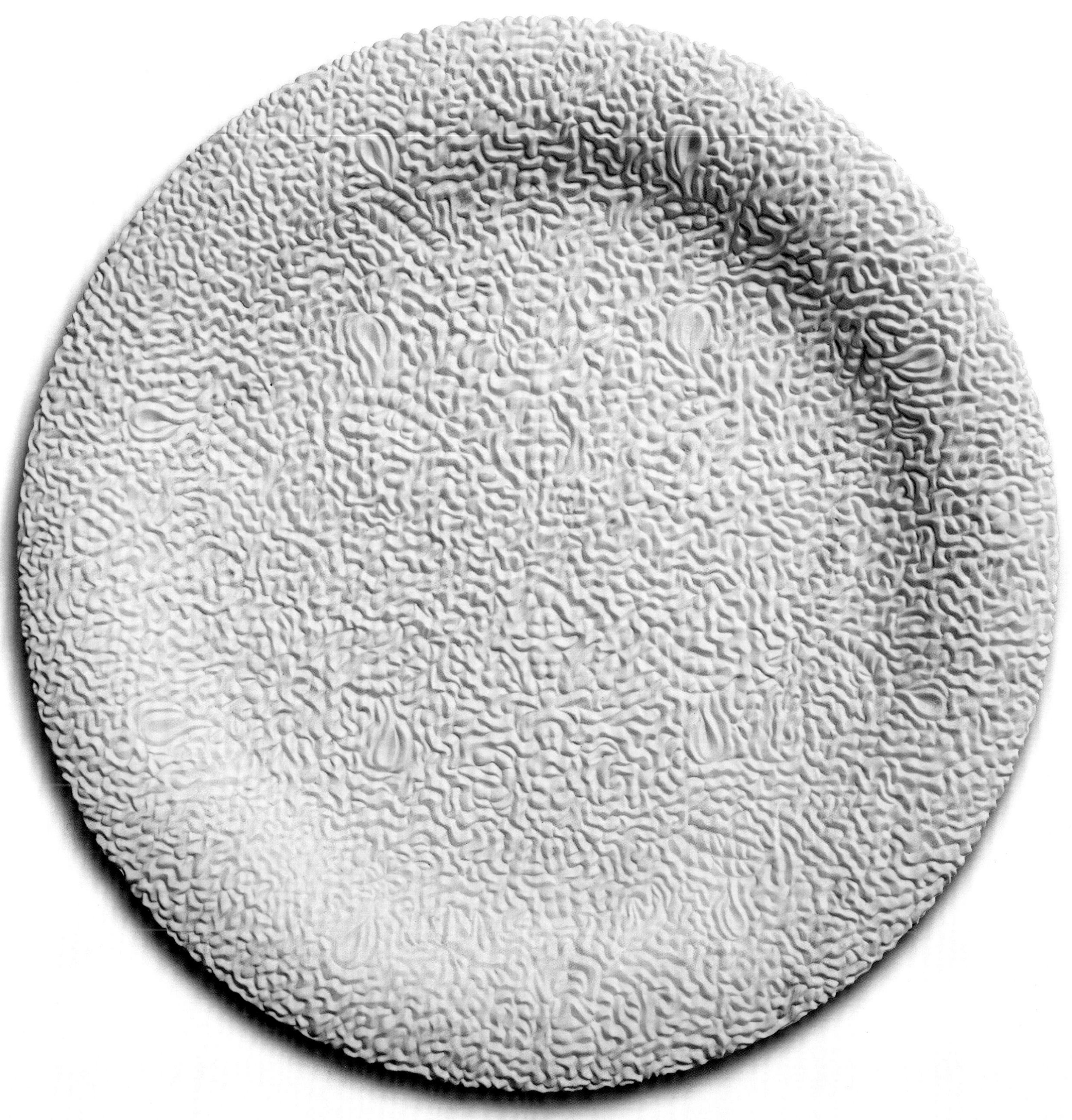

Vija Celmins *Web #5*, 2009

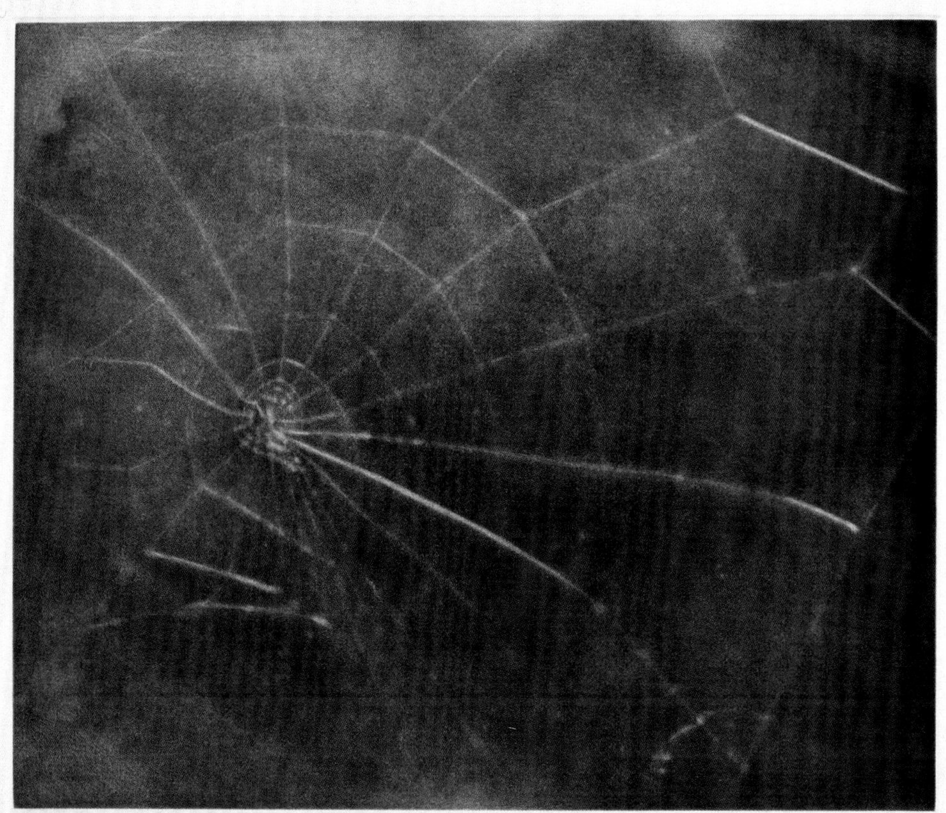

AP 22/30

V. Celmins '09

Philip Guston *Daisies*, 1973–1974

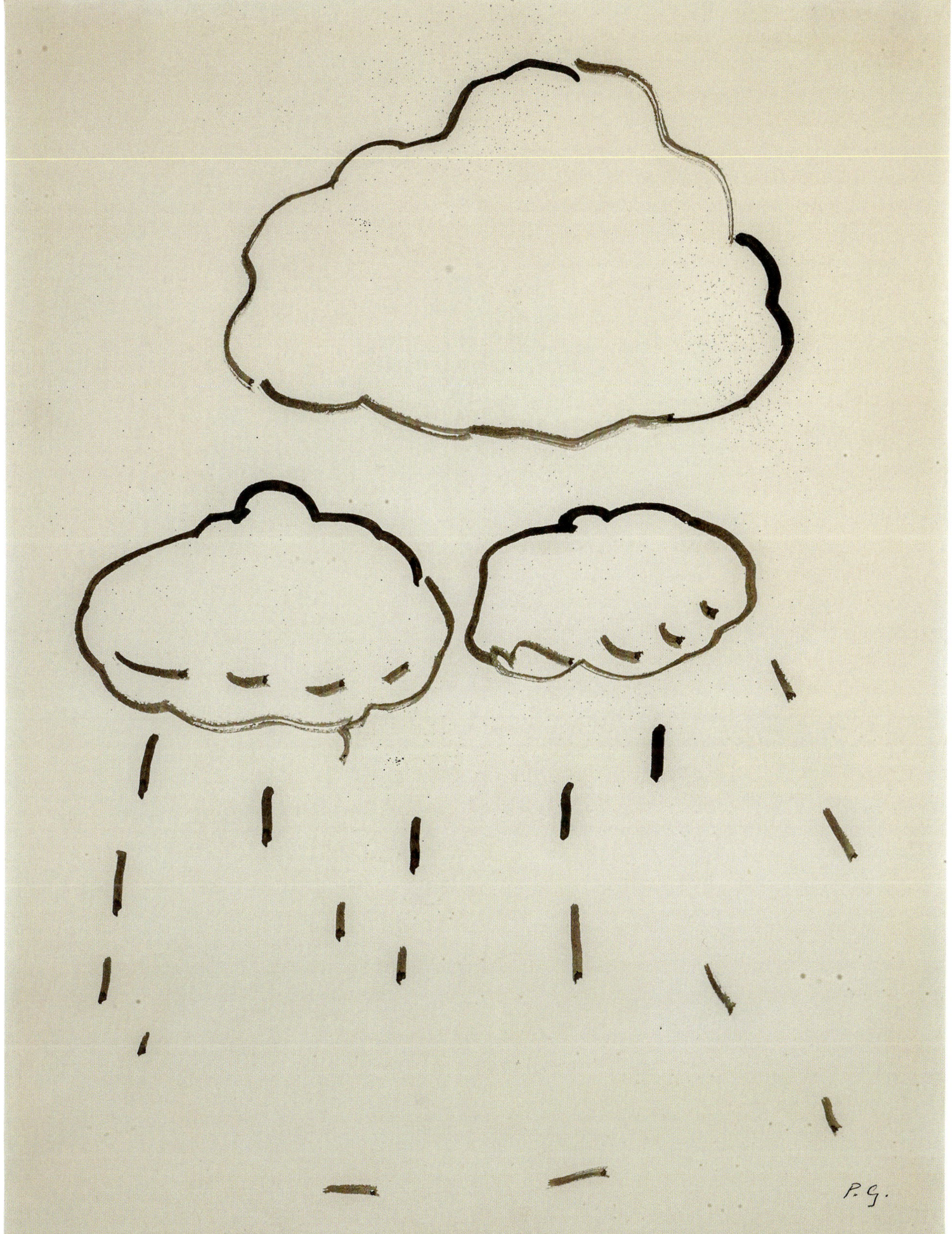
P. G.

Born in Montreal as Philip Goldstein, Guston (1913–1980) moved with his family to Los Angeles in 1919. As a young artist he was involved in the mural movement, and upon moving to New York in the mid-1930s, he created large-scale paintings as part of the Works Progress Administration's Federal Arts Project. Throughout this period, Guston particularly admired the work of Giorgio de Chirico, James Ensor, and Max Beckmann. While those references are not evident in his abstract work—which he made from 1948 until the mid-1960s—the influence of these artists resurfaced when he returned to figuration. This dramatic turn in his practice was met coolly by critics; when Guston first showed his cartoony, pink and cadmium red grisaille paintings at Marlborough Gallery in New York in 1970, the blunt, heavily drawn figures and objects were met with derision.

For the remaining decade of his life, Guston pursued a personal vocabulary and iconography, frequently combining still-life elements such as boots, cigars, paintbrushes, and easels with figures he called "hoods." These representations of Ku Klux Klan members were often engaged in banal scenes. As Guston wrote in a studio note, they are "dumb, melancholy, guilty, fearful, remorseful, reassuring one another."[3] As a child in Los Angeles, Guston had run-ins with Klansmen, and as early as 1930 made works probing their anti-Black racism and antisemitism. (One of Guston's early paintings was destroyed by a Klansman.) The triviality of many of these scenes with "hoods" belies the constant threat of violence.

Untitled (1979)—which represents a disembodied head seen in profile, the figure's eye bloodshot and straining up—was made the year before Guston's death. These figures, often shown with exaggerated, unblinking eyes, have been read as self-portraits. The strong and characteristic use of red exaggerates our sense of the subject's turmoil, anxiously living in a turbulent world.

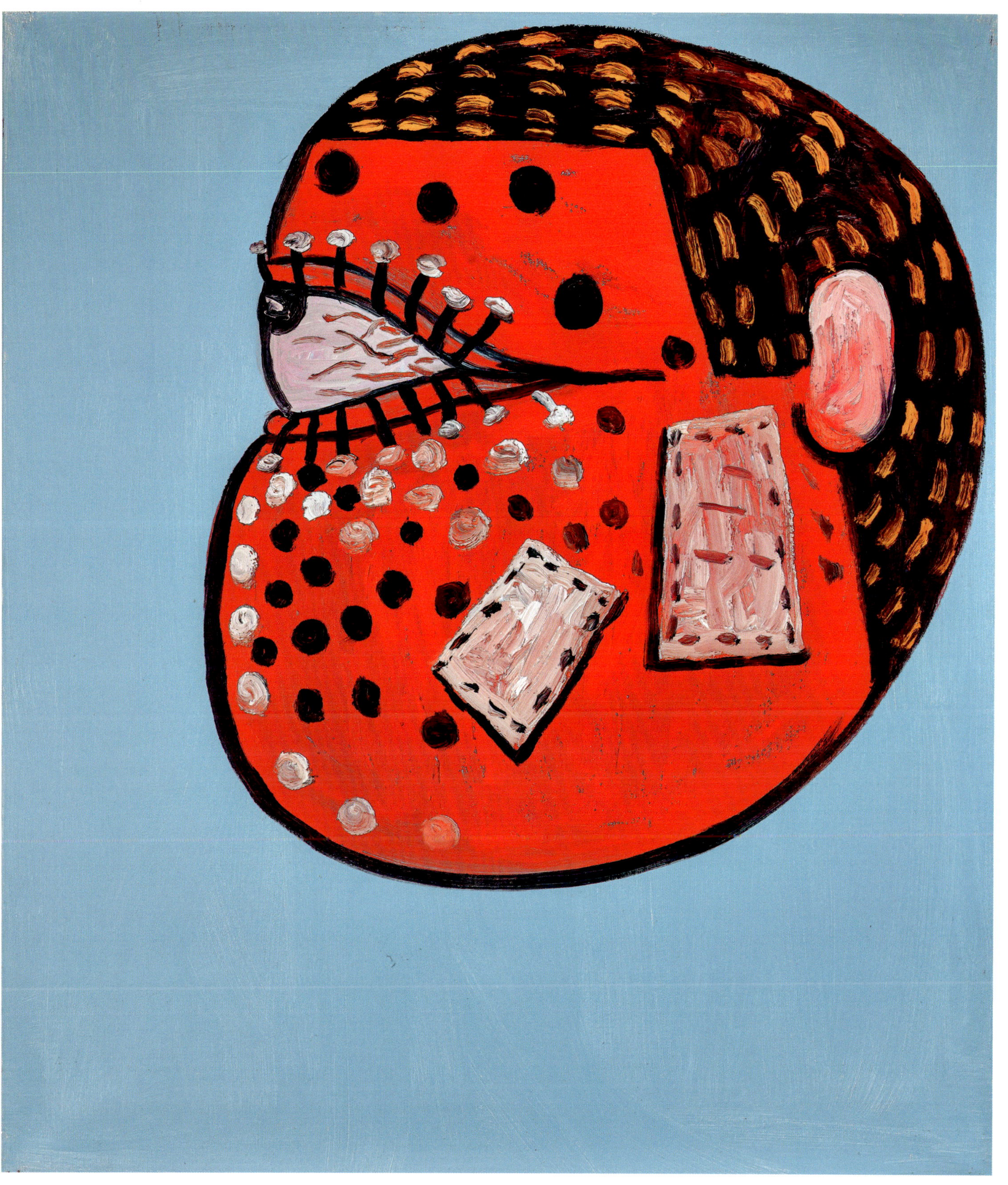

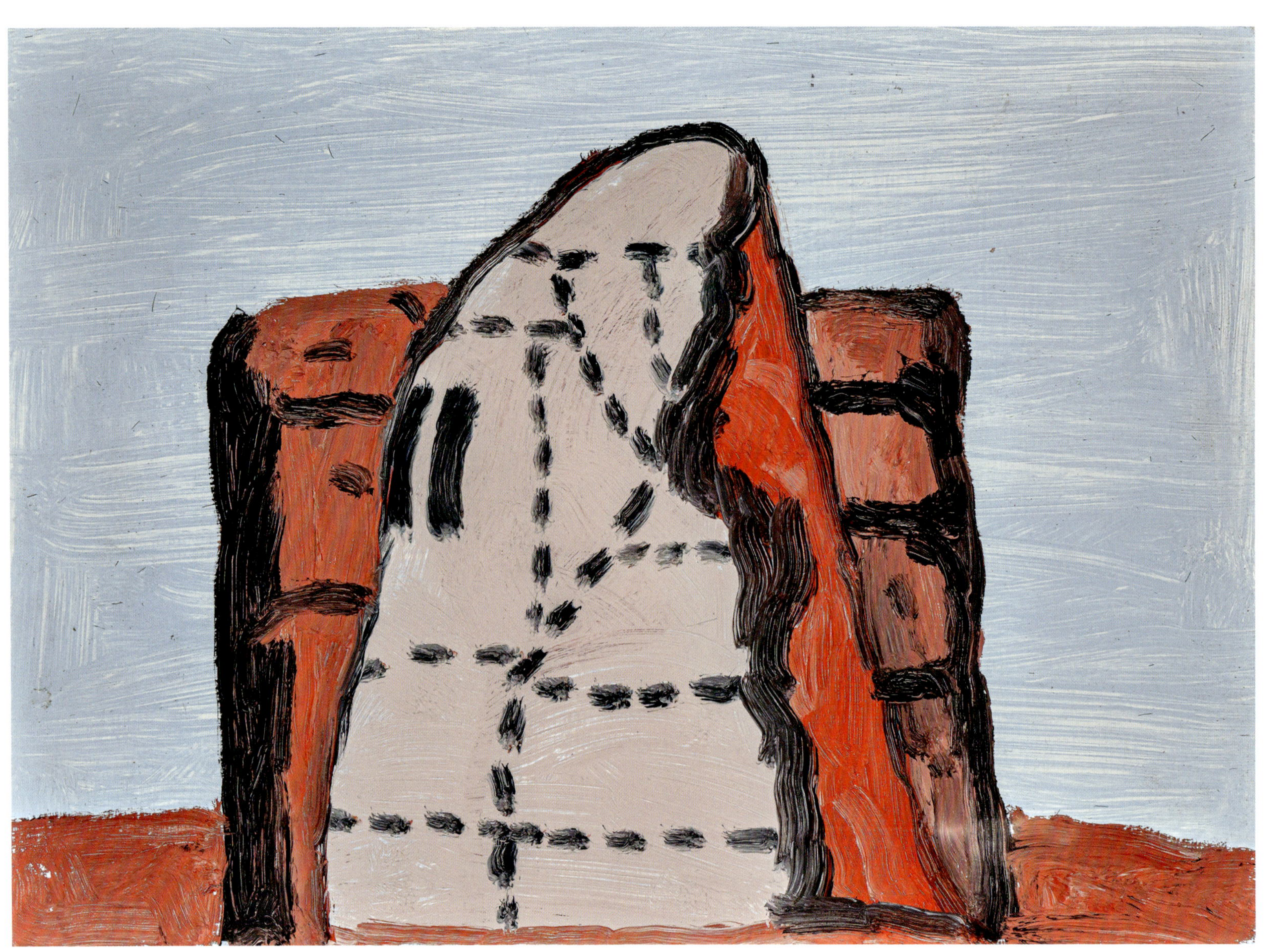

Philip Guston *Untitled*, c. 1968

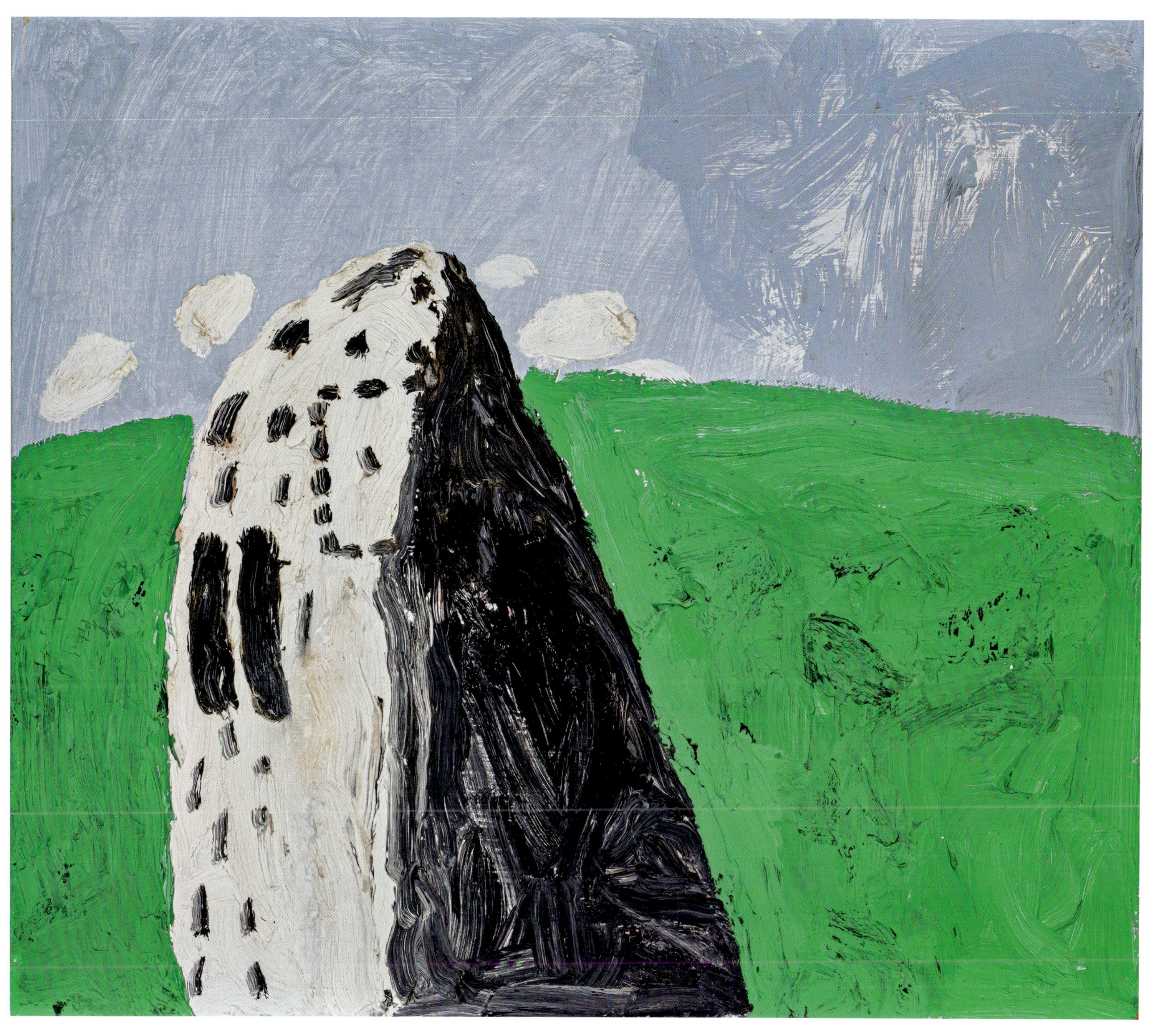

Philip Guston *Untitled,* 1970

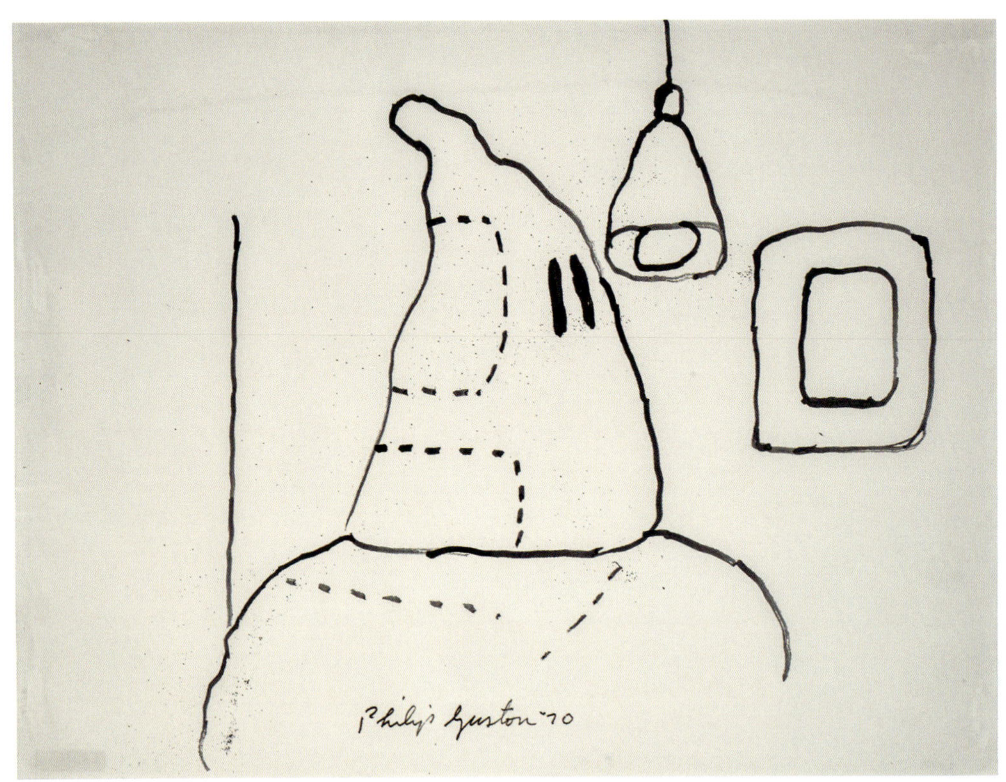

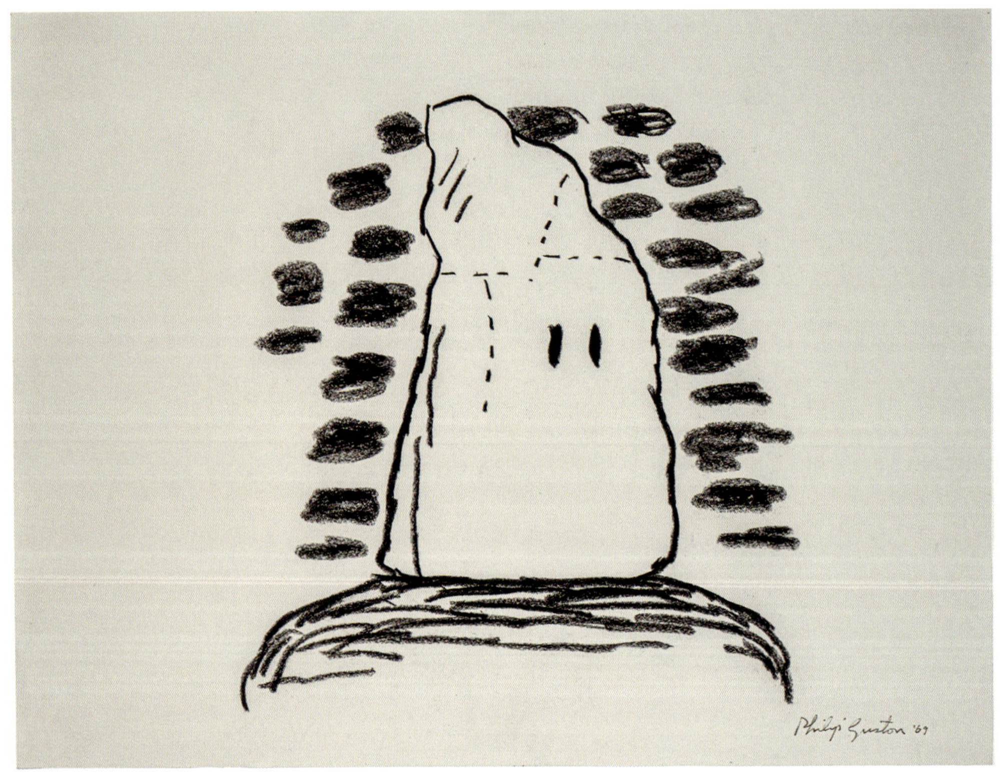

Philip Guston *Untitled*, 1970 *Untitled*, 1969

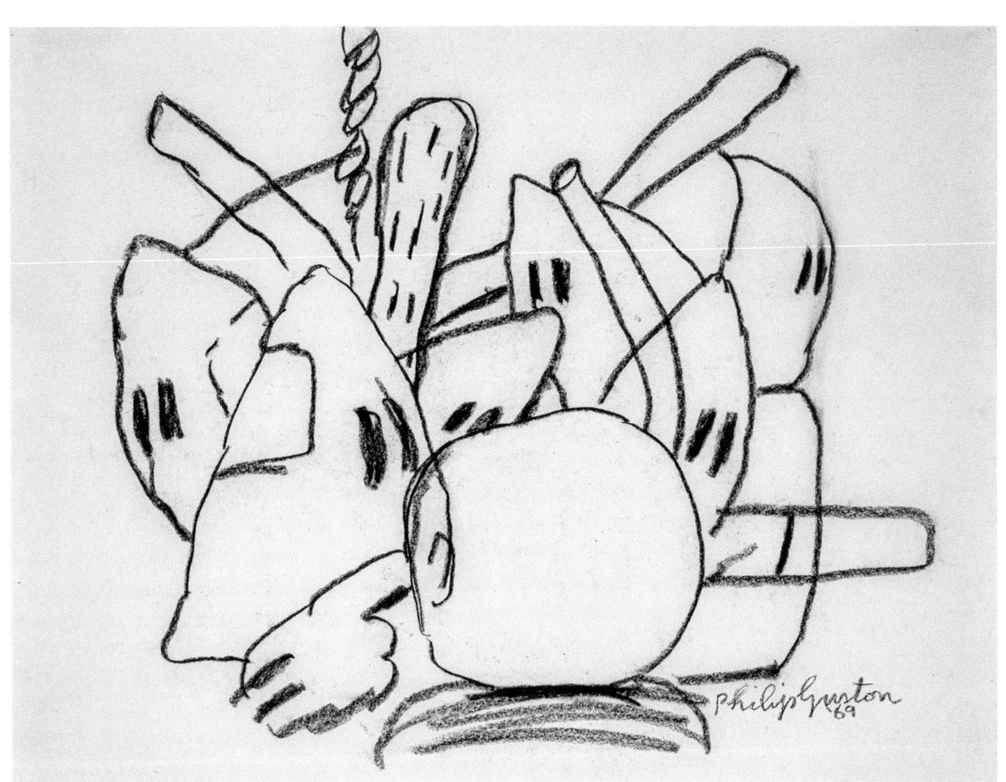

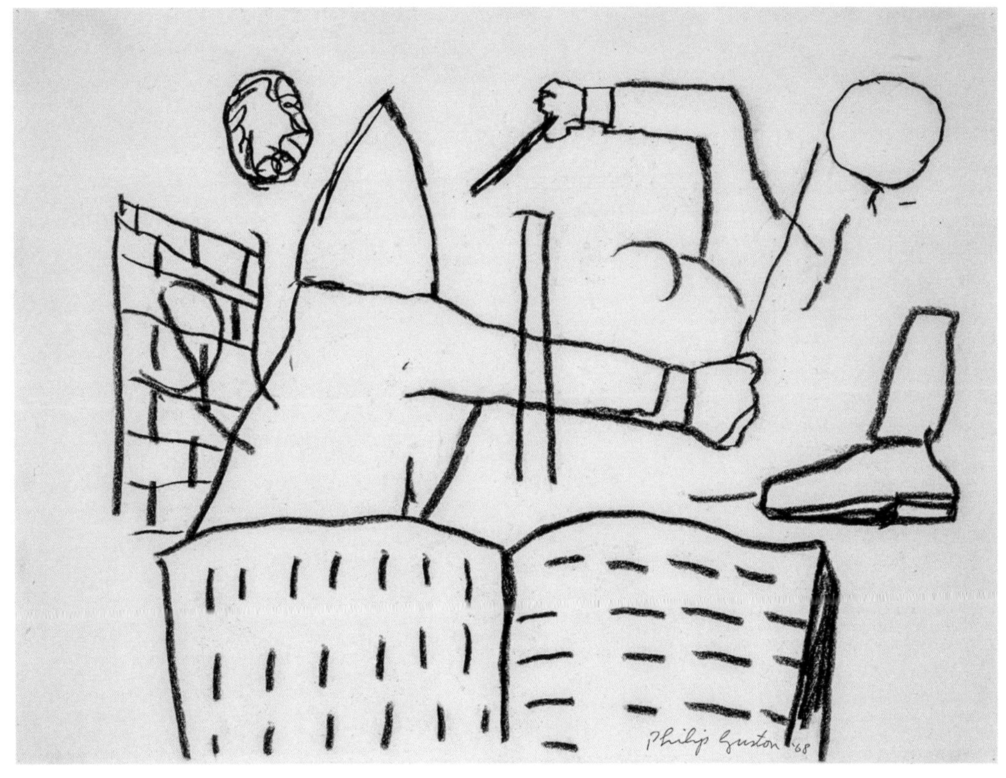

Philip Guston *Untitled (Hoods with Sheriff)*, 1969 *Untitled*, 1968

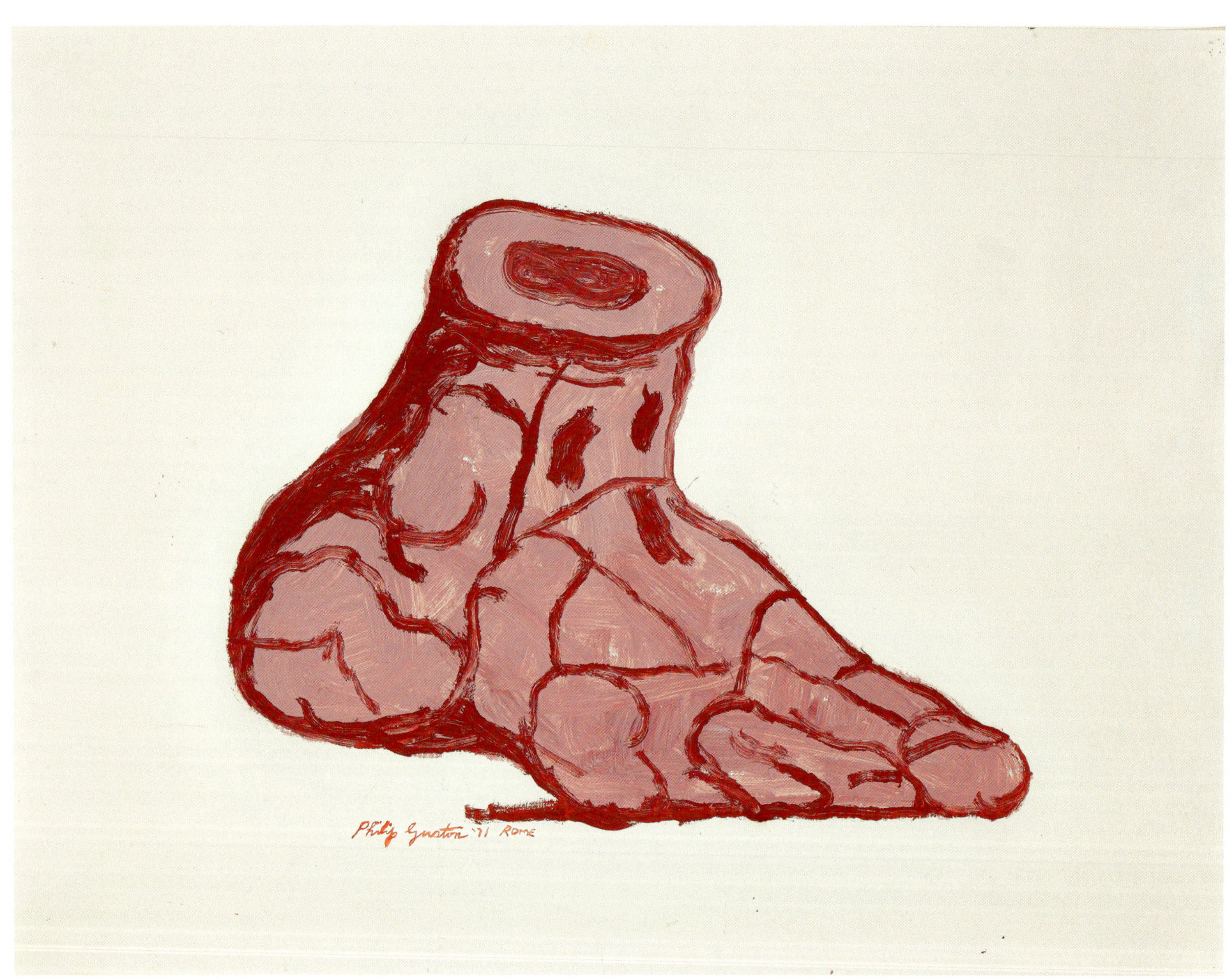

Philip Guston *Rome*, 1971

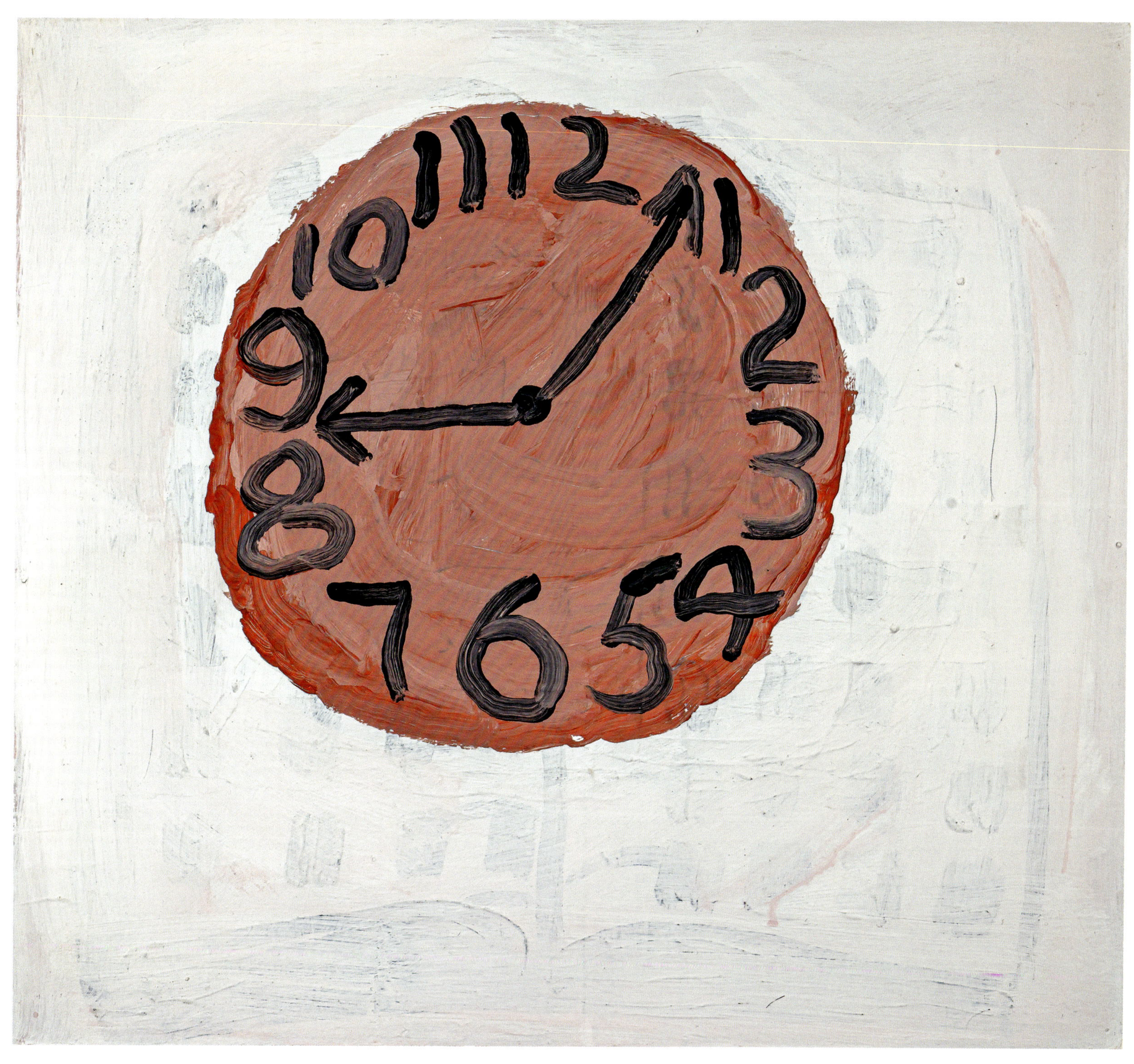

Philip Guston *Untitled,* 1968

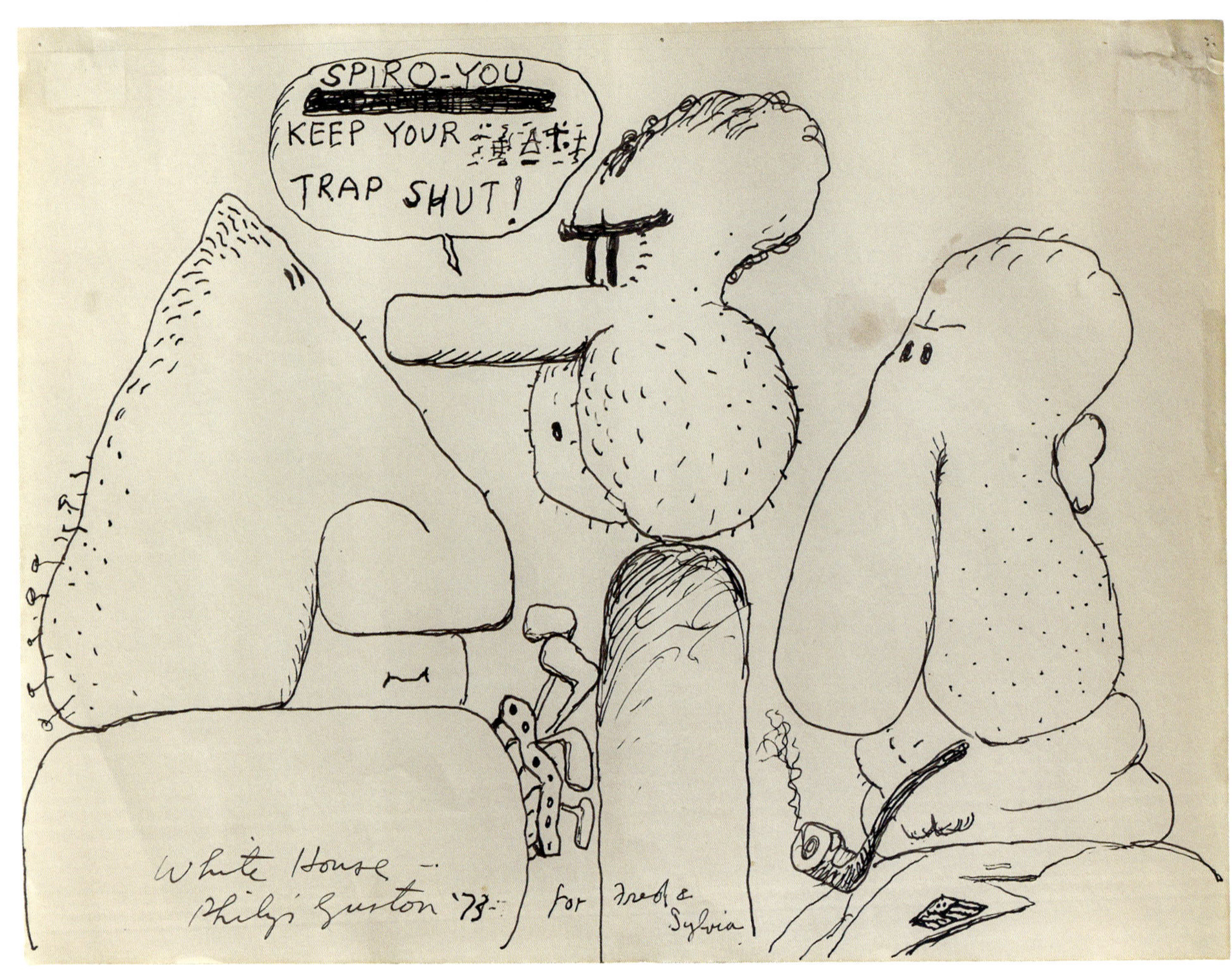

Philip Guston *White House*, 1973

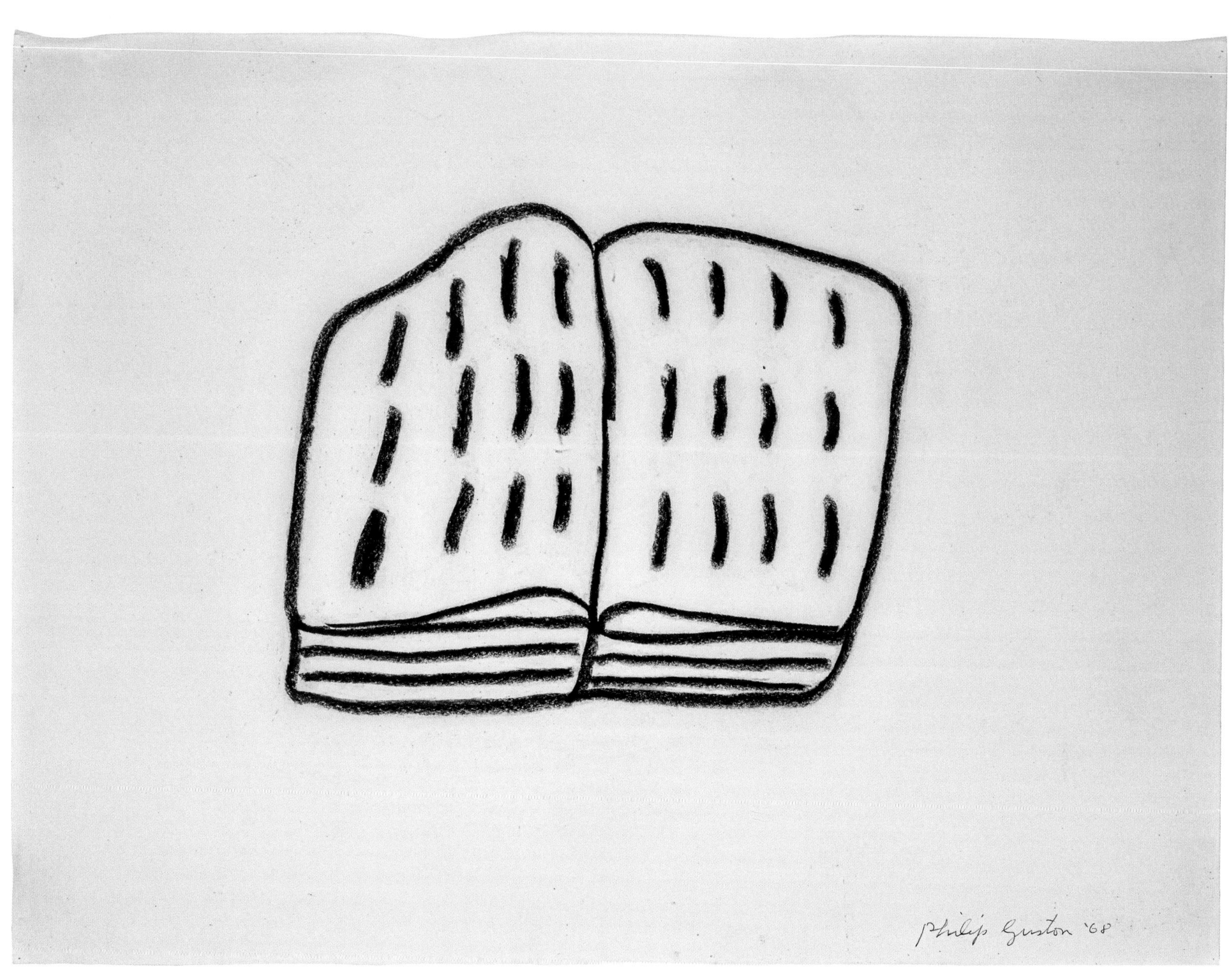

Philip Guston *Untitled (Book)*, 1968

Born in Johannesburg to a prominent anti-apartheid lawyer, William Kentridge (b. 1955) has long engaged with South Africa's violent history. The social and political drive in his practice is also inflected by his family's history—specifically his German, Jewish, and Lithuanian roots. While at university in the late 1970s Kentridge studied theatre and designed sets. Whether in his drawings, stop-animation films, or his ongoing dramaturgy, Kentridge maintains a strong interest in narrative and its potential to address social and political failings.

Kentridge drew *Another Country* (1994) shortly after apartheid ended. The flooded city street half-submerges a slave bell, a device used to regulate and control enslaved Africans in Cape Colony (present-day South Africa). Smudges and signs of erasure are characteristic of Kentridge's drawing style, and his drawings are often preparatory to—or, in the case of his stop-animation films, an integral part of—his time-based works. Kentridge's style, which alludes to the work of earlier politically minded artists such as Honoré Daumier, William Hogarth, and Francisco Goya, conveys a certain restlessness. Always open to revision and reworking, he understands drawing as a compelling vehicle to express injustice. Conceived as a prop for the video installation *More Sweetly Play the Dance* (2015), *Small Silhouette 35* (2014/2015) was derived from a charcoal drawing and later realized as a stainless-steel sculpture. The line drawing of the bird was the basis for a large floating standard, carried aloft in the lively procession which structures the thirty-five-metre-long moving frieze. *Silhouette* conveys something of the multidimensional and varied materials Kentridge keeps at his disposal.

William Kentridge *Drawing for Another Country (Flooded Street)*, 1994

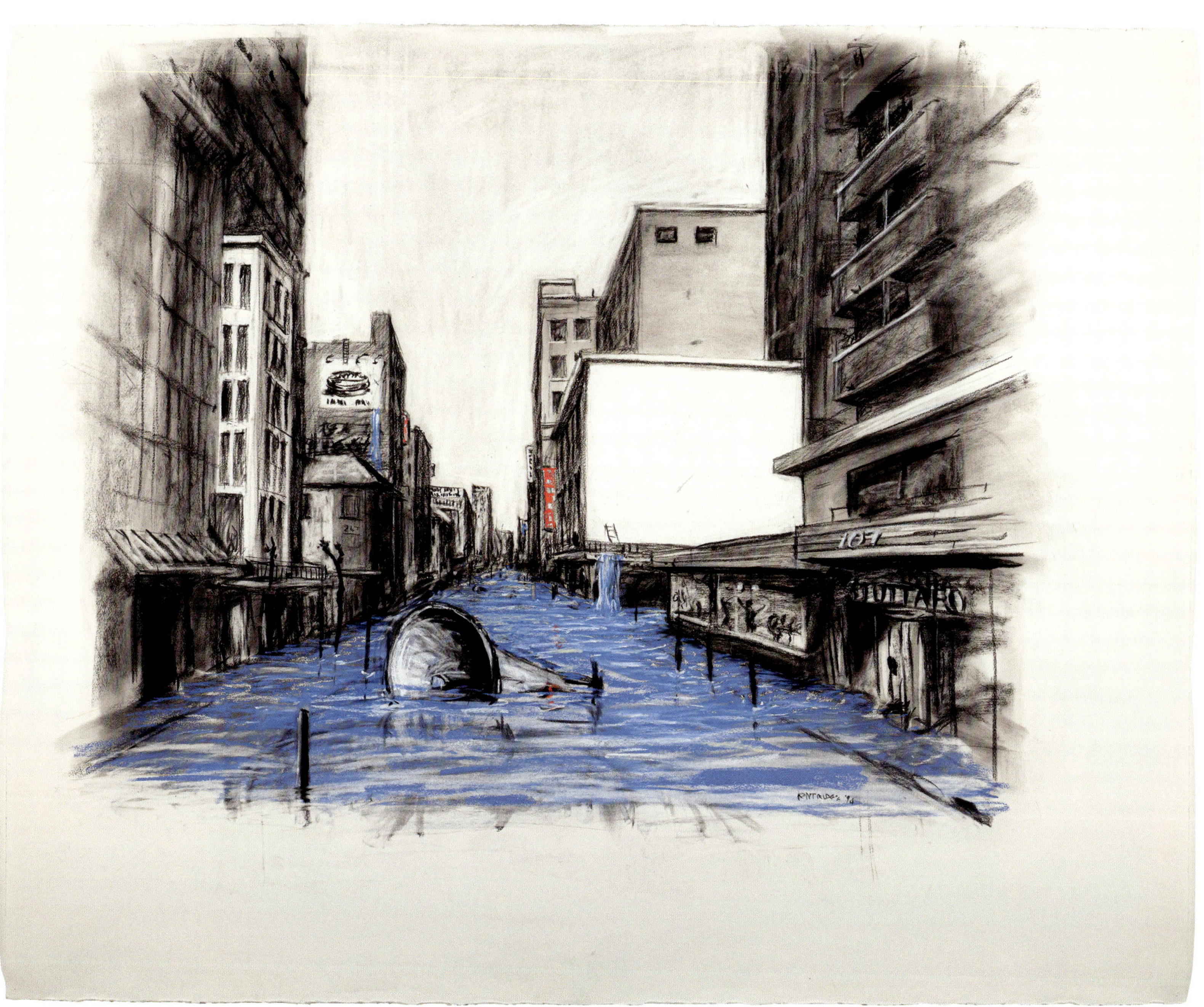

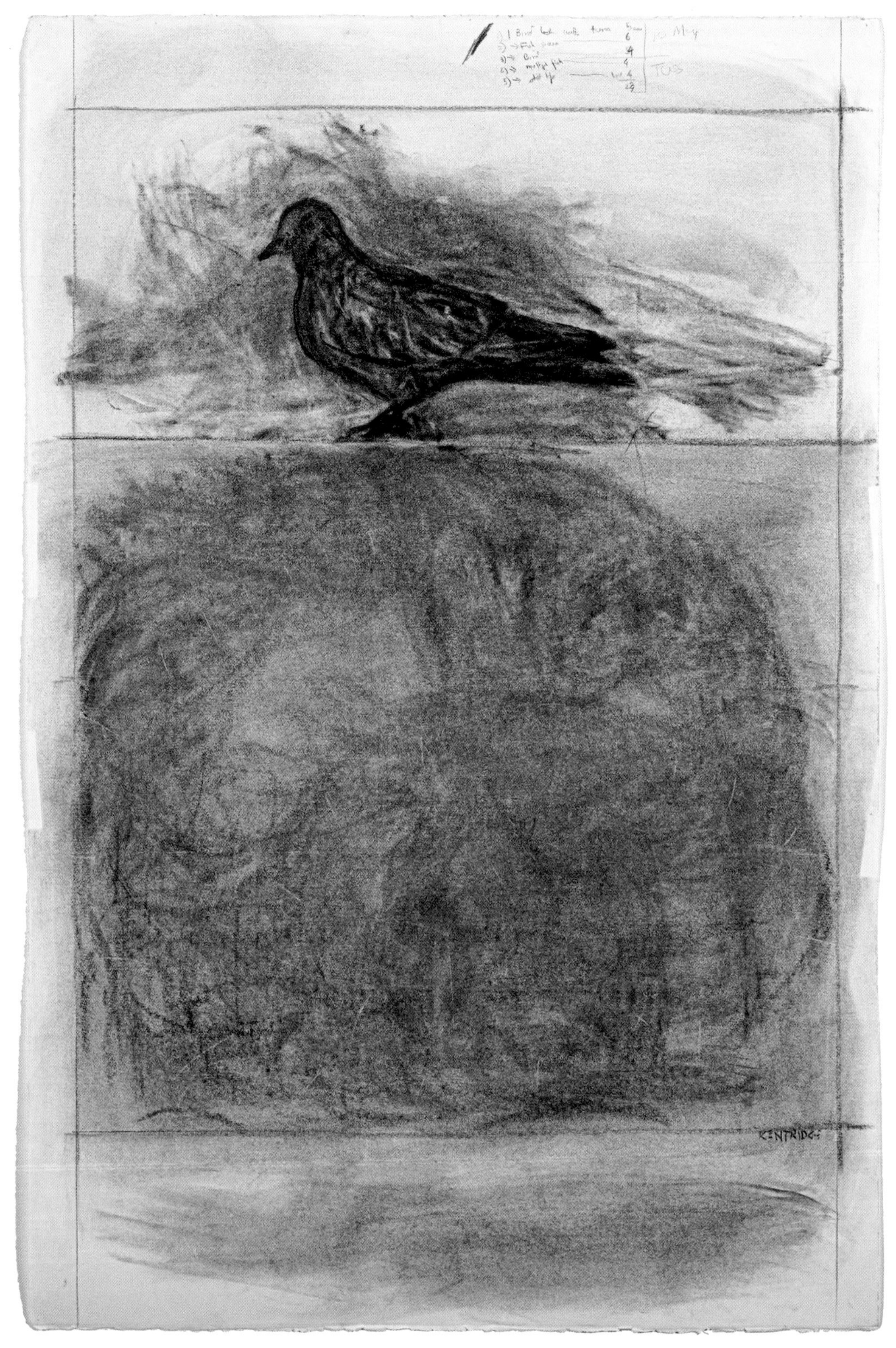

William Kentridge *Drawing for Medicine Chest,* 2000–2001

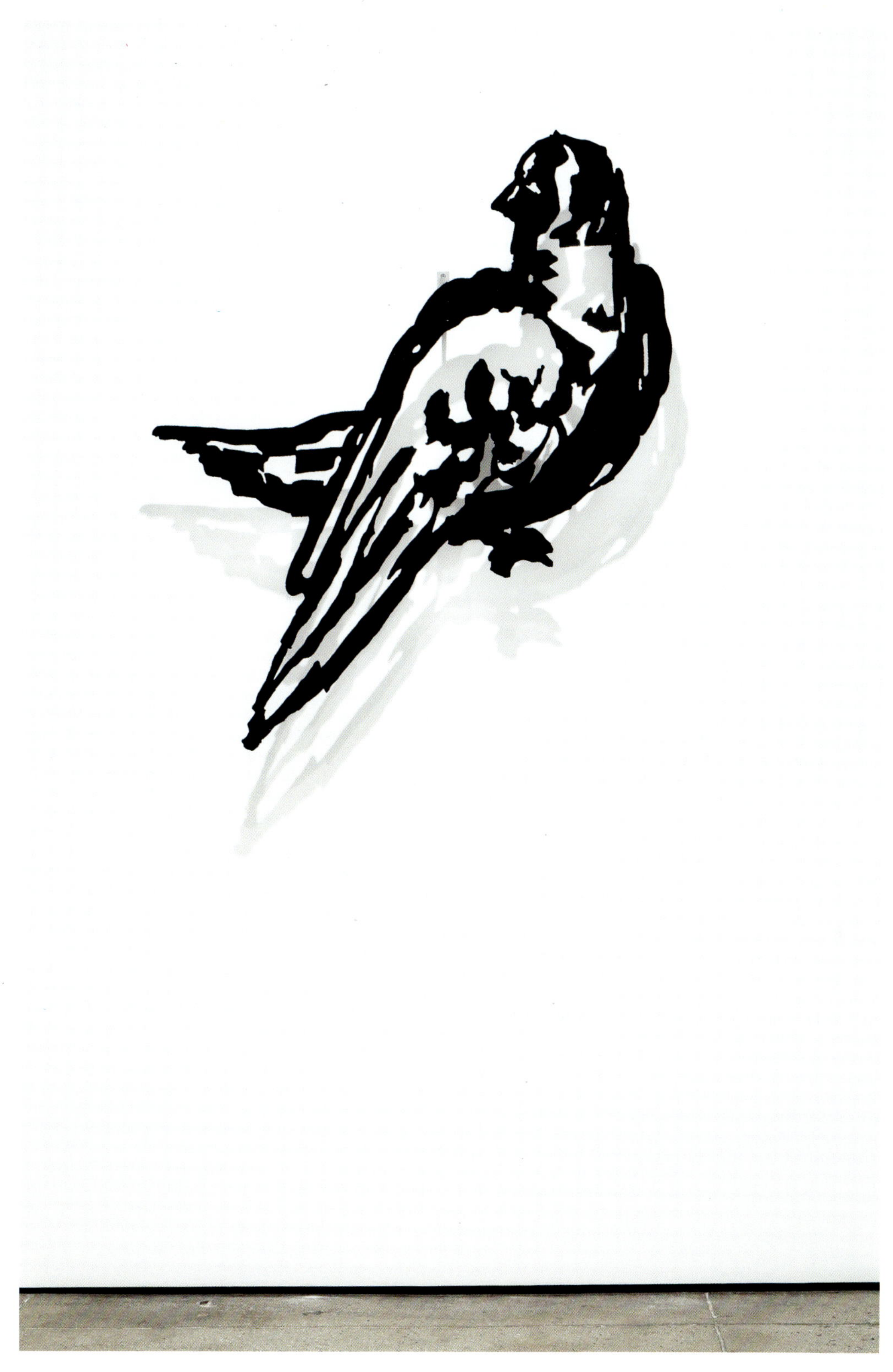

William Kentridge *Small Silhouette* 35, 2014/2015

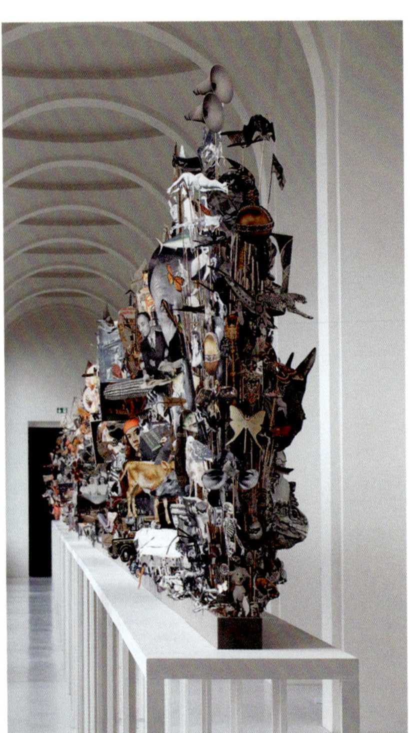

Installation view of Geoffrey Farmer's *Leaves of Grass* (2012) at *dOCUMENTA (13)*, Neue Galerie Kassel, Kassel, Germany, 2012.

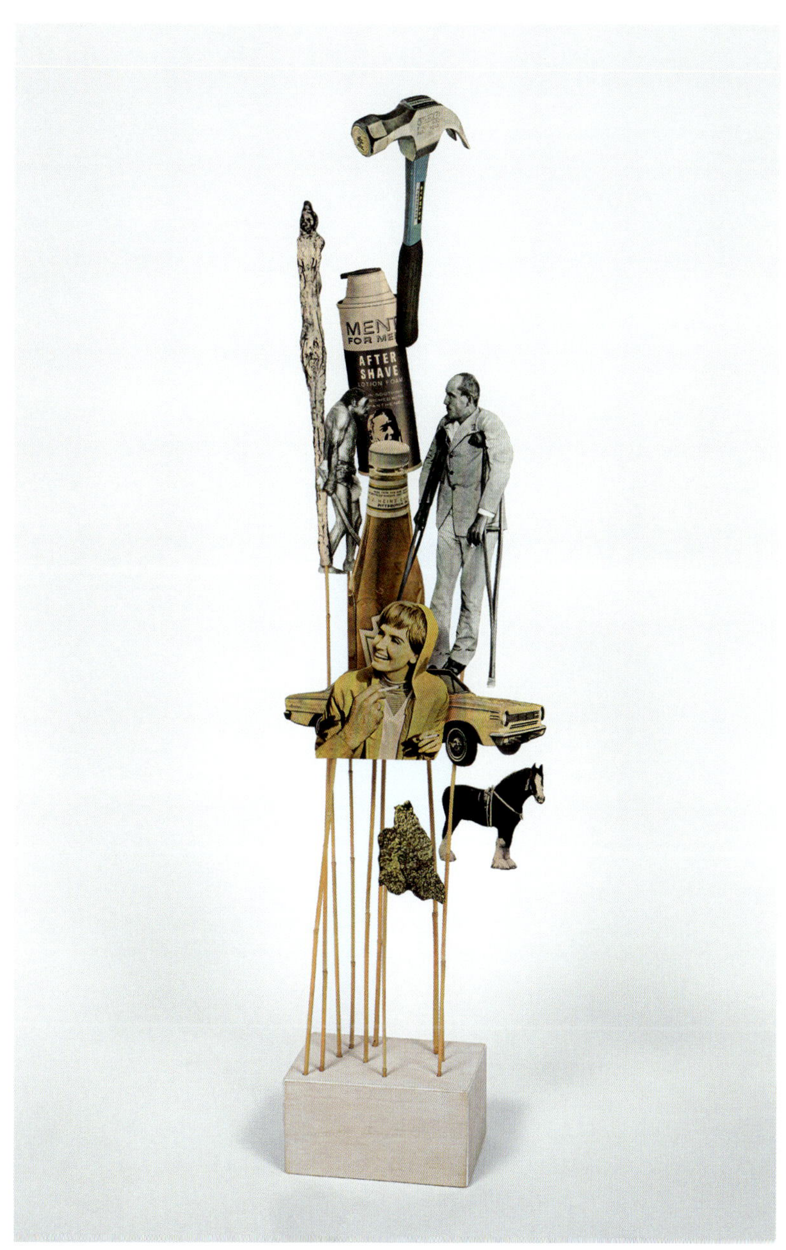
MENT
FOR ME
AFTER
SHAVE

John Massey *Number 16, Witness* (from the series *Studio Projections 1979*), 2008

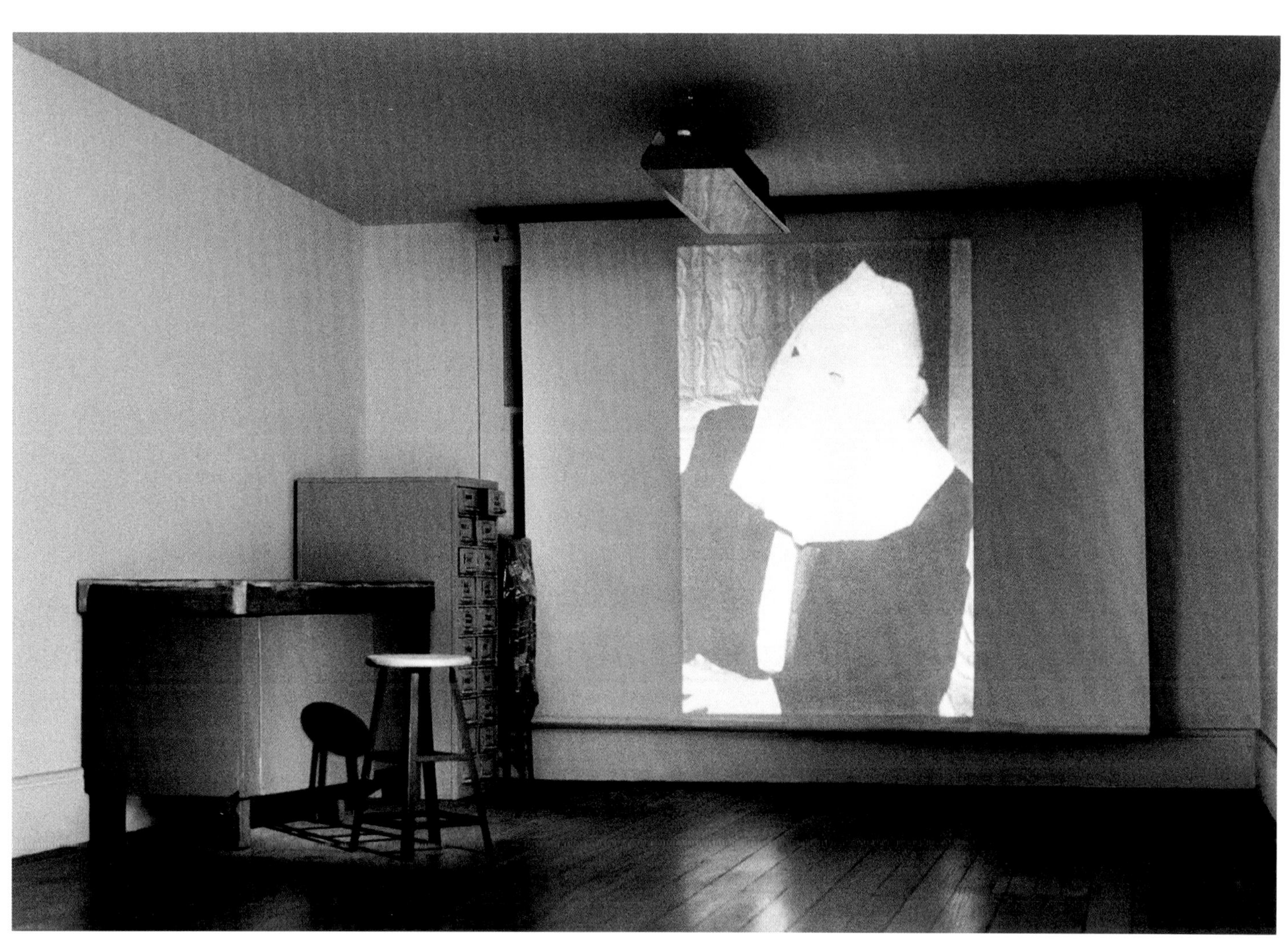

Thomas Houseago *Quaked Mask*, 2008

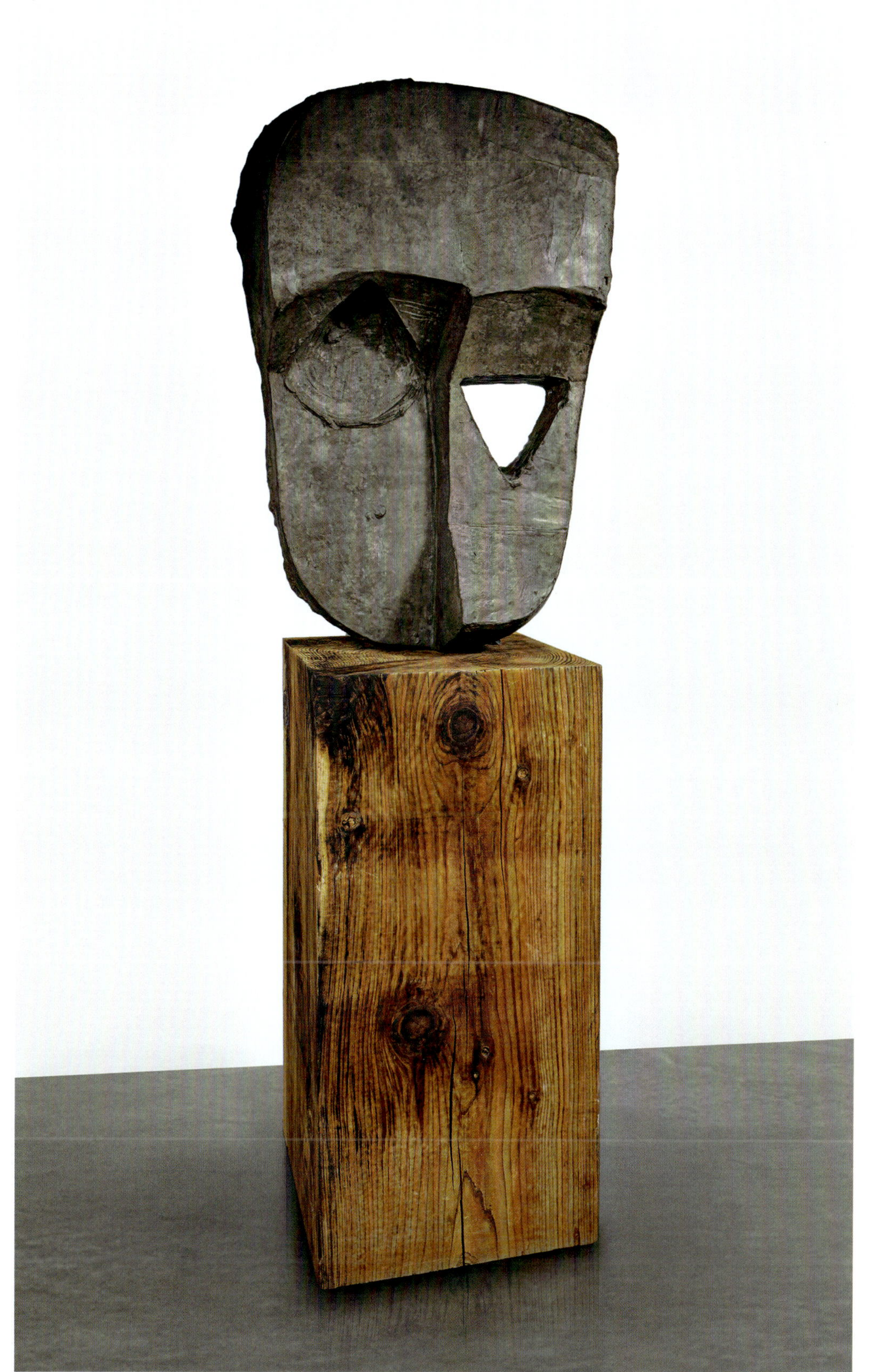

Andrew Grassie *Art Fabrication,* 2013

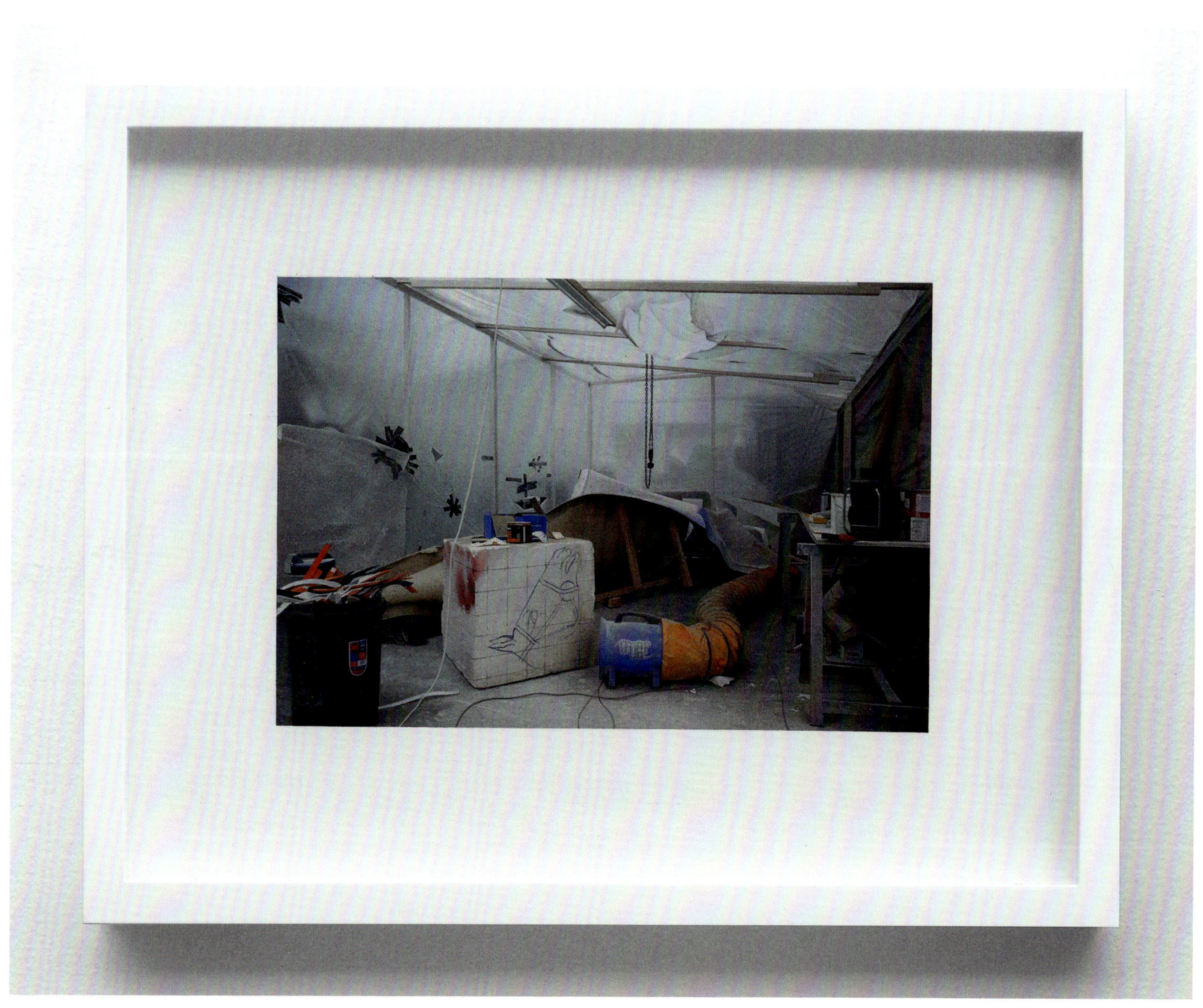

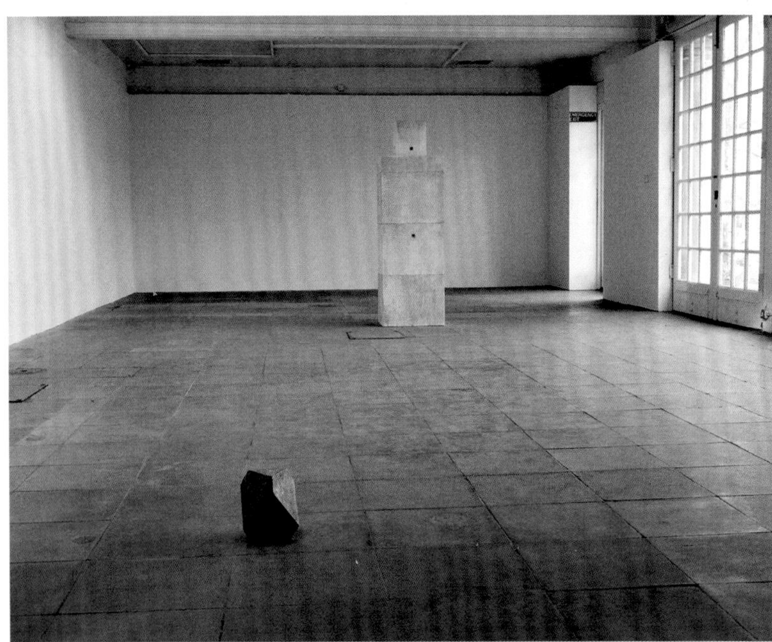

Installation view of Antony Gormley's *Heart* (1987) and *Room II* (1987) from *Five Works,* Serpentine Gallery, London, 1987.

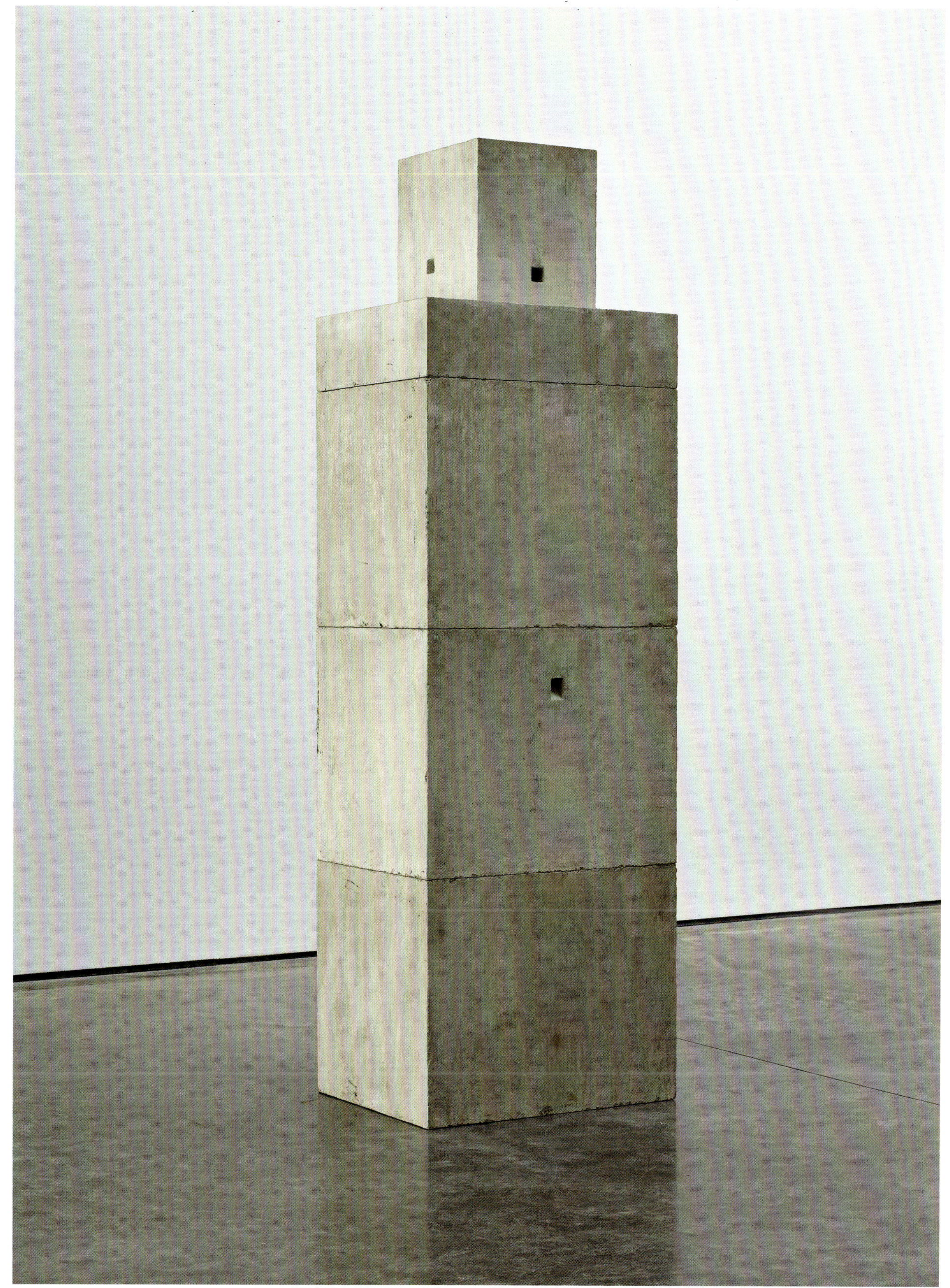

English sculptor Antony Gormley (b. 1950) is best known for works based on his own body. Following his studies in archaeology and art history at Cambridge University and Buddhist meditation in India and Sri Lanka, he began to make sculptures that questioned his own relationship to the world. Less interested in representing his own likeness, the castings and enclosures from and around his body are meant to reflect a universal human experience. Although they are made of different materials—concrete and cast iron—*Room II* (1987) and *Another Time X* (2008) are modelled directly from the artist's body.

Room II's concrete surface recalls a building facade, and the space within the hollow form perfectly accommodates Gormley's 6′4″ frame. The enclosing structure is intimately scaled for the body, at the same time protective and confining. *Another Time X* stands as a solitary figure but is identical to those in the related work *Another Place* (1997), a group of one hundred cast-iron figures facing the sea on Crosby Beach, Merseyside, near Liverpool, England. Temporarily installed on the beach in 2005, they were made permanent in 2007. These figures are based on casts from Gormley's body that were made in seventeen different sessions between May and July 1995. Although *Another Place* is permanently positioned on the coast, another one hundred related works of *Another Time* have been dispersed around the world in public and private collections. "The work asks where the human being sits within the scheme of things," Gormley said in 2008. "Each work is necessarily isolated and is an attempt to bear witness to what it is like to be alive, alone in space and time."[4]

Antony Gormley *Another Time X*, 2008

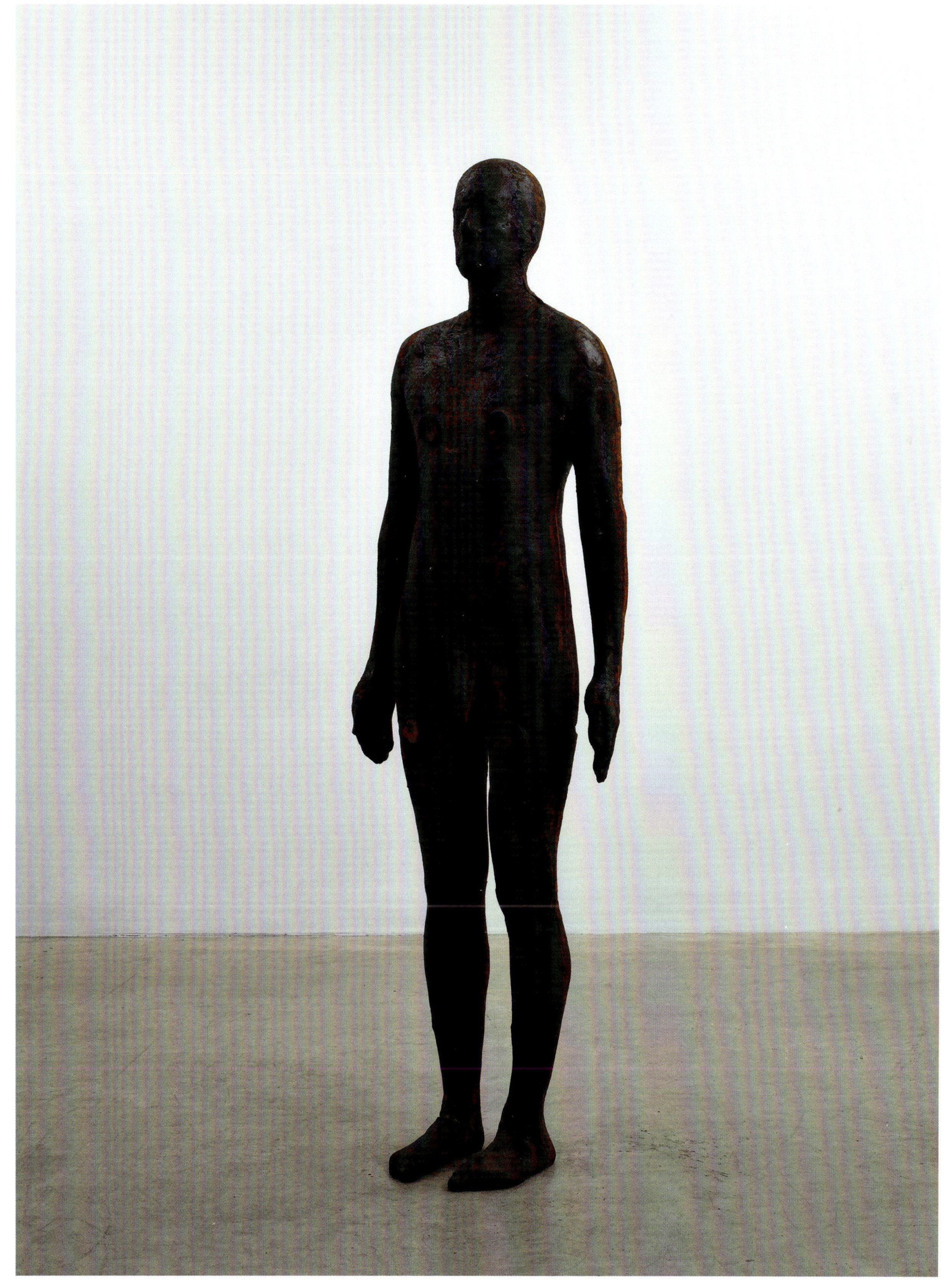

Wolfgang Tillmans *window, Sebastian Street*, 2017

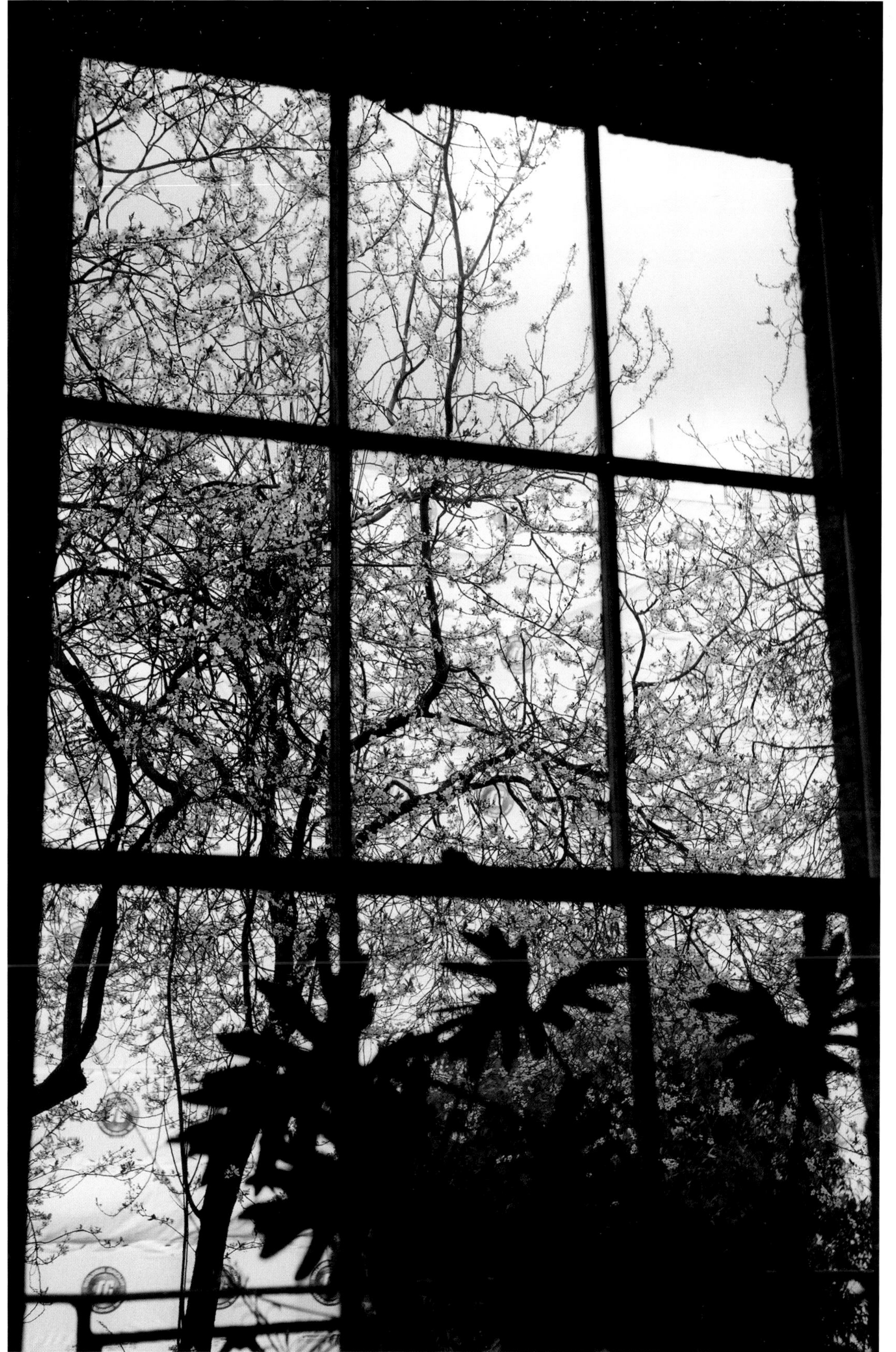

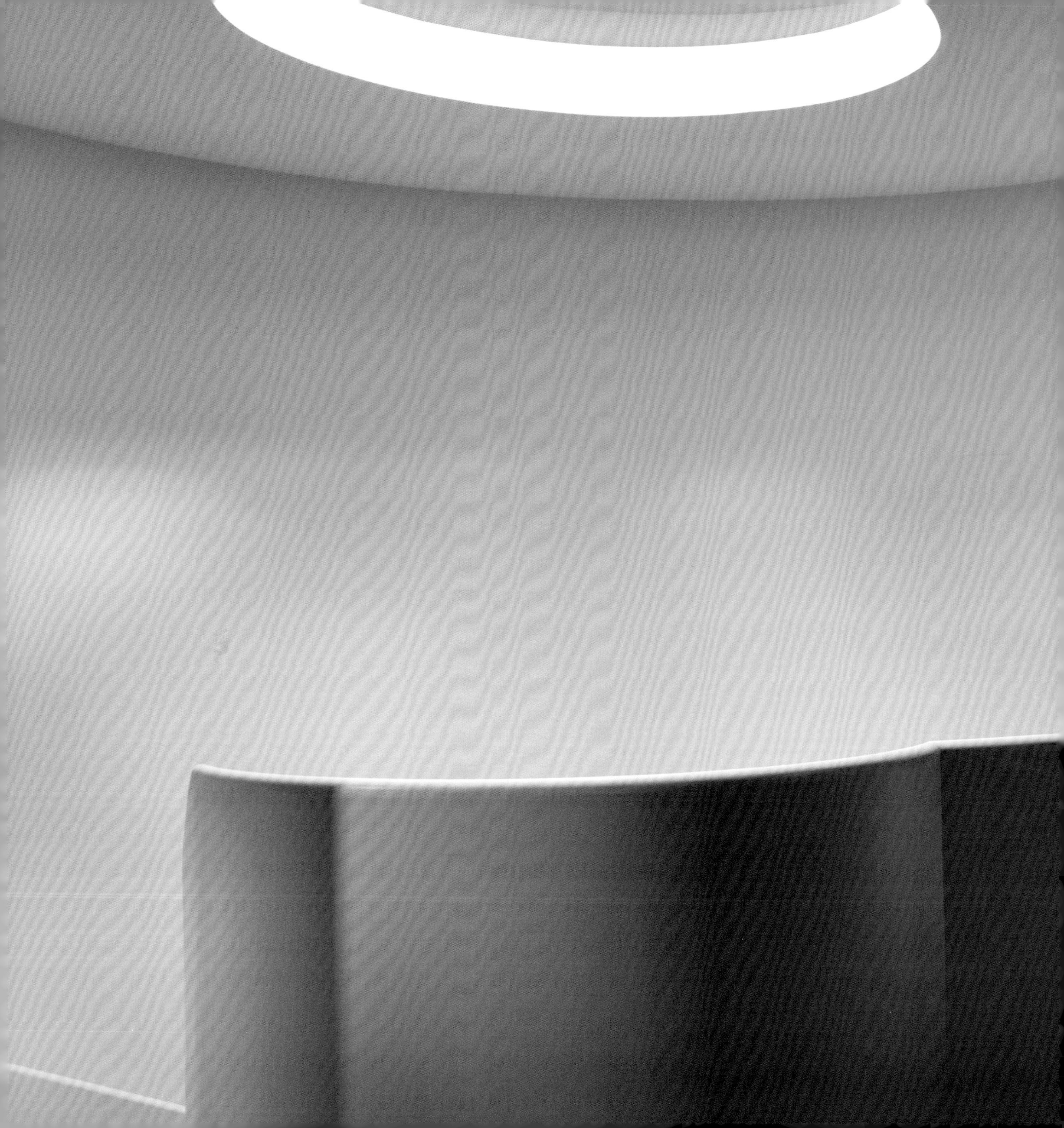

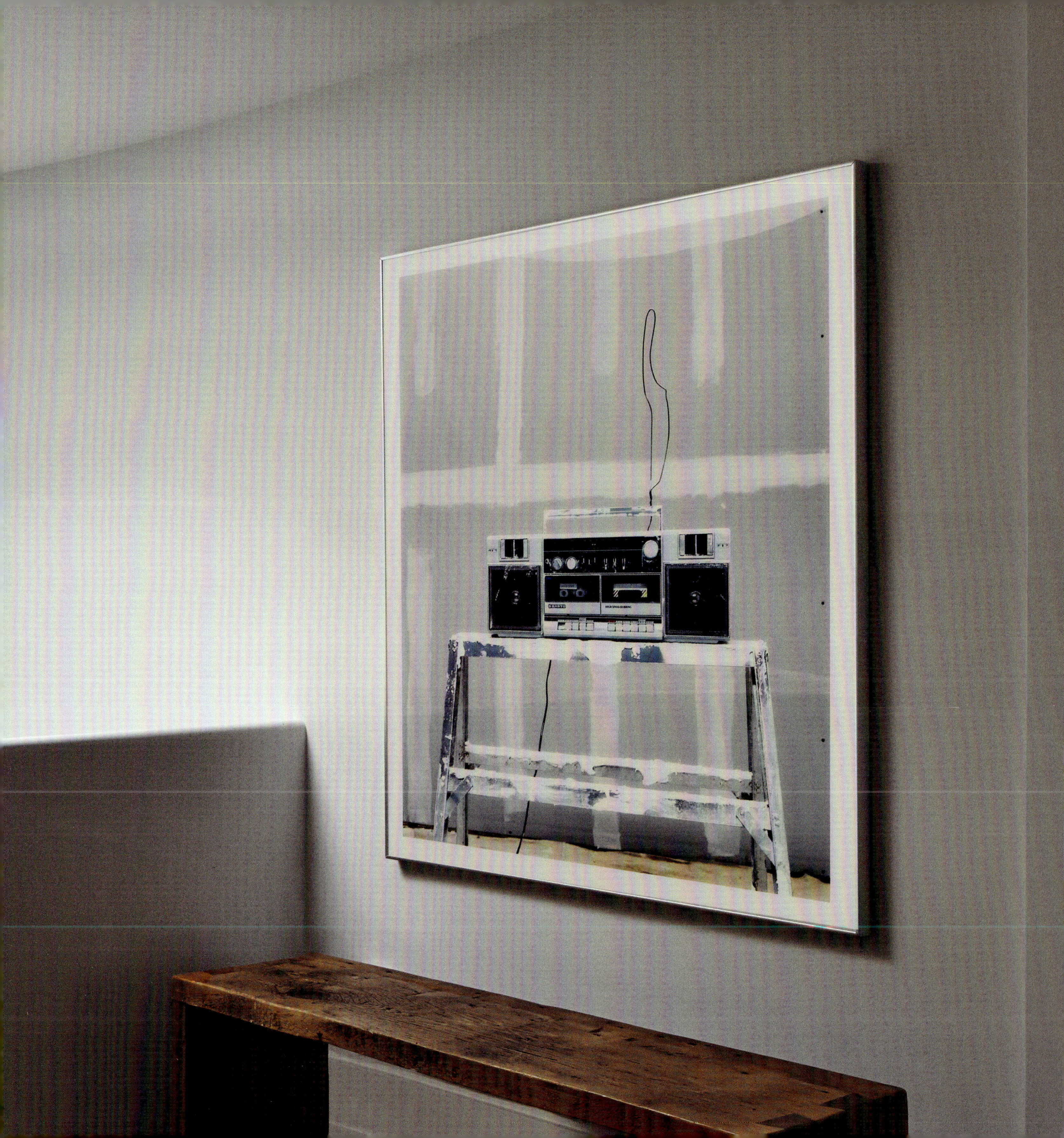

LIST OF WORKS

Works on display at the Art Gallery of Ontario for the exhibition *Light Years* (November 1, 2024–November 2, 2025) are marked with an asterisk.

All images are courtesy of the Art Gallery of Ontario and photographed by Toni Hafkenscheid, unless otherwise noted.

Ai Weiwei
born Beijing, China, 1957

* *Marble Plate*
2010
marble
100 cm diameter
Art Gallery of Ontario, Gift of Phil Lind, 2023
2023/297
© Ai Weiwei Studio;
Courtesy of Ai Weiwei Studio and Lisson Gallery.
Photography by Ken Adlard.
Page 96
Courtesy of Ai Weiwei Studio and the AGO.
Photography by Sean Weaver.
Page 97

Roy Arden
born Vancouver, British Columbia, Canada, 1957

Locked-Out Workers, (diptych) Vancouver, BC
1994
chromogenic print
99.1 × 64.8 cm
Art Gallery of Ontario,
Gift of the Estate of Philip B. Lind, 2024
2024/36
© Roy Arden
Image courtesy of the artist
Page 24

Bernd Becher
born Siegen, Germany, 1931
died Rostock, Germany, 2007

and

Hilla Becher
born Potsdam, Germany, 1934
died Düsseldorf, Germany, 2015

* *Chemical Plant, Wesseling/Cologne, Germany 1992*
1992
gelatin silver print
91.4 × 73.7 cm
Art Gallery of Ontario,
Gift of the Estate of Philip B. Lind, 2024
2024/37
© Estate Bernd and Hilla Becher, represented by Max Becher; courtesy Die Photographische Sammlung/SK Stiftung Kultur–Bernd and Hilla Becher Archive, Cologne
Page 77

Chris Burden
born Boston, Massachusetts, United States, 1946
died Topanga, California, United States, 2015

Trapezoid Bridge
2003
stainless steel
36.2 × 60 × 21.6 cm
Art Gallery of Ontario,
Gift of the Estate of Philip B. Lind, 2024
2024/38
© Chris Burden / Artists Rights Society (ARS), New York / CARCC Ottawa 2024
Page 93

Vija Celmins
born Riga, Latvia, 1938

Web #5
2009
mezzotint on paper
25.1 × 30.2 cm (image); 53.3 × 44.5 cm (sheet)
Art Gallery of Ontario, Gift of Philip B. Lind, 2019
2019/2487
© Vija Celmins, Courtesy Matthew Marks Gallery
Photo: AGO
Page 99

Greg Curnoe
born London, Ontario, Canada, 1936
died Delaware, Ontario, Canada, 1992

Canada
1962
paper collage
64.8 × 35.6 cm
Estate of Philip B. Lind
© Estate of Greg Curnoe / CARCC Ottawa 2024
Page 20

Diefenbaker, Canada
1962
paper collage
53.3 × 31.8 cm
Estate of Philip B. Lind
© Estate of Greg Curnoe / CARCC Ottawa 2024
Page 21

Andrew Dadson
born White Rock, British Columbia, Canada, 1980

* *White Tree*
2017
inkjet print mounted on aluminum
243.8 × 121.9 cm
Art Gallery of Ontario,
Gift of the Estate of Philip B. Lind, 2024
2024/39
© Andrew Dadson
Image courtesy of the artist and
Daniel Faria Gallery
Page 65

Thomas Demand
born Munich, Germany, 1964

* *Brennerautobahn*
1994; reprinted 2024
inkjet print mounted on aluminum
150 × 120 cm
Art Gallery of Ontario,
Gift of the Estate of Philip B. Lind, 2024
2024/40
© Thomas Demand / VG Bild-Kunst,
Bonn / CARCC Ottawa 2024
Image courtesy of the artist
Page 69

Stan Douglas
born Vancouver, British Columbia, Canada, 1960

* *Abbott & Cordova, 7 August 1971*
2008
chromogenic print mounted on aluminum
177.8 × 290.8 cm
Art Gallery of Ontario,
Gift of the Estate of Philip B. Lind, 2024
2024/41
© Stan Douglas
Page 31

* *MacLeod's Books, Vancouver*
2006
chromogenic print mounted on aluminum
178 × 305 cm
Estate of Philip B. Lind
© Stan Douglas
Pages 32–33

Masonic Lodge, Barkerville
2006
chromogenic print
84 × 83.5 cm
Estate of Philip B. Lind
© Stan Douglas
Page 28

Set for Win, Place or Show
(East View, West View, Overview)
1998
silver dye bleach prints (cibachromes)
71 × 98.5 cm each
Art Gallery of Ontario, Gift of Phil Lind, 2007
2007/386.1-.3
© Stan Douglas
Photo: AGO
Page 29

William Eggleston
born Memphis, Tennessee, United States, 1939

* *Sumner, Mississippi*
c. 1970
dye transfer print
38.1 × 55 cm
Art Gallery of Ontario,
Gift of the Estate of Philip B. Lind, 2024
2024/43
© Eggleston Artistic Trust
Image courtesy Eggleston Artistic Trust
and David Zwirner
Page 95

* *Untitled*
1971
dye transfer print
50.8 × 60.3 cm
Art Gallery of Ontario,
Gift of the Estate of Philip B. Lind, 2024
2024/42
© Eggleston Artistic Trust
Image courtesy Eggleston Artistic Trust
and David Zwirner
Page 94

Geoffrey Farmer
born Eagle Island, British Columbia, Canada, 1967

Collage
2012
Life magazine cutouts (1935–1985), archival glue,
miscanthus grass, floral foam and wooden base
approx. 60 cm
Estate of Philip B. Lind
© Geoffrey Farmer
Page 117

Leaves of Grass
2012
Life magazine cutouts (1935–1985), archival glue,
miscanthus grass, floral foam and wooden base
dimensions variable
National Gallery of Canada, Ottawa, Purchased
2012 with the generous support of the Audain
Endowment for Contemporary Canadian Art of
the National Gallery of Canada Foundation
45632
© Geoffrey Farmer
Installation view at *dOCUMENTA (13)*,
Neue Galerie Kassel, Kassel, Germany, 2012
Photo: Anders Sune Berg,
Courtesy Catriona Jeffries, Vancouver
Page 116

General Idea
active 1969–1994

2-024: Pan Over Drafting Table, Scattered with
Precision Instruments and Occasional Sketches
October 18, 1975
gelatin silver print mounted on serigraph print
and ink on card
45.8 × 35.6 cm
Estate of Philip B. Lind
© General Idea
Page 71

Liquid Assets
1980
Plexiglas, glass
33 × 18 × 13 cm
Estate of Philip B. Lind
© General Idea
Page 75

* *Three Men #1–#4*
1977
gelatin silver print mounted on cardboard
76.2 × 50.8 cm each
Estate of Philip B. Lind
© General Idea
Pages 72–73

Antony Gormley

born London, England, 1950

* *Another Time X*
2008
cast iron
edition 5/5 + 1 AP
191 × 59 × 36 cm
Art Gallery of Ontario,
Gift of the Estate of Philip B. Lind, 2024
2024/45
© Antony Gormley
Photo © Stephen White. Courtesy White Cube.
Page 127

* *Room II*
1987
concrete
208 × 51 × 66 cm
Art Gallery of Ontario,
Gift of the Estate of Philip B. Lind, 2024
2024/44
Installation view of *Room II* in *Five Works,*
Serpentine Gallery, London, 1987 with
Heart (1987), lead, 15 × 28 × 19 cm in foreground.
Page 124
© Antony Gormley
Photo © Stephen White. Courtesy White Cube.
Page 125

Rodney Graham

born Abbotsford, British Columbia, Canada, 1949
died Vancouver, British Columbia, Canada, 2022

Can of Worms
2000
chromogenic transparency mounted in aluminum
lightbox with walnut surround and silk electric cord
58.4 × 47 × 12.1 cm
Art Gallery of Ontario,
Gift of the Estate of Philip B. Lind, 2024
2024/46
© Estate of Rodney Graham
Page 49

* *Cedars, Stanley Park, #7*
1991–1993
gelatin silver print mounted on acrylic board
127 × 101.6 cm
Estate of Philip B. Lind
© Estate of Rodney Graham
Page 45

Fishing on a Jetty
2000
two transmounted chromogenic prints
234 × 123 cm (each);
248.9 × 393.7 cm (installed)
Art Gallery of Ontario,
Gift of the Estate of Philip B. Lind, 2024
2024/47
© Estate of Rodney Graham
Pages 50–51

* *Media Studies '77*
2016
two painted aluminum lightboxes with
transmounted chromogenic transparencies
232.2 × 182 × 17.8 cm (each);
232.2 × 376 × 17.8 cm (installed)
Art Gallery of Ontario,
Gift of the Estate of Philip B. Lind, 2024
2024/48
© Estate of Rodney Graham,
Courtesy Lisson Gallery
Image courtesy Lisson Gallery
Pages 54–55
Photo: Gieves Anderson
Page 10

Studies for Smoke Break 2 (Plaster): Boombox
2012
transmounted chromogenic print
121.9 × 101.6 cm
Estate of Philip B. Lind
© Estate of Rodney Graham
Page 57
Photo: Gieves Anderson
Page 131

Studies for Smoke Break 2 (Plaster): Box of Tapes
2012
transmounted chromogenic print
101.6 × 76.2 cm
Estate of Philip B. Lind
© Estate of Rodney Graham
Page 56

Tree with Bench, Vancouver, B.C.
1996
transmounted chromogenic print
132 × 158.7 cm
Estate of Philip B. Lind
© Estate of Rodney Graham
Page 46

Typewriter with Flour
2003
chromogenic transparency mounted in steel
lightbox with fabric-wrapped electrical cord
40 × 50.2 × 10.2 cm
Estate of Philip B. Lind
© Estate of Rodney Graham
Photo: Christine Burgin Gallery and
Donald Young Gallery
Page 52

Weathervane
2002
enameled stainless steel
67.9 × 63.5 × 54.6 cm
Estate of Philip B. Lind
© Estate of Rodney Graham
Page 53

Welsh Oaks #5
1998
gelatin silver print
91.5 × 122 cm
Estate of Philip B. Lind
© Estate of Rodney Graham
Page 47

Andrew Grassie

born Edinburgh, Scotland, 1966

Art Fabrication
2013
egg tempera on paper, on board
12.5 × 18.8 cm (unframed);
23.2 × 29.6 × 3.8 cm (framed)
Art Gallery of Ontario,
Gift of the Estate of Philip B. Lind, 2024
2024/49
© Andrew Grassie,
courtesy Maureen Paley, London
Photo: Andy Keate
Page 123

Philip Guston

born Montreal, Quebec, Canada, 1913
died Woodstock, New York, United States, 1980

* *Daisies*
1973–1974
ink on paper
41.9 × 31.8 cm
Estate of Philip B. Lind
© The Estate of Philip Guston,
courtesy Hauser & Wirth
Page 101

* *Rome*
1971
oil on paper
45.1 × 54.6 cm
Estate of Philip B. Lind
© The Estate of Philip Guston,
courtesy Hauser & Wirth
Page 108

* *Untitled*
1968
acrylic on panel
45.7 × 50.8 cm
Estate of Philip B. Lind
© The Estate of Philip Guston,
courtesy Hauser & Wirth
Page 109

* *Untitled*
1968
charcoal on paper
45.7 × 61 cm
Art Gallery of Ontario,
Gift of the Estate of Philip B. Lind, 2024
2024/50
© The Estate of Philip Guston,
courtesy Hauser & Wirth
Page 107

* *Untitled*
c. 1968
oil on panel
25.4 × 35.6 cm
Estate of Philip B. Lind
© The Estate of Philip Guston,
courtesy Hauser & Wirth
Page 104

* *Untitled*
1969
charcoal on paper
45.7 × 61 cm
Estate of Philip B. Lind
© The Estate of Philip Guston,
courtesy Hauser & Wirth
Page 106

* *Untitled*
1970
ink on paper
45.7 × 61 cm
Estate of Philip B. Lind
© The Estate of Philip Guston,
courtesy Hauser & Wirth
Page 106

* *Untitled*
1970
oil on hardboard
30.5 × 35.6 cm
Art Gallery of Ontario,
Gift of the Estate of Philip B. Lind, 2024
2024/51
© The Estate of Philip Guston,
courtesy Hauser & Wirth
Page 105

* *Untitled*
1979
oil on canvas
91.4 × 81.3 cm
Art Gallery of Ontario,
Gift of the Estate of Philip B. Lind, 2024
2024/53
© The Estate of Philip Guston,
courtesy Hauser & Wirth
Page 103

* *Untitled (Book)*
1968
charcoal on paper
45.7 × 61 cm
Estate of Philip B. Lind
© The Estate of Philip Guston,
courtesy Hauser & Wirth
Page 111

* *Untitled (Hoods with Sheriff)*
1969
charcoal on paper
45.4 × 58.4 cm
Art Gallery of Ontario,
Gift of the Estate of Philip B. Lind, 2024
2024/52
© The Estate of Philip Guston,
courtesy Hauser & Wirth
Page 107

* *White House*
1973
ink on paper
26.4 × 35.2 cm
Estate of Philip B. Lind
© The Estate of Philip Guston,
courtesy Hauser & Wirth
Page 110

Thomas Houseago

born Leeds, England, 1972

Quaked Mask
2008
bronze and redwood base
109.2 × 83.8 × 25.4 cm (excluding base);
243.8 × 83.8 × 61 cm (including base)
Estate of Philip B. Lind
© Thomas Houseago
Page 121

William Kentridge

born Johannesburg, South Africa, 1955

* *Drawing for Another Country (Flooded Street)*
1994
charcoal and pastel on paper
131.4 × 161.3 cm
Art Gallery of Ontario,
Gift of the Estate of Philip B. Lind, 2024
2024/54
© William Kentridge
Page 113

Drawing for Medicine Chest
2000–2001
charcoal and pastel on paper
119.4 × 78.7 cm
Estate of Philip B. Lind
© William Kentridge
Page 114

* *Small Silhouette 35*
2014/2015
acrylic paint on laser-cut stainless steel
144.8 × 126.4 cm
Art Gallery of Ontario,
Gift of the Estate of Philip B. Lind, 2024
2024/55
© William Kentridge
Image courtesy of Marian Goodman Gallery,
photo: Cathy Carver
Page 115

Anselm Kiefer

born Donaueschingen, Germany, 1945

Die Argonauten
2014
lead
7.6 × 35.6 × 24.1 cm
Estate of Philip B. Lind
© Anselm Kiefer
Page 79

Voyage au bout de la nuit
2006
mixed media on paper
49.5 × 106 cm
Estate of Philip B. Lind
© Anselm Kiefer
Page 78

John Massey

born Toronto, Ontario, Canada, 1950

Number 16, Witness
2008
from the series *Studio Projections 1979*
archival digital print
11.4 × 16.5 cm
Art Gallery of Ontario,
Gift of the Estate of Philip B. Lind, 2024
2024/56
© John Massey
Page 119

John McCracken

born Berkeley, California, United States, 1934
died New York City, New York, United States, 2011

* *Hyko-Ra*
1987
polyester resin, fibreglass, plywood
304.8 × 53.3 × 7 cm
Art Gallery of Ontario,
Gift of the Estate of Philip B. Lind, 2024
2024/57
© The Estate of John McCracken
Courtesy The Estate of John McCracken
and David Zwirner
Page 67
Photo: Gieves Anderson
Page 148

Scott McFarland

born Vancouver, British Columbia, Canada, 1975

Cabin with Motion Light
2001
digital chromogenic print
109.2 × 137.2 cm
Estate of Philip B. Lind
© Scott McFarland
Image courtesy of the artist
Page 25

Sugar Bush, Caledon Ontario (study)
2009
archival inkjet print
111.8 × 304.8 cm
Estate of Philip B. Lind
© Scott McFarland
Image courtesy of the artist
Pages 26–27

Jonathan Monk

born Leicester, England, 1969

Rew-Shay Hood Project VI
2008–2009
airbrush paint and a 1970 Dodge Charger
automobile hood
144.8 × 137.2 cm
Estate of Philip B. Lind
© Jonathan Monk; Image courtesy the artist
and Casey Kaplan, New York
Page 91

N.E. Thing Co.

active Vancouver 1966–1978

ACT # 13 – Fallen Logs, 30 Miles, East of Hope, B.C. Canada (1968)
1968
mixed media on photograph
61 × 91.4 cm
Estate of Philip B. Lind
© N.E. Thing Co.
Page 16

ACT # 17 – Simulated Tree Structures, North Vancouver, B.C. Information Booth, Foot of Capilano Road, N.V. B.C. Canada (1968)
1968
mixed media on photograph
61 × 91.4 cm
Estate of Philip B. Lind
© N.E. Thing Co.
Page 16

ACT # 32 – Seven Steel Pilings, Gravel Filled, White Lake Narrows, Ontario, Canada (1968)
1968
mixed media on photograph
61 × 91.4 cm
Estate of Philip B. Lind
© N.E. Thing Co.
Page 16

ACT # 73 – Ski Line Track, Anonymous Mountain, (1968)
1968
mixed media on photograph
61 × 91.4 cm
Estate of Philip B. Lind
© N.E. Thing Co.
Page 16

ACT # 74 – Andy Warhol's Brillo Boxes, Coll. National Gallery of Canada, Ottawa, Canada (1968)
1968
mixed media on photograph
61 × 91.4 cm
Estate of Philip B. Lind
© N.E. Thing Co.
Page 17

ACT # 106 – Target for Axe Training, Loggers Fair, Pacific National Exhibition, Vancouver, B.C. (1968) (Note Arrow)
1968
mixed media on photograph
61 × 91.4 cm
Estate of Philip B. Lind
© N.E. Thing Co.
Page 16

ACT # 112 – Microwave Tower, Middle of Saskatchewan, (1968) As Seen In Rear View Mirror On Netco Vehicle
1968
mixed media on photograph
61 × 91.4 cm
Estate of Philip B. Lind
© N.E. Thing Co.
Page 16

Double Light Casts – 1969 Seymour River N. Vancouver, B.C.
1968–1969; assembled 1981
cibachrome, map, felt pen, ink, pencil, crayon, paper
96.5 × 94 cm
Estate of Philip B. Lind
© N.E. Thing Co.
Page 19

Julian Opie
born London, England, 1958

* *This is Julian walking.*
2002
computer film on plasma screen
105 × 66 × 15 cm
Art Gallery of Ontario,
Gift of the Estate of Philip B. Lind, 2024
2024/58
© Julian Opie
Images courtesy of Julian Opie studio and Lisson Gallery
Pages 86–87

Bettina Pousttchi
born Mainz, Germany, 1971

Vancouver Time
2018
from the series *World Time Clock*
chromogenic print
120 × 149.9 cm
Art Gallery of Ontario,
Gift of the Estate of Philip B. Lind, 2024
2024/59
© Bettina Pousttchi
Page 89

Thomas Ruff
born Zell, Germany, 1958

* *jpeg gs02*
2007
chromogenic print with Diasec
246.1 × 185.1 cm
Art Gallery of Ontario,
Gift of the Estate of Philip B. Lind, 2024
2024/60
© Thomas Ruff / VG Bild-Kunst, Bonn / CARCC Ottawa 2024
Image courtesy the artist and David Zwirner
Page 63

Allan Sekula
born Erie, Pennsylvania, United States, 1951
died Los Angeles, California, United States, 2013

Volunteer watching, volunteer smiling (Isla de Ons, 12/19/02)
2002–2003
from the series *Black Tide/Marea Negra*
diptych, cibachrome print
67.3 × 171.4 cm (both panels)
Art Gallery of Ontario,
Gift of the Estate of Philip B. Lind, 2024
2024/61
© Allan Sekula Studio
Image courtesy of Marian Goodman Gallery, photo: Thierry Bal
Pages 80–81

Laurie Simmons
born Long Island, New York, United States, 1949

* *Lying Objects (Set of Four)*
1992
offset lithographs on Somerset Satin paper
38.1 × 50.8 cm each
Art Gallery of Ontario,
Gift of the Estate of Philip B. Lind, 2024
2024/62
© Laurie Simmons
Image courtesy of the artist
Pages 82–83

Ron Terada
born Vancouver, British Columbia, Canada, 1969

* *Entering City of Vancouver*
2002
3M reflective highway vinyl, extruded aluminum, industrial lights, galvanized steel, wood
305 × 305 × 152 cm
Collection of the Vancouver Art Gallery,
Gift of Phil Lind
2014.45.1 a-j
© Ron Terada
Photo: Linda Chinfen,
Courtesy Catriona Jeffries, Vancouver
Page 23

Wolfgang Tillmans
born Remscheid, Germany, 1968

* *window, Sebastian Street*
2017
inkjet print on paper mounted on Dibond aluminum in artist's frame
212 × 145 × 6 cm
Art Gallery of Ontario,
Gift of the Estate of Philip B. Lind, 2024
2024/35
© Wolfgang Tillmans
Courtesy of the artist, David Zwirner, New York/Hong Kong, Galerie Buchholz, Berlin/Cologne, and Maureen Paley, London
Page 129

Jeff Wall
born Vancouver, British Columbia, Canada, 1946

* *Basin in Rome 1*
2004
transparency in lightbox
31 × 31 cm
Art Gallery of Ontario,
Gift of the Estate of Philip B. Lind, 2024
2024/67
© Jeff Wall
Image courtesy of the artist
Page 40

* *Concrete Ball*
2002
chromogenic print
183 × 244.4 cm
Art Gallery of Ontario,
Gift of the Estate of Philip B. Lind, 2024
2024/66
© Jeff Wall
Image courtesy of the artist
Page 35

* *Double Self-Portrait*
1979; printed 2012
inkjet print
50.8 × 61 cm
Estate of Philip B. Lind
© Jeff Wall
Image courtesy of the artist
Page 37

* *Park Drive*
1994; printed 2014
inkjet print on paper mounted on aluminum
119 × 136 cm
Estate of Philip B. Lind
© Jeff Wall
Image courtesy of the artist
Page 38

* *River Road*
1994; printed 1997
transparency in lightbox
90.3 × 119 cm
Art Gallery of Ontario,
Gift of the Estate of Philip B. Lind, 2024
2024/65
© Jeff Wall
Image courtesy of the artist
Page 41

* *Steves Farm, Steveston*
1980; printed 1988
chromogenic print
40.6 × 131.4 cm
Art Gallery of Ontario,
Gift of the Estate of Philip B. Lind, 2024
2024/63
© Jeff Wall
Page 43

* Test print for *In the Public Garden*
1993
chromogenic print
41 × 51.1 cm
Art Gallery of Ontario,
Gift of the Estate of Philip B. Lind, 2024
2024/64
© Jeff Wall
Page 42

* *The Pine on the Corner*
1990; printed 2016
inkjet print
119 × 149 cm
Estate of Philip B. Lind
© Jeff Wall
Image courtesy of the artist
Page 39

Christopher Williams
born Los Angeles, California, United States, 1956

* *180HR15 Michelin XAS*
Manufactured by: Tigar Tyres d.o.o., Pirot, Serbia, Est. 1935
Parent Company: SCA Compagnie Générale des
Établissements Michelin, Clermont-Ferrand, France,
Est. 1889 Studio Rhein Verlag, Düsseldorf February 22, 2016
2016
selenium-toned silver gelatin print
50.5 × 60.6 cm
Art Gallery of Ontario,
Gift of the Estate of Philip B. Lind, 2024
2024/70
© Christopher Williams
Image courtesy the artist, David Zwirner,
and Galerie Gisela Capitain, Cologne
Page 59

* *Cutaway model Switar 25mm f1.4 AR.*
Glass, wood and brass.
Photography by the Douglas M. Parker Studio, Glendale,
California, November 17, 2007–November 30, 2007
2008
gelatin silver print
50.8 × 61 cm
Art Gallery of Ontario,
Gift of the Estate of Philip B. Lind, 2024
2024/68
© Christopher Williams
Image courtesy the artist, David Zwirner,
and Galerie Gisela Capitain, Cologne
Page 60

* *Fig. 4: Changing the shutter speed Exakta Varex IIa 35 mm*
film SLR camera
Manufactured by Ihagee Kamerawerk Steenbergen & Co,
Dresden, German Democratic Republic Body serial no.
979625 (Production period: 1960–1963)
Carl Zeiss Jena Tessar 50mm f/2.8 lens Manufactured by
VEB Carl Zeiss Jena, Jena, German Democratic Republic
Serial no. 8034351 (Production period: 1967–1970)
Model: Christoph Boland Studio Thomas Borho,
Oberkasseler Str. 39, Düsseldorf, Germany June 19, 2012
2012
inkjet print on cotton rag paper
55.9 × 44.5 cm
Art Gallery of Ontario,
Gift of the Estate of Philip B. Lind, 2024
2024/69
© Christopher Williams
Image courtesy the artist, David Zwirner,
and Galerie Gisela Capitain, Cologne
Page 61

Erwin Wurm
born Bruck an der Mur, Austria, 1954

Disobedience
2014
acrylic and fabric
45 × 23 × 23 cm (left figure),
47 × 24 × 25 cm (right figure)
Art Gallery of Ontario,
Gift of the Estate of Philip B. Lind, 2024
2024/71
© Erwin Wurm / Bildrecht / CARCC Ottawa 2024
Photo: Eva Würdinger
Page 85

This book was published on the occasion of the exhibition *Light Years: The Phil Lind Gift* at the Art Gallery of Ontario from November 1, 2024, to November 2, 2025.

Unless otherwise noted in the list of works (pages 133–140), all photography courtesy of the Art Gallery of Ontario, and all artworks collection of the Art Gallery of Ontario or the Estate of Philip B. Lind.

Every effort has been made to trace ownership of visual and written material used in this catalogue. Errors or omissions will be corrected in subsequent printings provided notification is sent to the publishers.

Printed and bound in Canada.
Printed on GardaMatt Art FSC White 100 lb Text.
Case bound with Milbank Linen (MBL 952).
Typeset in *Orleans* by Paul Barnes, Commercial Type.

ISBN: 9781773104393

10 9 8 7 6 5 4 3 2 1

Library and Archives Canada Cataloguing in Publication

TITLE: Light years : the Phil Lind gift / Adam Welch.

OTHER TITLES: Phil Lind gift

NAMES: Welch, Adam, author, organizer | Art Gallery of Ontario, publisher.

DESCRIPTION: Co-published by the Art Gallery of Ontario. | Catalogue of an exhibition held at the Art Gallery of Ontario from November 1, 2024 to November 2, 2025. | Includes bibliographical references.

IDENTIFIERS: Canadiana 20240438930 | ISBN 9781773104393 (hardcover)

SUBJECTS: LCSH: Lind, Philip B., 1943-2023—Art collections—Exhibitions. | LCSH: Art—Private collections—Exhibitions. | LCSH: Art, Modern—20th century—Exhibitions. | LCSH: Art, Modern—21st century—Exhibitions. | LCGFT: Exhibition catalogs.

CLASSIFICATION: LCC N6488.C3 T67 2025 | DDC 709.040074/713541—dc23

Art Gallery of Ontario
317 Dundas Street West
Toronto, Ontario
M5T 1G4
Canada
ago.ca

Goose Lane Editions
500 Beaverbrook Court, Suite 330
Fredericton, New Brunswick
E3B 5X4
Canada
gooselane.com

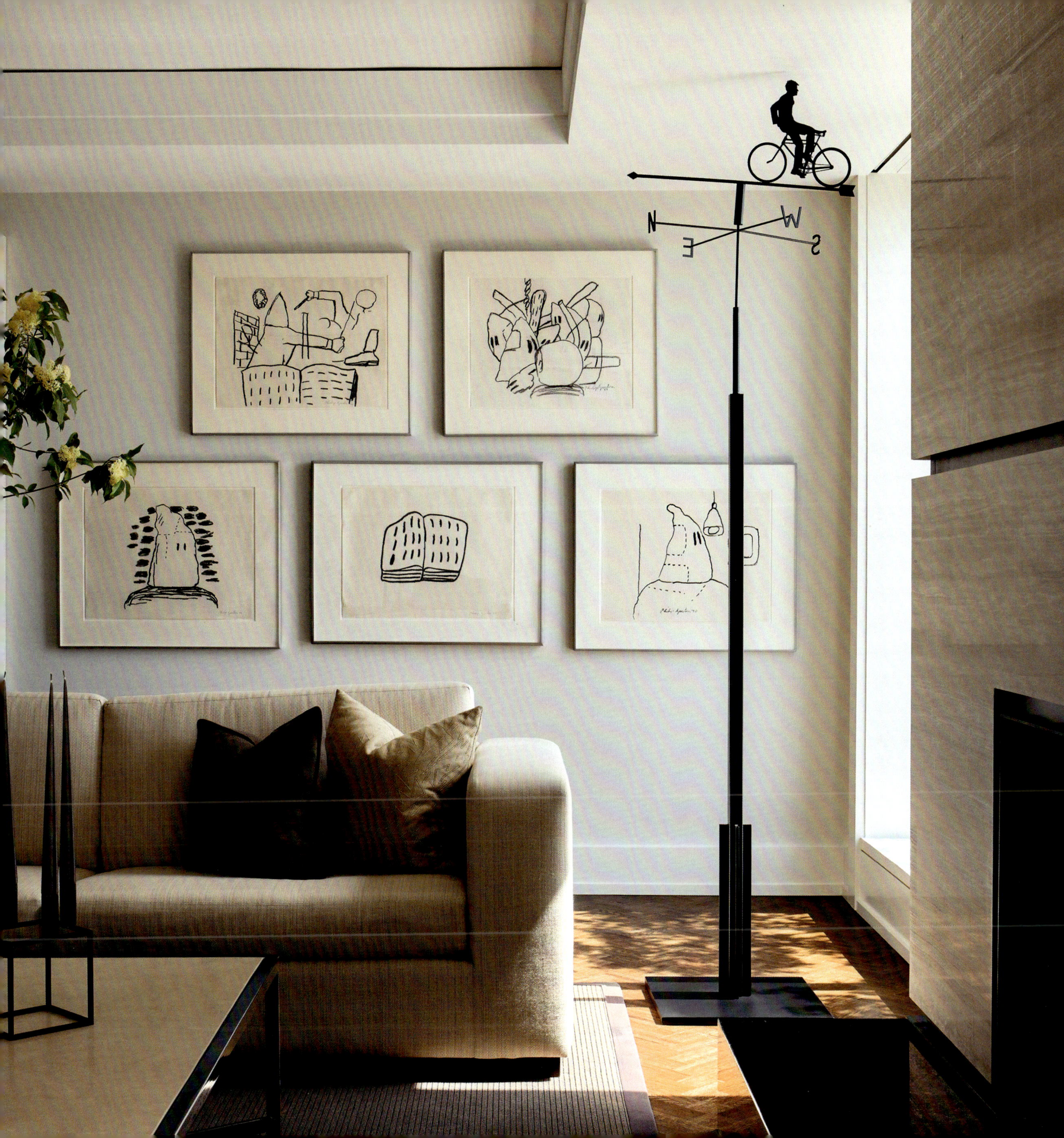
N
W
E
S

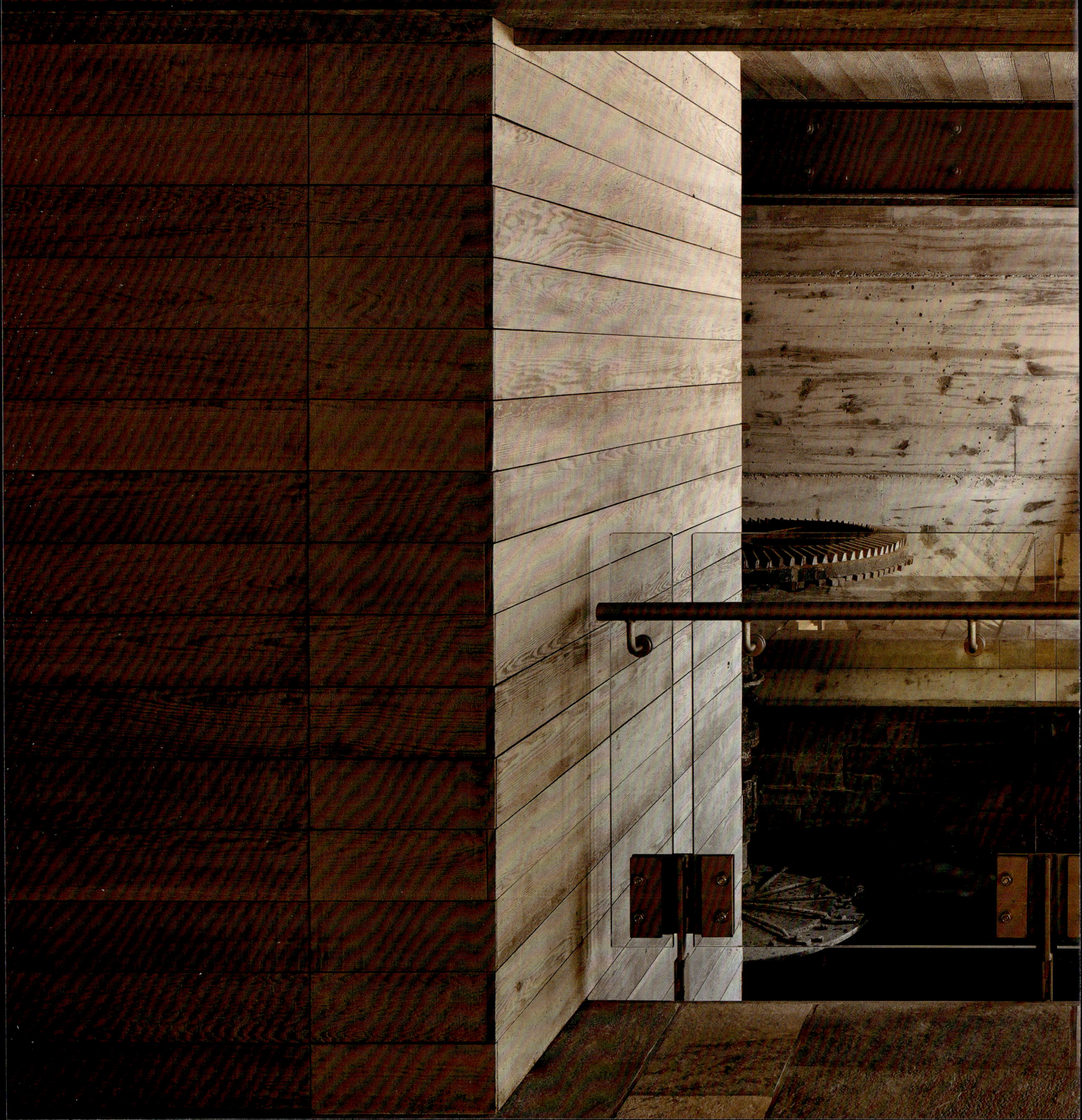

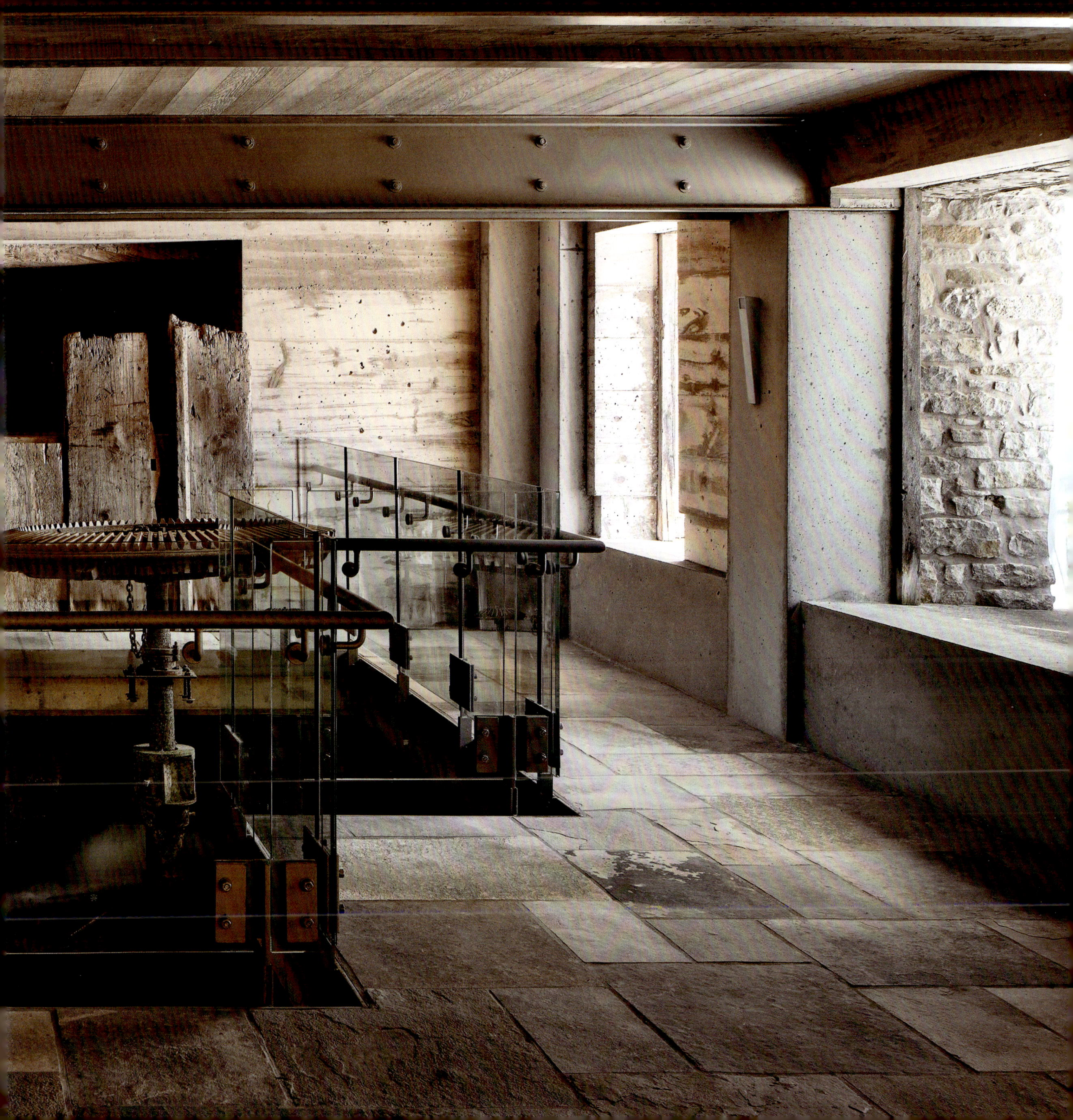